THE CALIFORNIA CLUB

THE CALIFORNIA CLUB

A Modern Contract Bridge Bidding System

Vic Sartor

ARCHWAY
PUBLISHING

Archway Publishing books may be ordered through booksellers or by contacting:

Archway Publishing
1663 Liberty Drive
Bloomington, IN 47403
www. archwaypublishing. com
1 (888) 242-5904

Because of the dynamic nature of the Internet, any web addresses or links contained in
this book may have changed since publication and may no longer be valid. The views
expressed in this work are solely those of the author and do not necessarily reflect the views
of the publisher, and the publisher hereby disclaims any responsibility for them.

Any people depicted in stock imagery provided by Thinkstock are models,
and such images are being used for illustrative purposes only.
Certain stock imagery © Thinkstock.

ISBN: 978-1-4808-5742-1 (sc)
ISBN: 978-1-4808-5743-8 (e)

Library of Congress Control Number: 2018900872

Print information available on the last page.

Archway Publishing rev. date: 7/18/2018

To my loving wife Kerry

Introduction

The California Club is a personal bidding system developed over 40 years of playing experience. It combines some elements of Schenken, Precision, and other well-known systems as well as many of my own inventions and adaptations. As the great comedian Jack Benny once said the first time he was introduced as the master of ceremonies on a radio variety show, "There will now be a brief pause for any of you who wish to say "Who cares?""

Like all strong club systems, the California Club uses a one club opening for most strong hands, thus limiting bids of one diamond, one heart, one spade, and two clubs. The 1C bid shows 17+HCP, not 16. Positive responses show a good 8/9+ HCP and are game-forcing. The 1D bid is usually, but not always, 11-16 HCP and may be short in diamonds. The 1H, 1S, and 2C bids show 11-16 HCP and at least 5-card suits. The 2D, 2H, and 2S bids are non-standard (covering both weak two bids and big 4441 hands) in the advanced version of the system, but more standard alternatives are also outlined for less adventurous bidders.

One area where the California Club differs markedly from Precision and other systems is in many of the responses to, and rebids after, the one club opening bid. Many of the responses follow Jeff Rubens' "useful space" principle; they have more than one meaning or cover a whole group of hands of a certain type. Whenever possible, transfers or suit switches are used so that a high percentage of no trump and major suit contracts are played by the one club opener.

Standard 2NT openings are handled by the 1C opening bid and described at a level lower than that of standard systems. This allows minor suit exploration and signoffs at the two and three level. Rebids of 1H and 1S after a 1C opening are forcing for one round. Therefore jump rebids of 2H, 2S, and 2NT are available for special purposes. This in turn changes the meaning of jump rebids at the three level.

These changes are not made frivolously. They allow descriptions of hands in ways not possible in most systems without sacrificing the ability to bid hands covered adequately by standard bidding.

Each of these topics will be described in detail in subsequent chapters, but first let's look at a simple outline of the system's constructive bidding sequences:

BALANCED HANDS

12-13 HCP-open 1D, rebid 1NT
14-16 HCP-open 1NT
17-19 HCP-open 1C, rebid 1NT
20-21 HCP- open 1C, rebid 2H***
22-24 HCP- open 2NT
25-27 HCP- open 1C or 3NT(check text)

SUIT-ORIENTED HANDS

11-16 HCP- open 1D, 1H, 1S, or 2C(natural)
17-21 HCP- open 1C, rebid 1H, 1S, 2C, or 2D
Special case- open 1D, then reverse or
jump shift (17-20 HCP)
Very strong (21/22+)- open 1C,
rebid 1H or 1S(forcing 1 round),
2S(clubs), or 2NT(diamonds) – essentially
game-forcing

4-4-4-1 HANDS

11-15 HCP- open 1D (even with short diamonds)
16+ HCP- open 2D or 2H (see text)

MAJOR SUIT WEAK TWO_BIDS

5-10 HCP, 6 hearts- bid 2D (see text)
5-10 HCP, 6 spades-bid 2H (see text)

PREEMPTS

Weak suits- open 3C, 3D, 3H, 3S
Good or solid suits- open 2S (see text)

Contents

Section 4
Defense, Carding, Appendices

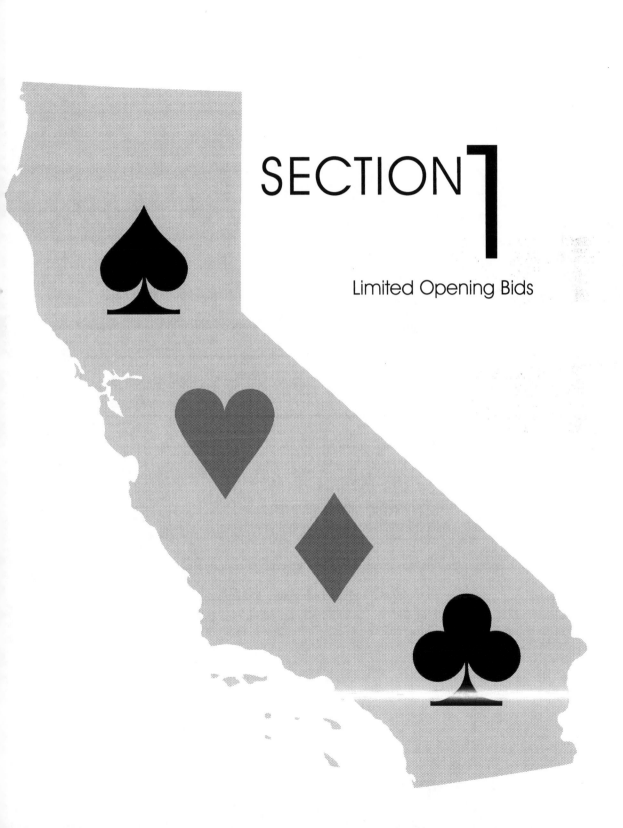

SECTION 1

Limited Opening Bids

CHAPTER 1

The All-Purpose 1-Diamond Opening Bid

I am going to start with the lowliest bid in a strong club, 5-card major system: 1 diamond. The 1D bid must feel like the old comedian Rodney Dangerfield—it gets no respect. I'll admit I'm guilty of this attitude myself. In friendly games, when I explain the alert for a 1D opening, I sometimes say, "He's got 13 cards and the delusion he's looking at an opening bid."

It's not quite as bad as all that, however. The California Club has some standards even for a 1D bid. With a balanced hand, it requires 12–13 high card points (HCP). Balanced 11-point hands should usually be passed. In essence, 1D is a weak no-trump (NT) bid.

Of course, the 1D opening is also used for a lot of suit-oriented hands that don't fit any other opening. A better definition might be "usually a limited hand (11–16 HCP), lacking a 5-card major, which may occasionally be very short in diamonds and may on rare occasions have as many as 20 HCP." We should probably concede that when the bidding begins with 1D, responder really has only a vague notion of what it may mean.

Although its vagueness may cause an occasional problem, the 1D bid also has its advantages. It allows you to open a weak NT-type hand without missing a possible 4-4 major suit fit when responder is too weak to try Stayman. It gives an immediate idea of the total partnership assets (though occasionally that idea may have to be adjusted if opener's rebid reveals the sole exceptional strong holding, which we'll discuss later). Of course, it sometimes allows an opponent to overcall in a major when he wouldn't have risked a 2-level overcall, but even that can occasionally work to our benefit.

The 1D opening not only serves as a form of weak NT, it also starts many sequences describing limited hands with no 5-card major and unbalanced distribution. This makes it the most common opening bid in the system. Here are some of the many hand-types that are opened 1D:

1. A balanced hand with 12–13 HCP (with or without a 4-card major)
2. A hand with 11–16 HCP and 6+ diamonds
3. A hand with 11–16 HCP, 5-4 or 4-5 distribution in the minors, and a major-suit singleton (2-2-5-4 hands with 12–13 HCP open 1D; 2-2-4-5 and 2-2-5-4 hands with 14–16 HCP have the option of opening 1NT)
4. A hand with 5-5+ distribution in the minors
5. Any hand with 11–15 HCP and 4-4-4-1 distribution, even if the singleton is in diamonds
6. A hand with 4-3 distribution in the majors and a *bad* 5-card club suit (avoiding a 2C opening with a bad suit)
7. A hand with 5+ diamonds, a 4-card major, and 17–20 HCP (a natural reverse or jump shift).*Alert:* Not opening 1C on this hand is unique among strong-club systems. It probably comes up less than 5 percent of the time, so responder always assumes he is facing a limited opening bid until the auction proves otherwise.

Balanced 1D Openings

Here are some typical balanced 1D openings:

A.	♠ Axx	B	♠ QJxx	C.	♠ Kxxx	D.	♠ Kx
	♥ Kxxx		♥ xx		♥ QJxx		♥ Q10x
	♦ KJx		♦ KQx		♦ xx		♦ Axxx
	♣ Qxx		♣ AJ10x		♣ AQx		♣ KJxx

Notice that the diamond suit may be shorter than 3 cards long. When we discuss suit-oriented hands, we will see occasional 1D openers that contain a singleton diamond. On the example hands, how will the auction commonly go?

- With A, if responder bids 1H, we have a simple 2H raise. If he bids 1S, we rebid 1NT. Over 2C or an inverted 2D (10+ HCP, 4–5+ diamonds), we would bid 2NT, showing a typical 12–13 HCP balanced hand.
- With B, we rebid 1S over 1H, raise 1S to 2S, and raise 2C to 3C. After an inverted 2D, we would raise to 3D showing a minimum with a diamond fit. With an extra queen, we would rebid 2S after 2D, showing a better hand, a spade stopper, but no heart stopper for NT.

- With C, we would raise either major to two, raise 2C to 3C, and bid 2NT after the inverted 2D.
- With D, we would rebid 1NT over either major, pass 1NT, and bid 2NT over 2C. Over a forcing 2D, we could bid 2NT or 3D.
- With all of these hands, we would pass a 1NT (6–10 HCP) response to our 1D opening. A jump response to 2NT would show 11-12 HCP in a balanced hand with no 4-card major. Raises to 3NT will depend on your aggressiveness, your opponents, and your sanity. A 3NT response shows anywhere from 13–16+ HCP with scattered stoppers and both majors stopped.

Continuations After 1D Opening, 1NT Rebid

After a 1D-1 of a major-1NT auction, two different response systems can be used. The first is simply a standard setup using 2C as new minor forcing (NMF). After 2C, opener shows one of the following:

- a bypassed 4+-card heart suit
- 3-card support for responder's presumed 5-card suit
- a NT rebid with no useful holding in either major

Since this is pretty standard these days, I won't spend time discussing it. The second possible scheme is a modified version of two-way NMF, which we will treat as the default method for our system.

Two-Way New Minor Forcing

After 1D-1 of a major-1NT, both 2C and 2D are artificial. A bid of 2C is forcing for one round. It begins game invitational sequences. It is *not* a relay to 2D. Opener bids 2H or 2S as described in simple NMF, but bids 2D as an artificial denial of 3-card support for opener's suit or a biddable second major. Responder can then invite in a 6-card major, a 5-card second suit, or 2NT. A bid of 2D is game-forcing, again seeking useful information. Opener's negative answers are 2NT or 3 of a 5-card minor. Simple rebids in the same suit or in the second major, without going through 2C or 2D, are strictly non-forcing.

Up to this point, these sequences are quite mundane, but now we come to my own adaptation of the convention. Direct rebids of 2NT, 3C, or 3D by responder are *transfers*.

A bid of 2NT is no longer needed as a natural invitation. To invite in NT, one starts with 2C, invitational NMF. So 2NT is now a transfer to clubs, showing 5 of opener's major and 5 clubs, either weak or very strong. Opener takes a choice of suits with the assumption that the bidding will end with the chosen partscore.

However, if responder has the strong (game-forcing and possibly slam-invitational) hand, he shows it by taking another bid. That may be a cue bid or a simple raise. The sequence 1D-1 of a major-1NT-3C shows 5-5+ with diamonds as the second suit. A sequence of 1D-1S-1NT-3D shows at least 5 in each major. The immediate 5-5 bids could also be used to show differences in concentration of values or distribution from sequences using the 2D force before bidding a second suit. That should be a matter of partnership discussion.

In summary, after 1D-1 of a major-1NT, the following bids are possible:

- 2C-forcing, invitational (opener bids a 4-card heart suit, shows 3-card support for responder's major, or bids 2D, 2NT, or 2 or 3 of a 5-card minor)
- 2D-forcing to game (same responses by opener)
- 2H, 2S-non-forcing (either as rebid of same suit or 2H as second suit after initial 1S response)
- 2NT-transfer to clubs (shows 5+ clubs, 5+ cards in the initial major, either non-forcing or slam try)
- 3C-transfer to diamonds (shows 5+ diamonds, 5+ cards in the initial major, either non-forcing or slam try)
- 3D-transfer to hearts (shows 5+ hearts, 5+ cards in an initial spade suit, either non-forcing or slam try)
- 2C and 2D can also begin invitational and game-forcing rebids of 6+ card majors

Several other invitational hands can be bid by means of the 2C NMF rebid over 1NT. For instance, 1D-1H-1NT-2C-2D-3C would show an invitational hand with 5 hearts and 5 clubs, while 1D-1H-1NT-2C-2 of anything-3H can show an invitational hand with 6+ hearts. A simple jump rebid can show the same type of hand—an invitation with a 6+ card suit—so I suggest that the NMF sequence show a poor to fair suit and the direct jump show a good suit. Partnerships will have to decide what constitutes a good suit.

The game-forcing 2D bid (rather than one of the secondary transfers) over opener's 1NT rebid could also be used to show 5-5 hands with values that are not concentrated in the long suits.

Examples might be:

♠ Kxxxx	♠ Q10xxx
♥ AQ	♥ K
♦ K10xxx	♦ AK
♣ K	♣ AJxxx

Knowing that the main suits may not be solid might help the partnership avoid a bad slam or steer the contract into NT.

Alternatively, a partnership might decide that bidding 2D and then a second suit at the 3-level only guarantees a 4-card suit, foregoing any differentiation between concentrated and non-concentrated 5-5 hands but probably showing interest in a slam. With 5 of a major and 4 of a minor but no slam interest, responder could bid or raise to 3NT rather than bidding a new suit after 2D. A final alternative, of course, is to play only the 2C bid as simple NMF with 2D natural. In my opinion, however, the double-barreled approach has many advantages and should be used.

1D-1 of a Major-1NT Rebid with Problem Hands

There are two types of hands that present an awkward rebid problem after an opening bid of 1D and a response of 1H or 1S. What do you do with a 1-4-4-4, 1-3-4-5, or 3-1-4-5 hand when partner bids one of your singleton? Some players have a religious conviction that a 1NT rebid here with a singleton constitutes a violation of at least three of the Ten Commandments. Another drawback is that if we do it with 14–15 HCP, we are understating our strength, since partner will generally expect a balanced 12–13 point hand.

But countering these objections is the fact that 1NT may be our best spot, especially at matchpoints. Furthermore, a rebid of 2C is no panacea. Even if we land in a good spot, we may get a bad score when 1NT makes 2 or 3. With 4-5 in the minors, we also have to hope partner doesn't correct 2C to 2D with 2-2 or 3-3 distribution in the minors.

My recommendation is to bid 1NT as long as the 3-card major is fairly strong. With absolutely no strength in either major, 2C is probably best. I wouldn't back up that opinion with a bet of more than a dime or two, however. As to the strength issue, an aggressive partner should give you a raise to 2NT (via 2C) with a decent 11–12 point hand on the statistically valid theory that two approximately equal hands will often make 3NT even when the total point count of the hands is only 23–24 HCP, so 2NT should be relatively safe. Opener can then bid game with his off-shape 14–15 point hand.

Other 1D Openers

As noted at the beginning of the chapter, the 1D opening covers several types of hands that aren't followed up by a 1NT rebid. Using that list as a reference point, let's discuss them in more detail.

#2: A hand with 11–16 HCP and 6+ diamonds

This is fairly obvious. The usual rebid will be 2D. With a maximum (15–16 HCP) and a good suit, you can jump to 3D.

#3: A hand with 11–16 HCP, 4-5 or 5-4 in diamonds and clubs, and 3-1 in the majors

As we discussed earlier, when responder bids the singleton, opener will have to choose between a 1NT and a 2C rebid. Should he decide on a 2C rebid, showing 9+ cards in the minors, responder now has a problem if he has a weak hand. Should he pass 2C or correct to 2D? Does opener have longer diamonds or clubs? Maybe Carnac the Magnificent would always be able to discern opener's exact distribution, but most of us will guess wrong a fair percentage of the time.

It might be a good idea to decide on one rule—"always pass 2C" or "always correct to 2D"—and stick to it. At least you won't go crazy second-guessing yourself. Another possible solution is for opener to rebid 2D when he has a good diamond suit and indifferent clubs. That would make it a better bet to pass 2C when he chooses that bid.

When responder has a better hand, the options are clearer. He can raise 2C to 3C or jump to 3D with invitational values. He can invite game with 2NT or just bid 3NT. He can force to game and solicit more information by using fourth-suit forcing. With a super fit in one minor, he may jump to 4 or 5 of that suit or make a splinter bid to show shortness and slam interest.

When responder bids opener's 3-card major, a raise is almost always the correct action. When the auction goes 1D-1H-2H or 1D-1S-2S, responder should never assume 4-card support for his suit. With only a 4-card suit, game-going values, and strength in the side suits, he may just jump to 3NT. Opener can correct to 4 of the major if there is a 4-4 fit.

When responder wants to investigate more slowly, we have a treatment that covers the situation. After 1D-1M-2M, responder makes the cheapest bid to show a 5-card suit. All other bids show he only had a 4-card suit. Bids of new suits are natural but may just show concentrations of strength. When 2S is the conventional bid, 2NT stands for spades.

Here are some example hands and auctions involving 5-4-3-1 1D openers:

A.	♠ x	♠ KQxx	1D	1S
	♥ AQx	♥ xxx	1NT	P
	♦ K10xxx	♦ Qx		
	♣ QJxx	♣ Kxxx		

Do we bid 1NT or 2C? It looks like an easy 110 in clubs. A bid of 1NT may score 120 for a good match point score; 2C is safer at international match points (IMPs).

B.	♠ AJx	♠ KQxx	1D	1S
	♥ x	♥ xxx	2S	P
	♦ K10xxx	♦ Qx		
	♣ QJxx	♣ Kxxx		

The 3-card raise gets us to a good spot. Let's hope we get a match point top with 140 or 170.

C.	♠ xxx	♠ Jxxx	1D	1S
	♥ x	♥ Axx	2C	P or 2D
	♦ AK109	♦ Qxx		
	♣ AQxxx	♣ Jxx		

With nothing in the majors,2C seems better than a 2S raise. That still leaves partner a guess between passing 2C or bidding 2D.

D.	♠ xxx	♠ Jxxx	1D	1S
	♥ x	♥ Qxx	2C	P or 2D
	♦ AK109x	♦ Qxx		
	♣ AQxx	♣ Jxx		

Here we have to make the same choices as in hand C.

E.	♠ Axx	♠ Qxx	1D	1H
	♥ x	♥ AQxx	2C	3C
	♦ AQ10x	♦ xx	3S*	3NT
	♣ A10xxx	♣ Kxxx		

*3S may be a little pushy, but 3NT looks makeable. If responder has no help in spades, he can retreat to 4C

F.	♠ QJx	♠ Kxx	1D	1H
	♥ x	♥ QJ9x	1NT?	2C*
	♦ AQxxx	♦ Kxx	2D	2NT
	♣ AJxx	♣ Qxx	3NT	

Both players bid a bit aggressively, but 3NT is a good contract.

Here are some hands involving our "cheapest suit" rebid to show a 5-card suit after 1D-one of a major-two of a major (1D-1M-2M) auctions. (*note- M means either major*)

G.	♠Kxx	♠ QJxxx	1D	1S
	♥ x	♥ Jxx	2S	2NT* (5 spades)
	♦ KQxxx	♦ Ax	4S (or 3C as a game try)	
	♣ AJ10x	♣ Kxx		

H.	♠ x	♠Axx	1D	1H
	♥ QJx	♥ K10xxx	2H	2S (5 hearts)
	♦ AQJx	♦ xx	3C	4H
	♣ Kxxxx	♣ AJx		

I.	♠ AQx	♠ Kxxx	1D	1S
	♥ xx	♥ AJ9	2S	3NT (only 4 spades)
	♦ Kxxx	♦ QJ	P	
	♣ KJxx	♣ Q10xx		

J.	♠ x	♠ xxx	1D	1H
	♥ Axx	♥ KQJx	2H	3D (only 4 hearts)
	♦ KQ10xx	♦Jxxx	4D	4H
	♣ Axxx	♣ Kx	P (or 5D)	

K.	♠ 10xx	♠ x	1D	1H
	♥ AKxx	♥ Qxxx	2H	3C only 4 hearts)
	♦ QJ	♦ A10xx	4H	
	♣ Kxxx	♣ AJxx		

#4: A hand with 11–16 HCP and 5-5+ distribution in the minors

This hand is easy to describe. With most 11–16 HCP hands, you open 1D and rebid 2C. Given a chance, you make a second rebid of 3C. With a very good 15–16 HCP and concentrated values in your two suits, you may open 1D and make a jump shift to 3C. The jump to 3C guarantees at least 5 cards in each of 2 *good* suits.

These hands would open 1D and rebid 2C over any 1-level response:

♠ x	♠ Kx	♠ xx	♠ AQ
♥ xx	♥ x	♥ Q	♥ x
♦ AQxxx	♦ KJ10xx	♦ QJxxx	♦ AKQxx
♣ AKxxx	♣ AJxxx	♣ AKJxx	♣ Jxxxx

These hands are good enough to jump shift to 3C:

♠ x	♠ xx	♠ x
♥ Kx		♥ A
♦ AQJxx	♦ AKxxx	♦ KQ10xxx
♣ KQJxx	♣ AKJ10xx	♣ KQJ109

We'll return to these hands later when we discuss the 2C and 2D responses to 1D.

#5: Any hand with 11–15 HCP and 4-4-4-1 distribution, even if the singleton is in diamonds

All minimum 4-4-4-1 hands are opened 1D. Even with shortness in diamonds, the rebids are generally not a problem. Bigger (16+ HCP) 4-4-4-1 hands are opened conventionally at the 2 level. They will be discussed later. Here are some 11–15 HCP 4-4-4-1 hands along with some possible responding hands and appropriate auctions:

A. ♠ A10xx	♠ Kxxx	1D	1S
♥ x	♥ Qxx	2S	3C (only 4 spades)
♦ KQxx	♦ Ax	4S	P
♣ KJxx	♣ Qxxx		
B. ♠ x	♠ QJxx	1D	1S
♥ AJxx	♥ 10x	1NT	P
♦ AQxx	♦ Jxx		
♣ Kxxx	♣ QJxx		
C. ♠ x	♠ Qxxx	1D	1H
♥ AQxx	♥ KJxx	2H	2NT (4 spades, only 4 hearts)
♦ KQxx	♦ Jx	3H	P
♣ QJxx	♣ Axx		
D. ♠ Kxxx	♠ Q10x	1D	1NT
♥ AQxx	♥ Jx	P	
♦ x	♦ Jxxxx		
♣ AJxx	♣ Kxx		
E. ♠ J10xx	♠ KQxx	1D	1S
♥ AKxx	♥ Qx	3S*	4S
♦ AKxx	♦ Qxx		
♣ x	♣ Jxxx		

*3S=Absolute maximum, non-1C opener, 4 trump

Looking at hand E, about the only hand opener can logically have is a maximum (15–16 HCP) with 4 good trump and a good 4-5 card minor (probably diamonds) or this kind of 4-4-4-1 hand. We'll see what would be bid with a similar, slightly bigger hand when we discuss hand type #7.

#6: A hand with 4-3 distribution in the majors and a bad 5-card club suit (avoiding a 2C opening with a bad suit)- a 2D bid in many Precision partnerships

I have a strong personal prejudice against opening a Precision-style 2C on hands such as these:

♠ KQx ♥AQxx ♦ x ♣ Jxxxx   ♠ AJ10x ♥ AQx ♦ x Qxxxx

Just as we occasionally open 1D with 4-4-1-4 distribution (see hand D above), we also sometimes open 1D in a hand with a bad 5-card club suit and a singleton diamond. Again, the rebids are generally very comfortable. If responder bids a major, we can make a 3- or 4-card raise. If he bids 1NT, we can bid 2C.

I may have neglected to mention a very important rule: if a 1D opener pulls a 1NT or 2NT bid to 2C or 3C, responder must never correct to diamonds, in order to allow for a case like this. The odds are very high that responder has at least 3 clubs. Even under the worst circumstances, you'll wind up in a 5-2 trump fit. When opener has a maximum 1D opener and 5 bad clubs, he can raise 1NT to 2NT or raise 2NT to 3NT.

#7: A hand with 5+ diamonds, a 4-card major, and 17–20 HCP (a natural reverse or jump shift in standard bidding)—"the 1D bid with muscles"

Finally, we come to a unique feature in this system's handling of unbalanced hands with real diamond suits. In most big club systems, this is just another 1C opener. When responder replies 1D, as often happens, opener bids 2D. As the auction proceeds, he often winds up bidding his major at the 3 level. All of this is very inefficient. It also results in wrong-siding any diamond contract and exposing the strong hand as dummy.

This is one situation where natural bidding is much more efficient, and there is no good reason for not incorporating it into a strong club system. The only legitimate objection is that including these hands in our 1D opening overloads that bid, but I think that is nonsense. Responder does not have any extra burden when replying to 1D. He simply bids naturally as if playing Standard American. When opener shows great strength with a natural reverse or jump shift, he continues with a few conventional rebids, but they aren't much more complex than those used by experts in standard frameworks.

Here are some typical "1D with muscles" opening bids:

A.	♠ AKxx	B.	♠ xx	C.	♠ Axx	D.	♠ x
	♥ x		♥ KQJx		♥ AKxx		♥ AQ10x
	♦ AKQxx		♦ KQJxx		♦ AQJxxx		♦ AKJxx
	♣ Qxx		♣ AK		♣ ---		♣ AQx

With each of these hands, we open 1D rather than 1C.

An obvious question occurs: what if responder passes? The answer is simple: we play 1D, unless the opponents balance. If they do, we can double or bid our major. In any case, we should be in a makeable contract. If partner can't find a bid in response to 1D, it is highly unlikely we can make game. Actually, the only remote chance for us to bid game is when our super-weak partner has a long major, and an opponent's bid allows us a chance to bid again and find a big secondary fit.

The following are some typical auctions that show "diamonds with muscles":

- 1D-1H-2S
- 1D-1S-2H
- 1D-1NT-2H
- 1D-1NT-2S

We'll discuss the continuations after forcing 2C or 2D bids later.

You may recall that in our discussion of 4-4-4-1 and 5-4-3-1 1D openers, we said a sequence of 1D-1H-3H or 1D-1S-3S shows a maximum limited opening bid (15–16 HCP). So another obvious question arises: what happens if you start a planned "muscle" sequence and responder bids your 4-card major?

It just so happens I have a fiendishly clever answer: you jump to 2NT, which is not needed to show a standard 18–19 point hand. Any balanced or semi-balanced hand in that range would be opened with a big club. The 2NT rebid is entirely conventional and says,"I have a 17–20 HCP hand, and you bid my 4-card major!"

Continuations after the big reverse or jump shift fall into two groups. If the sequence is standard and natural, we will use a form of Ingerman. All suit bids are forcing for one round. This allows responder to rebid his suit or support opener's diamonds without worrying about being passed. A bid of 2NT is artificial and weak, suggesting but not forcing 3C and allowing responder to follow with a sign-off in 3D or 3 of the major. Opener may ignore the suggestion and bid 3D or 3NT with maximum length or strength. New suits introduced after the first two rounds of bidding are forcing.

If opener uses the artificial jump to 2NT, there is a set of artificial 3-level responses.

The 3C bid is used to show any hand that has no interest in slam. It may show a very weak initial response, planning to sign off at 3 of the agreed-upon major, or a hand good enough to go to game if opener has a maximum hand. All other 3-level and 4-level bids show extra values—at least enough to suggest slam. Armed with the information from these bids, opener can try for slam or sign off in game.

Let's start with the 3C reply to opener's 2NT rebid. When responder bids 3C, opener simply clarifies his strength. He bids 3D with the worst possible hand (17–bad 18 HCP), bids 3H with the medium range (good 18–19 HCP), and jumps to game in the major with a maximum (good 19–20 HCP). Responder can sign off in 3 of the major or bid 4 himself after a 3D or 3H answer to 3C.

When responder has at least some slam interest (probably requiring a minimum of 11 HCP or great distribution), he makes a conventional response other than 3C. Any bid other than 3C is game-forcing. The bids from 3D to 3NT give information about trump strength. If the combined trump holding is not likely to be strong enough to hold trump losers to 1, opener will sign off in game. Any other bid indicates no more than 1 prospective trump loser. The following are the responses after 1D-1M-2NT:

Opener	Responder
1D	1H or 1S
2NT*(17–20 HCP,	3C—no slam interest; may want to sign off at 3M or 4M
5+ diamonds, 4 of	3D—some slam interest; poor suit
responder's major)	3H—some slam interest; Q-high suit
	3S—some slam interest; A- or K-high suit
	3NT—some slam interest; AK, AQ, or KQ

Assuming the trumps are satisfactory, opener can now bid 3NT (if available) or 4D (if responder has bid 3NT) to ask for aces (simple Blackwood). If responder's holding in specific suits is crucial, opener can bid one of the side suits as an asking bid. He can also ask about diamonds if 4D is not needed as Blackwood.

The responses would be three simple steps: no control, second-round control, or first-round control. If there's room, a fourth step could show AK. A follow-up in another suit would be a second asking bid. If the answer to the first asking bid prevents a convenient ask in the other, a second bid in the same suit can be used to ask in the other side suit. A follow-up of 4NT would ask for key cards..

If opener has asked for and received information about aces or key controls and then makes the cheapest bid in the agreed-upon trump suit, that is a sign-off. However, responder can overrule the sign-off if he knows the partnership assets exceed 33 HCP.

Here are some sample auctions featuring the conventional 2NT rebid:

Opener	Responder	Auction	
A. ♠ AKxx	♠ QJxx	1D	1S
♥ x	♥ Axx	2NT (4 spades,	3H (slam interest, Q-high suit)
♦ AKQxx	♦ xx	17–20 HCP)	
♣ Qxx	♣ Axxx	4C (asking bid)	4S (first round control)
		4NT (aces?)	5H
		5NT	6C
		6S	P
B. ♠ AKxx	♠ xxxx	1D	1S
♥ x	♥ Qxx	2NT	3C (no slam interest)
♦ AKQxx	♦ Jx	3H (18–19 HCP)	3S (bare minimum, 5–6 HCP)
♣ Qxx	♣ Kxxx	4S (aggressive but reasonable)	P
C. ♠ AKxx	♠ Qxxx	1D	1S
♥ Qx	♥ xxx	2NT	3H (slam interest, Q-high suit)
♦ AKQxxx	♦ x	4H (asking)	4S (no control)
♣ x	♣ AKQxx	P	
D. ♠ x	♠ xxx	1D	1H
♥ KQJx	♥ xxxx	2NT	3C*
♦ AKQxx	♦ x	4H (good 19-20 HCP)	P
♣ Axx	♣ KQxxx		
E. ♠ x	♠ xxxx	1D	1H
♥ AQxx	♥ KJxx	2NT	3C*
♦ AQJxxx	♦ Kx	3H (18-19 HCP)	4H
♣ KQ	♣ xxx	P	

All of these combinations could be bid adequately by opening a strong club, but the natural reverses and jump shifts are so descriptive that it seems silly not to use the natural bids. Besides, opponents may not be quite as frisky in competition if they know a 1D opening might contain 20 HCP. In standard bidding, opener might open 1D and then jump to 4H or 4S with several of our example hands, leaving only the 5-level for slam exploration. With our system, we can often get crucial information at the 3 or 4-level.

F.	♠ Qx	♠ xxx	1D		1H
	♥Axxx	♥ KQxx	2NT		3NT (slam interest, 2 of 3 top honors)
	♦ AKQ10x	♦ xx	4C (asking)		4S (first round control) or 4NT (AK)
	♣ Qx	♣ AKxx	5C (now asks in in spades)		5D (no control)
			5H		P
G.	♠ x	♠ Qxx	1D		1H
	♥ Axxx	♥ KQxx	2NT		3NT (slam interest, 2 of 3 top honors)
	♦ AKJ10xx	♦ xx	4D (aces?)		4S (1)
	♣ KQ	♣ Axxx	6H		P

Non-Major Responses to a 1D Opening

So far, our partner has been very cooperative. In almost every case, he has responded to our 1D opening by bidding 1 of a major suit. Unfortunately, this will not always be the case. Partners have been known to bid 1NT or even go to the 2 or 3-level. In this section, we will cover these situations.

1D-1NT

Let's start with a response of 1NT. When responder has a fairly balanced hand and 6–10 HCP, he has an easy response of 1NT. Opener's rebid choices are fairly simple. He will often pass. With a long diamond suit, he may rebid 2D or even 3D with a maximum and a suit that may run in 3NT. A rebid of 2H or 2S would be the strong reverse just discussed He may also rebid 2C. This would ordinarily show both minors. However, a special case occurs when opener has opened 1D with short diamonds and 5 clubs (say

At the risk of redundancy, let me repeat our ironclad rule:*If a 1D opener corrects a 1NT response to 2C, responder must pass.* Responder will almost always have at least 3 clubs and is a favorite to have 4 or 5. Even if a better diamond fit exists, 2 clubs will be playable. That also applies if responder has both minors, although with 5 good diamonds and 4 weak clubs, a 2D rebid would often be better. If opener has 4-4-1-4 distribution, he can use his judgment. I would generally pass 1NT, but 2C might be right.

Before going on to 2-level responses, I'd like to discuss one particularly awkward situation involving the club suit. When opener bids 1D and responder has a weakish hand with clubs as his only long suit, his choice of responses can be quite unappealing. With a very weak hand and short diamonds, pass can be scary (especially vulnerable), but it is often necessary. Luckily, the opponents will usually bid something and save the day. With 6–10 HCP and 2-2 or 3-1 in the majors, the usual reponse of 1NT could put him in a terrible contract. If he has no sure side entries, he may never get a trick from his clubs. Even with 6–10 HCP, the best option may sometimes be to pass in hopes of later making a delayed 2C bid.

Here's where one of my cockamamie ideas comes in. With something like 1-3-4-5, 3-1-4-5, 1-3-3-6, or 3-1-3-6 distribution, it could be right to bid a 3-card major. If opener raises you to 2, a 4-3 fit may play pretty well. If he makes the most likely rebid of 1NT, you haven't lost anything, and at least his hand may get some benefit from concealment and the opening lead. If he bids 1S over your 1H, you can bid 1NT. And if a disaster occurs, you'll have an interesting story to share.

Even if you decide to ignore this possibly boneheaded idea, the suggested 2-level system responses I'm going to propose do offer at least some help in this area. We will get to them presently. First, I'd like to discuss all of the 2-level responses to 1D in general.

2-Level Responses to 1D: A Basic Scheme

I will first present a rather sane, comfortable bidding scheme that shouldn't cause anyone a great deal of mental discomfort. It is, in fact, a basic scheme I have used for years in many of my strong club partnerships.

The main features are rather simple: 1D-2C is standard, forcing for at least one round. It may contain a 4-card major if it has game-forcing values. Rebids of 2NT or 3C show minimum hands and may be passed. 1D-2D is an inverted raise, showing 10+ HCP and 4-5+ diamonds but not forcing to game. It denies a 4-card major. Opener can show a minimum by rebidding 2NT or 3D or probe for game by bidding a major suit feature.

Jumps to 2H and 2S can be weak or strong, depending on partnership preferences. I prefer traditional strong jump shifts here. It allows responder to immediately alert partner to the possibility of a slam. 1D-2NT is invitational, showing 11–12 HCP and at least half-stoppers in both majors, 1D-3C is preemptive, and 1D-3D is essentially the same—an inverted weak diamond raise. Invitational hands can be shown by a bid of

2C or 2D followed by 2NT or a rebid of the suit. With game-forcing hands, responder has to bid a new suit at his second turn or simply bid game (usually 3NT).

After a 2C response, opener can rebid 2D, bid 2NT, or raise to 3C to show a "normal"(11-16 HCP) 1D opener. These bids are non-forcing, though 3C is highly invitational. 2D is a waiting bid, covering a variety of the 1D openers discussed on pages 6-10. It may or may not show a real diamond suit, but it often does, since there are alternative bids available. 2D takes up little bidding room and allows responder to bid a major (forcing) or 2NT or 3C (invitational).It ensures a 4-4 major fit will be found whenever one exists. If responder bids 2H or 2S, that bid is forcing to game but may only show a feature. Opener can raise with 4 trump or temporize with a 2S or 2NT bid, waiting for responder to confirm or deny possession of a real 4-card suit.(That process will be discussed in more detail in the next two sections). With maximum values (15-16 HCP) and a normal 1D opening, opener may sometime jump to 3D or 3NT.

A 2NT rebid after a 1D-2C sequence usually shows balanced distribution and at least partial stoppers in both majors. It tends to deny a 4-card major and often shows the weak NT (12-13 HCP) type of 1D opener.

That leaves the rebids of 2H and 2S. These bids could be treated as showing big reverses in "1D with muscles" hands. It would allow extra room for slam exploration. However, having them available as a natural way to show a 4-card major in a "normal"1D hand seems a much more efficient use of bidding space. The combination of a big 1D opener facing a 2C response will be relatively rare. For this system, therefore, opener will be able to rebid 2H or 2S after a 1D-2C auction without showing a huge hand. When he does have the big reverse, he will have to rebid 3H or 3S.

Opener's options after an inverted 2D response to 1D are similar in some ways to those used after 1D-2C. He also has to jump to 3H or 3S to show the 17–20 HCP "1D with muscles" hand. This is because the entire 2-level is needed to describe various "normal" 1D hands. There is one major difference. Responder's 2D bid denies a 4-card major. Opener 's 2H or 2S rebid may simply show a stopper for NT rather than a real 4-card suit." He can bid 2NT or 3D with appropriate minimums. He can bid 2H, 2S, or 3C in order to probe for 3NT with extra values in a "normal" 1D hand (14–16 HCP) or just jump to 3NT.

Now that I have outlined the general structure, I think it would be useful to have a more complete discussion of responses in the minor suits. It is important to understand the various continuations which apply after an initial 1D opening bid. Some of the following review may be redundant, but you never know when it might be helpful for a pop quiz.

Responses to 1D with 5+ Clubs

When responder holds 5+ clubs and 6–10 HCP, he will usually not be able to bid his long suit. He also has to realize that game is not very likely. Remember that 1D is not usually a strong opener. If balanced, it will often have only 12–13 HCP. It will rarely have more than 16 HCP. In order for us to have any higher ambitions than a 9-or 10-trick game, responder needs a very strong hand. So his first important objective in responding to a 1D opening will be to explore for any possible major-suit fit.

As mentioned in the previous section, that might even involve bidding a 3-card suit in extreme circumstances. (Don't get carried away with that ploy.) If no major fit is found, one of the partners will often bid 1NT, and the auction will end. A second possibility is that opener will rebid 2C or 2D, and the bidding will stop in a minor partscore.

With 11–12 HCP, 5 clubs, and no major, responder may be able to invite with 2NT. With that hand and a major, responder may be able to bid his major and then start an invitational sequence with an artificial 2C over opener's 1NT rebid. With 10–12 HCP and 4+ diamonds, he may make a direct 2D response to 1D. With no other choice, he may have to bid 2C and invite by rebidding 2NT or 3C (with 6). The following are some typical hands that will respond 1H or 1S to a 1D opening, despite holding longer clubs and 10+ HCP:

A.	♠ K10xx	B.	♠ x	C.	♠ 10xxx	D.	♠ Qx
	♥ Qxx		♥ AQxx		♥ KQx		♥ AKxx
	♦ x		♦ Kx		♦ x		♦ QJ
	♣ KQxxx		♣ J10xxxx		♣ AQJxx		♣ J10xxx

If he has no 4-card major and scattered honors, he may bid 2NT (11–12 HCP) or 3NT (13–16+ HCP) without mentioning a club suit. With a weakish 6–10 HCP and no major, he will often be forced to bid 1NT. Hands A and B above will pass a 1NT rebid by opener. Hand B may make a game try if raised. Hand C will probably make an invitational bid over 1NT or 1S. Remember that both 2C and 2D are artificial and forcing over opener's 1NT rebid. A bid of 2C is invitational; 2D is game-forcing. Hand D will force to game in either hearts or NT.

1D-2C and 3C Responses
(Assuming a normal 11–16 HCP opener)

As noted, responses to 1D on hands with length in clubs need special treatment. We have already seen how many semi-balanced invitational hands may be handled. We also have reasonable methods for handling intermediate hands with 4-card majors and longer club suits. We will now discuss a set of bids we can use to handle weak, intermediate, and strong club 1-suiters and strong hands with long clubs and a 4-card major side suit.

The 2C response will not be game-forcing, but responder's rebids may create a game force. The 2C responder may have a major side suit, but if so, he will have game-forcing values. With less, he would bid his major first and use one of the invitational sequences described in the previous section. The following response scheme covers the possible replies to a 1D opening by a hand with 5 or more clubs.

- **Weak (3–7 HCP) hand with 7+ clubs:**jump to 3C. (Be careful about –200 if vulnerable. The rules do allow you to pass.)

- **7–10 HCP hand with 6+ clubs**: bid 1NT or pass, and then bid 2C if given the chance.

- **11–12 HCP hand with 6+ clubs:**bid 2C, then rebid 3C (invitational)

- **11–12 HCP hand with 5 or 6 clubs, thoughts of NT game:**bid 2C, then bid 2NT or 3C if opener bids 2D. If opener's rebid is 2NT, pass or raise 2NT to 3NT

- **11–12 HCP with 5+ clubs and 4-card major:**bid the major suit first, then invite (see above)

- **13+ HCP with 5+ clubs and 4-card major:**bid 2C, then bid 2H or 2S (game-forcing) if opener's rebid is 2D. If his rebid is 2NT, raise to 3NT or bid a suit at 3-level.

- **13+ HCP with 5+ clubs and no 4-card major:** bid 2C and then bid 3-card major suit fragment (2H or 2S) over a 2D rebid. Opener will never raise to 4 since the auction is game-forcing. If he raises to 3, bid 3S or 3NT to deny a real 4-card suit.

- **13+ HCP with 6+ clubs, no singleton**: bid 2C, then 2H or 2S (feature) over a 2D rebid. Opener will never raise to 4 since the auction is game-forcing. If he raises to 3, you may bid 3NT to indicate you just bid a feature. Over a rebid of 2NT, a new suit at the 3-level is natural, so you just raise to 3NT unless you want to try for slam. With a slam-invitational hand, you can bid a suit feature and then 4NT or another suit later.

- **13+ HCP with 6+ clubs, singleton**:bid 2C, then jump to 3H. 3S, or 3NT (singleton diamond) over opener's 2D rebid. If opener rebids anything else, splinters would only apply at the 4-level. New suits at the 3-level are natural and game-forcing.

The following are some example hands with long clubs. Opener bids 1D and rebids 2D over 2C.

E.		F.		G.		H.		I.	
♠ x		♠ x		♠ AQ		♠ x		♠	
♥ Kxx		♥ Kxx		♥ xx		♥ QJxx		♥ AJx	
♦ J		♦ KJx		♦ A10x		♦ xx		♦ Kxxx	
♣ KQ10xxx		♣ AQxxxx		♣ KJ10xxx		♣ AKQxxx		♣ AQJxxx	

With E, bid 2C, then rebid 3C. With F, bid 2C, then 2H. With G, bid 2C, then 3D (2S is too likely to get raised).With H, bid 2C, then 2H. With I, bid 2C, then 3D, then 4H. An immediate 4S (void) is also reasonable. (A possible alternative 1D-2C scheme is outlined in Appendix A.)

Special Case:1D- 2C- 2H or 2S Rebid

. A 1D opener will sometimes rebid 2H or 2S after a 2C response. As has previously been discussed, this shows a hand with 5+ diamonds, a 4-card major, and 11-16 HCP.
The entire default rebid structure will be as follows :

- **After a 1D-2C sequence**, a 2H or 2S rebid by opener shows a "normal"1D opener (11-16 HCP) with a 4-card major. A 2NT rebid by responder is non-forcing. Any new suit bid is forcing.

- **After a 1D-2C sequence**, a 2NT rebid shows a "normal"(11–16 HCP)1D opening. It is usually a 12–13 HCP balanced hand and is non-forcing. With minimum values, responder may pass.

- **After a 1D-2C sequence**, a simple raise to 3C also shows a normal (11–16 HCP) 1D opener. It tends to show an unbalanced hand with at least some game prospects and is forcing to 3NT or 4C.

- **After a 1D-2C sequence**, opener's 2D rebid is a catchall waiting bid. It also shows a "normal" 1D opening. It may show a real diamond suit or simply a hand without a 4-card major that the opener feels does not have adequate stoppers in the majors for a 2NT bid. Unlike 2NT, it is absolutely forcing for one round. Responder must bid at least once more to complete a description of his hand.

- **A jump to 3D** has the same meaning as it would have had if opener had opened 1D and responder had replied 1H or 1S. It shows a maximum normal 1D opening (15–16 HCP) and a solid 6+ card diamond suit.

- **Jumps to 3H, 3S, and 3NT** may depend upon partnership preferences. **In our default structure, jumps to 3H or 3S are the way we show the"1D with muscles"** hand. A 3NT response here would indicate a poor fit and a desire to make that the final contract. New suit bids would show support for opener's major and slam interest. 4D would show interest in a diamond slam.

- **It is possible that some partnerships may develop more complex structures in which the 1D opener merely rebids 2H or 2S with the big reverse, waiting to show extra strength by means of late conventional bids.** They might use 3H, 3S, and 3NT as splinter bids to show specific. shortness and a "1D with muscles" hand. Those who might be interested in such creative developments may wish to look at Appendix A, which contains a few ideas which may be relevant." For now, however, the treatments outlined on the pages 14-16 will be the default structure for the system.

Before we discuss the continuations that follow various 1D-2C sequences further, we should first note that not all of the big hands with 5 diamonds, a 4-card major, and 2-2 distribution in a side suit need be opened 1D. With good NT stoppers in both short suits, it is certainly reasonable to open 1C, planningto rebid 1NT. A hand such as AQ

Kxxx KQxxx KJ would be a perfect example. An opener should probably favor a 1D opening bid on a big 5-4-2-2 hand when it contains at least one unstopped doubleton. Obviously, big 5-4-3-1, 6-4-2-1 or other unbalanced hands meet our criteria for a 1D opening, assuming they are not so strong that they would be opened 2C in Standard American bidding. This system has conventional treatments to handle those hands. They will be described in a later chapter,

1D-2C Revisited- Opener's Choice of Rebids and Continuations.

We have already described opener's possible rebids after a 1D-2C pretty thoroughly, but there are a few nuances that might be worth mentioning.

In choosing between 2D and 2NT, opener should look at the location of his honors and decide whether there are good reasons to play the contract from his side. Tenaces in the majors may make 2NT preferable to 2D. A holding like Kx or Qx is usually less vulnerable when the left-hand opponent is on opening lead. High honors with no intermediate cards (i.e. Axx) suggest making a waiting bid of 2D, allowing the responder a chance to declare the contract, which might be the best course. Of course, he may not have any better stoppers than opener, but it is worth the effort to attempt to right-side the contract.

A 2NT rebid is very descriptive. It should usually show the weak NT version (12–13 HCP) of a 1D opener. More importantly,, it should have least a partial stopper in both majors. If responder is at all nervous about his holdings in the majors he may pull 2NT to 3C (6+ card suit, 11-12 HCP), which is non-forcing. If he wants to force to game, he may bid 3D, 3H, or 3S, showing a stopper for NT or the beginning of a slam try. He may also just raise 2NT to 3NT, especially if he thinks he might provide 5 or 6 club tricks.

As previously described, a raise of responder's original 2C response to 3C is also narrowly defined. It should show at least 4-card support and is forcing to 3NT or 4C. It should suggest an unbalanced hand with some game (or even slam) prospects in clubs. With a less promising hand or only 3-card support, opener can bid 2D first and support clubs later.

The 2D rebid covers almost all of the other normal 1D openers. Obviously, that involves a pretty wide variety of hand types. The 2D bid basically lets the responder give a clearer picture of his hand before he commits himself to a particular course of action. Since opener would almost always bid a 4-card major if he had one, it allows the responder the freedom to use a 2H or 2S continuation to create a game-forcing auction even when he just has a fragment in that suit.

If opener has 4-card support for responder's major but no NT stopper in the other major, he has several possible continuations available. He may bid 3C to show a fit. He may bid 3D to show extra length. He may bid the fourth suit to ask opener to bid 3NT with a half stopper. He may also make a delayed raise of responder's major, showing decent 3-card support. This may establish a Moysian 4-3 fit (see note below) when partner has a real 4-card suit and neither partner can bid NT. If responder now bids 4C or 4D it is forcing, essentially telling opener to choose between the 4-3 major suit game and the 11-trick minor game.

In some cases, opener may bid the fourth suit as an artificial force. It may show a hand lacking a stopper for NT and lacking a better bid (i. e.,if the auction begins 1D-2C-2H, 2S is a convenient force over 2H if responder can't stop spades).Partner would be expected to bid NT with the right hand. A bid of 2S may also be a waiting bid, which may be followed by a delayed 3NT bid or a slam invitation at the 4-level.

In general, when the auction starts with 1D-2C and responder has an average game-forcing hand, the partners will aim for game in a major or 3NT. They will show their major if they have one, and then show stoppers in the side suits or bid NT directly if no 8-card major fit is found. Minor-suit games will be bid only as a poor alternative choice, and slams will be rare.

Unless opener shows a big hand with a jump reverse into a major, a responder will usually need at least 18 HCP to make slam even a fairly reasonable proposition. On those rare occasions when one of the partners wants to explore for slam, he will first have to establish a game force and then use a bid of 4 of a minor to indicate slam ambitions and ask for keycards. Many may play that pulling 3NT to 4C or 4D will suggest a trump agreement and simultaneously serve as the partnership key-card-asking mechanism. Others may prefer Kickback or Redwood (using the next higher suit to ask for key cards) in that situation. I will leave it to each partnership to establish any sophisticated agreements they feel comfortable with.

Note- The "Moysian Fit" was named for long-time Bridge World editor Sonny Moyse, who conducted a decades long campaign extolling the virtues of the 4-3 fit.

"1D With Muscles" Continuations After a Jump to 3H or 3S

Since our default agreement is that a big reverse after a 1D-2C auction is shown by a jump rebid of 3H or 3S, we need to have some sensible continations which will allow responder to either sign off in game or suggest slam without getting too high. I will stipulate for the record that the room for intelligent bidding is rather limited. We will need two slightly different sets of bids: one to handle a jump to 3H and another compatible with a bid of 3S.

If opener's major is hearts, responder has a bit of leeway. He has three bids which are not slam suggestions. The two most obvious are 3NT and 4H. Responder can make a simple raise to 4H based on several factors. He may have 4-card support and minimum values for his 2C bid. He may have very weak 4-card support (ie. all small cards). His own club suit not be very solid, or he may have three small cards in opener's diamond suit, suggesting possible losers there. He may even just instinctively not like his hand for slam.

He may bid 3NT for any or all of the same reasons, plus one that is even more basic: He may lack 4-card heart support. His one flexible option is a bid of 3S. That bid may show uncertainty about a 3NT contract or it may be the beginning of a delayed slam try in hearts. It asks opener to bid 3NT with a stopper. If opener bids 3NT over 3S and responder then bids 4H, that is a slam invitation. He could have bid 4H directly with no slam interest.

To show slam interest in one of the minors after opener's reverse to 3H, responder makes a direct bid of 4C or 4D. This is forcing to 4NT or 5 of a minor. Opener can then use Redwood (the next higher suit) to ask for key cards.

When opener jumps to 3S over 2C, responder's choices are more limited; He must immediately bid 3NT or 4S if he thinks that is likely to be the best final contract. Direct bids of 4C, 4D, or 4H (showing spades) would be slam tries. Opener could then use the next free suit (any suit not being considered as trump) to ask for keycards or he could sign off in 4S or 4NT. Partnerships will probably want to work out their own agreements. A useful agreement might be to make 3NT forcing to 4NT. That would give opener a chance to make a delayed slam try in a minor by bidding 4C or 4D. If responder had any slam interest he could then cue bid an ace to show support. With continued disinterest he could try to sign off by rebidding 4NT or 5 of the minor suit in question:

Other Invitational and Game-Forcing Sequences

With no major, the bidding may be as simple as 1D-2NT (invitational) or 1D-3NT. With game-forcing values and a 4-card major, responder can choose one of three routes. Unless slam seems likely, he will check for a 4-4 major fit first. If 5-4-2-2, he can bid the major first, and then use the artificial 2D to get to game after a 1NT rebid, or simply jump to 3NT if no 4-4 major fit is found. If more distributional or very strong, he can bid 2C first, bid his major, and then bid a feature, showing a genuine second suit. This route would tend to suggest slam interest.

When responder has 6+ clubs anda 5-card major, he must bid 2C, 2 of the major, and then later rebid the major. This sequence merely shows opening values, not super strength.

Here are some hands that show those situations:

J.	♠ KQx	K.	♠ Kxx	L.	♠ KQ	M.	♠ x	N.	♠ x
	♥ KJxx		♥ AJ		♥ K109		♥ AKxx		♥ AJ9xx
	♦ x		♦ xx		♦ Ax		♦ KJx		♦ Q
	♣ AJxxx		♣ A10xxx		♣ QJxxx		♣ AK109xx		♣ AK109xx

With hand J, responder will start with a 1H bid and then force to game, probably 4H or 3NT. With no major, hand K is a simple jump to 2NT. Hand L is stronger, but slam is unlikely. A jump to 3NT is probably best. Hand M is a hand that can be shown by bidding 2C and then 2H or 3H. A later bid of 4D or a splinter to 4S (if space allows) will describe the hand beautifully. On hand N, a 2C bid followed by 2H and then a subsequent rebid of hearts would show the 6-5 distribution.

Invitational and Weaker One-Suited Hands

As previously mentioned, a 2C response does not promise the world's fair. We can use it to show two kinds of 1-suited hands with less than game-forcing values. One type is an invitational 11–12 HCP 1-suited hand thatwould offer a good shot at 3NT if opener has a decent fit. With this hand, we simply bid 2C and rebid 3C. The second type has long clubs with scattered stoppers, making it suitable to declare a NT contract. With this hand, we can bid 2C and rebid 2NT.

With either of these 1-suiters, some partnerships may want to require a certain minimum suit quality. Others may choose to leave it to the bidders' judgment. Opposite the invitational hand, the 1D opener can look at his fit in clubs and his chances of stopping the other three suits and either pass or try 3NT. A bid of 3NT should usually have at least a fair chance when responder has the 11–12-type hand.

Finally, we have the kind of problem hands we discussed earlier—those with long clubs that need to be played in the suit but lack the values for a 2C response to 1D. There is a simple solution, but it needs to be used judiciously. We will describe subpar hands (3–9 HCP) with 6+ (preferably 7) card club suits with an immediate jump to 3C. The bid should be used with careful consideration of vulnerability and suit quality. Trying it with Q9xxxx vulnerable is not recommended with a possibly homicidal partner.

Here are some examples of weak and invitational 1-suited hands with long clubs:

	O.	♠ x	P.	♠ Qx	Q.	♠ xx	R.	♠ x
		♥ Jxx		♥ xx		♥ xxx		♥ xx
		♦ Jxx		♦ KJx		♦ K		♦ J10xx
		♣ AK109xx		♣ KQ10xxx		♣ Q10xxxxxx		♣ QJ109xx

With hand O, responder should bid 2C and then follow up with 3C. If opener has Qx of clubs, 3NT is a good bet. With hand P, responder might bid 2C and then rebid 2NT or 3NT. With hand Q, he can make a weak jump to 3C, assuming reasonable vulnerability conditions. With R, a pass of 1D is probably best, though an adventurous 3C might work.

Inverted Diamond Raises of a 1D Opening

Diamond raises of a 1D opening are inverted. The 2D raise shows 10+ HCP and denies a 4-card major. It should usually guarantee a 5-card suit, but sometimes must be made with 4. The raise to 3D is a little more risky than in other systems, since opener may occasionally have only 1 diamond. It should show from 5–9 HCP and a 6-card suit, though a decent 5-card suit may do in a pinch. It is not a good idea to get too frisky with the 3D bid, especially when vulnerable. Better to pass 1D than to go for 800 versus an opponent's partscore.

After 1D-2D

An important area for partnership discussion is the meaning of opener's rebids after the inverted raise to 2D. A bid of 2H or 2S after 1D-2D shows good values in a normal 11–16 HCP hand and a stopper, not necessarily a suit. Those bids usually show 14–16 HCP. Because of our default agreements, we have no choice but to jump to 3H or 3S in order to show the big 17–20 HCP hand. The sequence 1D-2D-2NT shows the 12–13 weak NT opener but does not absolutely guarantee sure stoppers in both majors.

The sequence of 1D-2D-3D shows a minimum with at least 3, and probably 4, diamonds. It also hints strongly that opener's majors may have weaknesses. It is non-forcing, as is 2NT. The sequence should show values in both minors, and it is again non-forcing. It is often up to responder to place the contract in 3NT if he is the one with the major suits under control and better than a minimum response.

Here are some typical auctions:

A.	♠ Kx	♠ Axx	1D	2D (10+ HCP)
	♥ Kxx	♥ xxx	2NT (12–13 balanced)	P or 3NT
	♦ Axxx	♦ KQxxx		
	♣ Kxxx	♣ Qx		
B.	♠ x	♠ Kxx	1D	2D
	♥ KJxx	♥ Qxx	3D (minimum with	P
	♦ KQxx	♦ Axxxx	3+ diamonds)	
	♣ Axxx	♣ Jx		
C.	♠ AQx	♠ xx	1D	2D
	♥ x	♥ KQx	2S (stopper,14+HCP)	3NT
	♦ AQxx	♦ Kxxxx	P	
	♣ Kxxxx	♣ QJx		
D.	♠ x	♠ xxx	1D	2D
	♥ Axx	♥ Kx	3C (minors, extra values)	3H (stopper)
	♦ KQxxx	♦ Axxxx	4S (splinter)	4NT (RKCB)
	♣ AKxx	♣ QJx	5C (0 or 3 KC)	6D

1D-3D

The raise to 3D shows less than 10 HCP and a long diamond suit. Because the 1D bid may be short, responder should have a 6-card suit vulnerable and a decent 5-card suit non-vulnerable. It may sometimes be preferable to bid 1NT or pass, hoping to bid diamonds later, rather than commit to a 3D contract.

These are possible 3D responses:

E.	♠ x		F.	♠ xx		G.	♠ x
	♥ Qx			♥ xxx			♥ xx
	♦ QJxxxx			♦ KQJxxx			♥ KQ109x
	♣ xxxx			♣ xx			♣ xxxxx

Inverted raises do not apply in competition. The simple raise to 2D over an overcall or double is standard. A cuebid shows the good raise over an overcall. Over a double, 2NT and 3D are available as limit and preemptive raises.

This scheme is relatively simple and has proved quite effective over the years. If the reader does not belong to the Mad Scientist Fan Club, he may want to just accept these methods as the default choice for the system and skip the next few pages. If, however, the discovery of a new convention or treatment causes you to salivate uncontrollably like one of Pavlov's dogs, you may be open to the alternate suggestions I am about to propose.

Alternative 2-Level Response Schemes

Some say I just can't leave well enough alone. I prefer to think of myself as full of new ideas. My friends seem to agree. They're always telling me I'm full of it. At any rate, I have some additional unconventional ideas for 2-level and 3-level responses to a 1D opening.

These generally involve using jumps to 2H or 2S as artificial rather than natural strong or weak jump shifts. By either making them part of our minor suit response scheme or giving them a purely conventional meaning, we may be able to improve the accuracy of the basic structure we have just outlined in this chapter.

For instance, using a jump to 2 of a major to show a game-forcing minor 1-suiter could eliminate the need for a 2C responder to bid a feature in a major in order to establish a game force. A 2C response followed by 2NT or 3C would be invitational, and a 2C response followed by a 2H or 2S rebid would almost always guarantee 4 cards in the major. Conversely, using that bid to show an invitational 1-suiter would allow the 2C bidder to make a forcing 2NT or 3C rebid—essentially a 2/1 GF treatment. Both 1D-3C and 1D -3D would continue to be weak.

Another possibility is to use jumps in the majors to show weak 5-5+ hands. A sequence of 1D-2H could show both majors and 5–9 HCP, while 1D-2S could show both minors and the same range. With a normal 1D bid, opener would simply sign off in the best part score. With super fits or a "1D with muscles" hand, he could jump in one of responder's suits or complete his reverse. This treatment would make it easy to find the best fits on some hard-to-describe hands and would also have some preemptive value.

It would also be possible to combine elements of both ideas. The 1D-2H sequence could show the weak hand with both majors, while 1D-2S could show either an invitational or forcing single-suiter in either minor. Opener could bid 3C (pass/correct) or 2NT to find responder's suit. With 17–20 HCP, he could just complete his reverse at the 3-level, bid 3NT, or bid 4 of responder's suit.

The following brief outline of each of these ideas offers three possible schemes:

A.	1D	2H=	good 6+ card club suit (invitational or forcing)
		2S=	good 6+ card diamond suit (invitational or forcing)
B.	1D	2H=	5/5+ in majors, 5–9 HCP
		2S=	good 6+-card club or diamond suit (invitational or forcing); opener bids 2NT (game interest) or 3C (pass/correct) to find responder's suit.
C.	1D	2H=	5/5+ in majors, 5–9 HCP
		2S=	5/5+ in minors, 5–9 HCP

Of course, using one of these schemes means losing whatever natural meanings a pair has assigned to a jump to 2H or 2S. I have always used them as old-fashioned strong jump shifts. An immediate strong jump often makes a slam auction simpler. Others prefer a Precision-like treatment, with the jump essentially showing a weak 2-bid, 5–9 HCP, and a 6-card suit. Each pair will have to decide if it is worth losing the natural bid in order to use one of these treatments.

CHAPTER 2

Major Suit Openings and Responses

It is not necessary to spend a lot of time describing the 1H and 1S openings in this system. These bids are very much like those in any standard system, except that they are limited to a range of 11–16 HCP. An opening bid of 1H or 1S guarantees a 5-card suit. The only important departures from standard bidding occur in opener's first rebid. Jump bids at opener's second turn (whether in the same suit or in a second suit) show 15–16 HCP, not 17+.

The big differences in our approach to the majors comes with our response scheme. There we find many nonstandard treatments and conventions. Some of them are fairly radical departures from standard practice. Because of this, at the end of the section, I will direct the reader to a brief outline of a more conventional alternative set of bids that work quite well with the system. They just aren't as much fun.(See Appendix D.)

The first section will introduce what I have modestly labeled "Sartor 2/1" responses. We start with this because these bids include the weakest raise of opener's major along with new suit responses. We will then proceed to constructive raises, "Sartor Raises"(limit or better), "Sartor Jump Shifts"(don't ask), and splinters.

You may have noticed that I have attached my name to several of my personal brainstorms. There are two reasons for this. First, I don't think that conventions should only be named after the Jacobys and Bergens of the world. We nobodies should be able to grab a little notoriety too. Secondly, after you've gotten into a couple of them, you may conclude that nobody else would allow their name to be attached to such flights of fancy. Anyway, as I mentioned before, I have provided more standard alternatives for those who don't recognize pure genius when they see it.

Sartor 2/1 Responses

Sartor 2/1 responses actually involve the use of transfer responses to an opening bid of 1H or 1S. These are not ordinary transfers, however. They are two-way bids. A 2-level suit bid either shows the bid suit with at least game-invitational values or a weakish, non-forcing transfer into the next highest suit. The latter hands may be either a weak raise of opener's major or a 6-card or longer off-suit—the type of suit standard bidders try to escape into via the forcing NT.

For those of you who haven't just tossed the book into the fireplace, let me clarify with specific examples. A 2C response to 1S would show either a club suit and 10+HCP, as in old-fashioned Goren, or a weak hand with a 6+card diamond suit. Opener is expected to accept the transfer unless he has a very good suit of his own or two 5+ card majors. Responder will then pass in what figures to be a reasonable partscore contract or describe an invitational or game-forcing hand with a second bid.

This type of two-way bidding scheme is especially suited to a strong club system, because opener's hand is limited to a specific range. When responder drops the bidding by passing the transfer, there is almost no chance that he is missing a game. On the rare occasions that game is possible despite responder's weakness, opener will refuse the simple transfer and show his extra strength and/or distribution.

Probably the best way to start the discussion of this scheme is to provide a summary. Here are responder's possible bids after a 1H or 1S opening bid (note that Appendix C outlines possible special 1S and 1NT responses to 1H):

- **With fewer than 8 HCP and 3+ cards in opener's suit, bid 2 of the suit below opener's major** (1H/2D or 1S/2H)—This is the weakest type of major suit raise. Opener *must* accept this transfer except with a very exceptional maximum. Responder will always pass if he has the weak raise. Since opener must (with few exceptions) bid 2 of his major, responder can risk very weak preemptive raises when they seem appropriate.

- **With fewer than 8 HCP and 4+ cards in opener's suit, bid 3 of opener's suit** (1S/3S or 1H/3H)—The bid suggests but does not guarantee side shortness.

- **With 8–10 HCP and 3+ cards in opener's suit, bid 2 of opener's suit** (1S/2S or 1H/2H)—Opener can then use short- or long-suit game tries to explore for game. Constructive raises will be discussed in detail in a separate section.

- **With 11–12 HCP and 2 or 3 cards in opener's suit, bid 2 of responder's best minor, and then 2M, 2NT, or a raise to 3M**—The minor suit may be a real suit or a weak 6+ card holding in the suit above it. It is a strong suggestion that opener should bid that suit with any normal opening.(The exceptions are a very strong rebiddable suit of his own or a second 5-card major.) After opener accepts the transfer, responder can bid 2M with either 3 small trump or a doubleton honor. He also has the option of bidding 2NT. If the transfer was into opener's major, a raise to 3M shows the hand and guarantees 3-card support. If opener has only 5 trump and wants to check on responder's holding after a raise to 2M, he bids 2NT or a suit at the 3-level. Responder bids 3M to confirm 3-card support. As a side note, should responder hold the same hand with 3-card trump support including the A, K,or Q, he bids a forcing 1NT and then makes an invitational jump to 3M.

- **With 10+ HCP, 4+ cards in opener's suit**—There are two choices here: a Sartor Raise or a Sartor Jump Shift. The Sartor Raise covers hands from limit raises to slam tries. It is a sort of modified Jacoby 2NT. The Sartor Jump Shift can show a kind of mini-splinter with 9–11 HCP when it doesn't show an old-fashioned slam try. I will go over these two bids in detail in their own separate sections.

- **With 11–12 HCP and balanced distribution**—Bid a forcing 1NT. After opener's forced rebid, make an invitational bid of 2NT or an invitational single raise in either major.

- **With 13–16 HCP, 3+ cards in opener's suit, and no slam prospects**—Bid 4M directly. Another option would be to bid a good 5-card minor and jump to 3M if possible (or 4M if opener rebids his suit). This would allow opener to bid 3NT occasionally if he thought that would be the best spot. Sometimes it might even allow slam exploration based on a perfect fit. Of course, 1M-4M may also just be a traditional distributional raise with 5+ trumps. Appendix B outlines an alternative to the 1M-4M bid with the balanced 13–16 HCP hand.

- **With 13-16+ HCP, 1–3 cards in opener's suit, and no slam prospects**—Bid a forcing 1NT, then 3NT (or 4H if a 4/4 fit is uncovered).Remember the forcing NT can be used with 11–12 HCP hands to make invitational bids in NT or either major.

- **With 9–11 or 15+ HCP, 4+ cards in opener's suit, and shortness in a side suit**—Use a Sartor Jump Shift. This bid is used to divide splinter bids into distinct HCP ranges for more accuracy in slam bidding (see page 49-50).

- **With 12–14 HCP, 4+ cards in opener's suit, and shortness in a side suit**—Use a standard splinter bid. The splinter may be a direct jump to 3S, 4C, 4D, or 4H or a delayed double jump after the bid of a good side suit (refinement on pages 49-50).

- **With 16–17+ HCP, 4+ cards in opener's suit, and no short suit**—Bid a forcing 1NT and jump to four of a good side suit for a sort of Swiss type iraise.

- **With 17–18+ HCP, 2 cards in opener's suit**—Bid a direct 3NT.

- **With 19+–20 HCP, 2 cards in opener's suit**—Bid a forcing 1NT, then 4NT.

- **With 17+HCP and unbalanced hand**—Make a Sartor Jump Shift (the strong natural part of a three-way bid; see pages 49-50) Your next bid will indicate a strong one-suited hand.

These bids form what I hope is a pretty seamless overall scheme. In some cases, the description in the outline is sufficient to play the system. Some bids require a more detailed discussion, however. I'll use the next few sections to go into more detail on some of the bids listed above. I'll start by revisiting two-way transfers, which form the underpinning of Sartor 2/1.

Two-Way Transfer 2/1 (Sartor 2/1)

The system's most obvious deviation from standard bidding is the set of bids I have labeled Sartor 2/1. As I outlined on pages 32–34, these bids allow responder to describe hands that range from anemic to slam-worthy. The most unorthodox feature of these bids is the use of what I have termed "two-way transfers." These were not created just for the sake of novelty. They allow responder to bid some weak hands that are handled awkwardly in standard and 2/1 bidding. They also allow both invitational and game-forcing sequences.

The reason these bids can work is because the opening 1H or 1S bidder is limited to 16 HCP. When a 2-level response is made to a major suit opening, the opener knows that he is in no danger of missing game if it is a weak bid. With any ordinary 1H or 1S bid, he can confidently accept the transfer to a new suit if he has any tolerance for it at all. He can be confident he will be playing in a reasonable contract, even though it may be based on a 6-1 trump fit. If the transfer is into his own suit, he *must* accept the transfer, because responder is often trying to set the final contract at 2 of opener's suit while also shutting out the opponents. The exceptions might be a jump acceptance or the bid of a second suit with extraordinary distribution.

Should the responder's bid be based on a better hand, he will always get a chance to make a second bid to make his intentions clear. He can then make a game-invitational or game-forcing second bid. In effect, these sequences mimic the standard responses that most players use when partner opens 1NT, though there are a couple of major differences.

The clearest difference, and the one that will probably cause ACBL directors apoplexy if you try to use this system in any event short of the Vanderbilt or the Reisinger, is that the transfers do not always show the next highest suit. They may actually show the bid suit and a good hand.

Specifically, a response of 2C shows either a weak hand with long diamonds or a good hand with a club suit or at least club values. A response of 2D to 1S shows a weak hand with 6+ hearts or a good hand with diamonds. If the opening was 1H, then the weak option is a transfer back to hearts—a weak raise of the suit. A 2H response to a 1S opening shows the weak spade raise or good hearts.

A minor glitch in the system is that there is no way to make a definite transfer into clubs (see Appendix C for a partial solution). The best we can do is to use the standard forcing NT with some slightly nonstandard responses. Opener bids 2C any time he has nothing special to show—no 6-card major or 4+-card side heart or diamond suit. If responder has a weak hand with long clubs, he may be able to pass opener in a 2C contract. I'll outline more forcing NT sequences in a little while.

Assuming opener bids the next higher suit after a 2-level response (in effect accepting a transfer), responder can then pass, make an invitational or game-forcing raise of opener's major, or even bid a new suit to create a game-forcing auction and perhaps explore slam possibilities. He can also bid an invitational 2NT or make a forcing rebid of his own suit. Probably the best way to continue the description of the entire scheme is to go through actual auctions using the 1NT, 2C, 2D, and 2H responses.

First, we'll take a brief detour as I give a few more details about the system's various uses of the forcing NT, as promised.

I have tried to blend the standard forcing NT into my system of transfer responses. As I already mentioned, I use 2C as a kind of default rebid for the opening bidder. Opener will rebid 2C unless he has a decent 6-card major, a 4+-card side heart suit, or a decent 4+ card diamond suit. Responder may pass with long clubs and a weak hand or raise to 3C, 2NT, or 3S with an invitational hand. He may also make an invitational raise of opener's 2D, 2H, or 2S second bid to 3D, 3H, or 3S. Beyond those fairly mundane options, the forcing NT is also used for several types of strong hands (refer to page 28). These include raises to game, slam invitational Swiss Raises of opener's suit, and slam-invitational bids in NT.

Now let's go through some illustrative auctions. In all of the first group, opener bids 1S. We'll start with a forcing NT and proceed on to 2C, 2D, and 2H responses. I won't try to give every possible variation, but I'll illustrate the variety of hands responder may have.

1S-1NT

1S	1NT	opener does not have 6 spades, 4 hearts, or 4 good diamonds
2C	P	responder has a weak hand with 6+ clubs
1S	1NT	opener has at least 4 decent diamonds/4 hearts
2D or 2H	P	responder chooses to play in the second suit (hand unclear) with better values, he could invite or jump to the 4 level
1S	1NT	opener has 6+ spades
2S	P	responder could raise to 3S or 4S with better values
1S	1NT	
2X	2NT	responder has 11–12 HCP, balanced
1S	1NT	
2X	3S	responder has a balanced 3-card limit raise (11–12 HCP)
2C/2D/2H	3C/3D/3H	responder has an invitational hand with at least 5 clubs, 4 diamonds, or 4 hearts (with a good 6-card suit he may bid 1NT and then jump to 3D or 3H directly over 2C or 2D)
1S	1NT	
2X	3NT, 4NT	responder has a balanced slam invitation
4C,4D,4H		responder has a balanced slam invitational raise in spades with strength in the bid suit

Special Situations Involving 1S-1NT

This special sequence can help find a heart fit after a 1S opening. Since responder would bid a direct 2C to show a weak hand with 6+ diamonds and would bid a direct 2D to show a weak hand with 6+ hearts, a delayed bid of these two suits after a forcing NT can be used as a way to find a better fit when responder has exactly 5 hearts. After a 1S-1NT-2C sequence, a bid of 2D shows a 5-card heart suit with 0-1 spades, while 2H shows a 5-card heart suit with exactly 2 spades. This serves the same purpose as the BART convention, which could certainly be used as an alternative here.

1S-2C

1S	2C	opener has nothing special and is willing to play 2D
2D	P	responder has a weak hand with 6+ diamonds
1S	2C	opener is willing to play 2D if responder has 6 diamonds
2D	2S	responder has good clubs, xxx or Hx in spades, 11–12 HCP
1S	2C	
2D	2NT	responder has good clubs, 0–2 spades, 11-12 HCP
1S	2C	a rebid of responder's suit can be treated as forcing to 3NT
2D	3D	or 4 of a minor-.He could invite with a 2H(1-round force),2S, or 2NT rebid here, or start with a forcing NT to show an invitational 1-suiter*
1S	2C	
2D	3S	responder has good clubs and forcing 3-card raise

---

*An alternative would be to use 3C as an artificial checkback bid. Opener could bid 3H with 3-card support, 3S with a 6+card card suit, and 3D with neither.

Many of the same continuations apply after 1S-2D.

1S-2D

| 1S | 2D | opener is willing to play 2H if responder has 6 hearts |
| 2H | P | responder has a weak hand with 6+ hearts |

| 1S | 2D | |
| 2H | 2S | responder has good diamonds, 11–12 HCP, and Hx or xxx in spades |

| 1S | 2D | |
| 2H | 2NT | responder has good diamonds, 11–12 HCP, and 0–2 spades |

| 1S | 2D | |
| 2H | 3S | responder has good diamonds and a forcing 3-card raise of spades |

| 1S | 2D | |
| 2H | 3D | responder has 6+ diamonds; the auction is forcing to 3NT or 4 of a minor |

Special Situation Involving 1S-2D

When responder bids 2D, it is possible that there is a game for us even when all he has is the weak hand with 6+ hearts. Therefore, he can't just meekly accept the relay to 2H when he has good hearts and/or extra values. He can use two special rebids to indicate good hearts and a non-minimum.

A bid of 2NT shows 3 good hearts and extra values. If responder has 6 hearts, he can retransfer with 3D or 4D. A jump to 3H (rather than a simple acceptance of the transfer) shows a 4-card suit and extra strength. If responder has hearts, he can pass or bid 4H. When responder really has diamonds and at least invitational values, he can always bid 3S or 3NT.

1S-2H

The 2H response to 1S is different from the minor-suit responses in one major respect. It is still a two-way bid. It may show a real heart suit and at least 11 HCP or serve as a relay to the next suit- spades. However, that relay is obviously not going to show a 6-card spade suit. I'm sure anyone with 6 or 7 spades opposite a 1S opener will be able to figure out some other sort of spade raise. When the 2H bidder has a spade raise, it will be a weak raise (0–7 HCP) not suitable for a preemptive jump. This allows us to make a bid that has at least some preemptive value without getting too high.

It may also allow us to exercise a little creativity. It might occur to certain devious types to make the bid with a doubleton, 7–8 HCP, and good side suit holdings in hopes of luring a vulnerable opponent into a rash balance at the 3 level. But we can't get too frisky if partner might bid a new suit at the 3-level himself.

In order to make sure that partner doesn't do anything rash, we need a firm rule:*opener must accept the relay unless he has really extraordinary distribution*. Our basic premise is that there will rarely be a game when opener has any ordinary sort of limited (maximum of 16 HCP) 1S opener opposite a weak raise. He can safely pass 2S without worrying about missing game. With a great hand and a solid suit, he may occasionally super-accept by bidding 2NT or 3S. With a big 2-suiter, he might be justified in bidding 3 of another suit. But 98 percent of the time, the auction will go 1S-2H-2S-P.

When responder actually has a heart suit, the auction will proceed similarly to those which follow 1S-2C or 1S-2D, with one exception:a response of 2H followed by a rebid of 3H is merely invitational, showing 6+ hearts and 11–12 HCP. With a forcing hand, responder can rebid 3C or 3D, showing a real heart suit and forcing to 3NT or 4 of the minor. That allows the opener to show 3+ card heart support or a 6+ card spade suit. A jump to 4S is a mild slam try, since responder could have just jumped to 4S to begin with.

| 1S | 2H | 2H forces opener to bid 2S in most cases |
| 2S | P | responder has a weak (0–7 HCP) spade raise |

| 1S | 2H | |
| 2S | 3S | responder has a heart suit, 3+ spades, and 11–12 HCP |

| 1S | 2H | |
| 2S | 3H | responder has a 6+ cardheart suit and 11–12 HCP |

1S	2H	
2S	3C or	responder has a heart suit, forcing values, and wants
	3D	opener to bid 3H, 3S, or 3NT if he can

Alternatively

1S	2H	
2S	3C (artificial checkback) responder has 5+ hearts, forcing values*
3D, 3H, 3S	see above	

1H-1NT

The sequences after 1H-1NT are essentially the same as those after 1S-1NT, with a couple of necessary adjustments. First, 1H-2C can show a weak hand with a long diamond suit, so 1H-1NT-2C-2D is available for another purpose. So is 1H-1NT-2C or 2D-2S, since responder would have bid 1S in response to 1H if he had a 4-card spade suit. My suggestion is that both 2D and 2S be used to show a need for a stopper in a hand that would otherwise qualify for a 2NT bid. Many use it as an "impossible" raise of opener's minor. Beyond those exceptions, both partners' rebids are familiar. Here are some example auctions:

| 1H | 1NT | opener doesn't have 6 hearts or 4+ diamonds |
| 2C (default) | 2NT | responder has 0–2 hearts, 11–12 HCP |

| 1H | 1NT | |
| 2C | 3H | balanced limit raise |

The following sequences are similar to those after 1S-2C:

1H	2C	
2D (default)	P	responder has a weak hand with 6+ diamonds

1H	2C	
2D	2H	responder has good clubs, Hx or xxx in hearts, 11–12 HCP

1H	2C	
2D	2S	responder has 11+ HCP, good clubs, and 4 spades or a spade stopper, searching for 3NT, 4S, or another game

A rebid of 3D and all new suit bids after this sort of sequence are forcing to 3NT or 4 of a minor. Responder may even be trying for slam.

1H-2D

The 2D response to 1H, just like the 2C response, begins many invitational and forcing sequences like the ones discussed in previous sections. With those hands, responder shows a good diamond suit and 11+ HCP. The 2D bid may also be a weak raise of hearts. Opener is required to accept the relay and bid 2H unless he has an extraordinary hand. Responder will pass with a weak raise. We can now consider better raises.

Constructive Raises (7+/ 8 – 10 HCP)

What about those 8–10 HCP hands (7 HCP hands with 4 trump and side shortness also qualify) that may produce game opposite a good major suit opener? For those hands, we use constructive raises with short- and long-suit game tries.

When responder raises opener's 1H or 1S directly to 2 of that suit, opener may want to try for game with a 15 or 16 HCP hand, or even a very shapely 13 or 14. He does so in one of two ways. If opener bids the next higher denomination, he is beginning a relay to a long-suit game try. If responder has a singleton or void, however, he may skip the relay and bid his short suit directly.

Assuming the relay is accepted, opener bids a suit of 3 or more cards where help is needed. If opener bids any of the denominations above the long-suit relay bid, that is a short-suit game try. Responder will usually accept opener's relay by bidding the next higher denomination. If he skips over that bid and bids one of the next three denominations, he is making a short suit game try of his own.

To clarify the last paragraph, the following is an outline of constructive raises:

Opener	Responder
1S	2S (7+/ 8-10 HCP)
2NT-long suit relay to 3C, then	3C-accepts 2NT relay
3D, 3H, or 3S (clubs) are	
long suit game tries (no singleton)	

If opener has a singleton

If responder has a singleton
Alternate Second Response
(bypassing relay to 3C)

Direct Short Suit
Try(bypassing 2NT)
3C=singleton club   3D=singleton diamond
3D=singleton diamond   3H=singleton heart
3H=singleton heart   3S=singleton club (relay suit)

The auction 1S-2S-3S is not defined. It is unlikely to be needed as a preemptive bid. Perhaps it would be best used to describe a maximum hand with a very weak trump suit.

Here is the scheme for hearts:

Opener		*Responder*
1H		2H (7+/8-10 HCP)
2S	long suit relay to 2NT, to be followed by 3C, 3C or 3H (no singleton) (3H=spades)	2NT-accepts 2S relay
		Direct Short Suit Try
Direct Short Suit Try		(bypassing relay to 2NT)
2NT- shows a singleton spade		3C=singleton club
(spades is the relay suit)		3D=singleton diamond
3C-singleton club		3H=singleton spade (relay suit)
3D-singleton diamond		

Again, to recap: if opener makes the cheapest bid over a single constructive major suit raise, he denies a singleton and wants to make a long-suit game try. Any other bid up to 3 of the trump suit is a short-suit game suit try, including 2NT, which shows short spades in a heart auction.

Here are some constructive raise auctions:

A.

♠ AKJxx	♠ Qxxx	1S	2S (7+/8–10 HCP)
♥ Axx	♥ xx	2NT(relay)	3C (accepting relay)
♦ xx	♦ xxx	3S (asking for	4S (I've got great help)
♣ KJx	♣ AQxx	help in clubs)	

B.

♠ AKJxx	♠ Qxxx	1S	2S
♥ Axx	♥ x	2NT	3H (ignoring relay-shows
♦ xx	♦ KJxxx		0-1 heart)
♣ KJx	♣ Qxx	4S	P

C.

♠ AKJxx	♠ Qxxx	1S	2S
♥ Axx	♥ Qxx	2NT	3S (stands for club
♦ xx	♦ KJxxx	P-(club singleton not	singleton-the relay suit)
♣ KJx	♣ x	helpful)	

D.

♠ x	♠ xxx	1H	2H
♥ AQxxx	♥ Jxxx	2NT (bypassing 2S	4H (perfect spade
♦ KJxx	♦ Ax	relay-shows singleton spade)	holding)
♣ AJx	♣ Kxxx	P	

E.

♠ xx	♠ QJx	1H	2H
♥AQxxx	♥ Jxxx	P (not maximum, no sin-	
♦ KJxx	♦ Ax	gleton, may just decide to	
♣ AJx	♣ xxxx	"protect the plus" at MP) or	
		2S, then 3C (LSGT if vul-	
		nerable at IMPS)	

Don't forget that if you have a standard raise to 2 of a major with less than 8 HCP, you must use the "suit under" Sartor 2/1 transfer; 1S-2H includes the weak raise in spades, and 1H-2D includes the weak raise in hearts. This actually can be used as a semi-psychic bid, since opener is not allowed to refuse the transfer without a very unusual hand. You can make the bid with 0 HCP if you think it might steal a contract or confuse the opponents. Against vulnerable opponents, you might do it with 7 HCP and a doubleton in partner's suit, hoping to get a shot at doubling a 3-level balance. In the hands of someone with a devious mind like mine, this bid could be a lot of fun.

Sartor Raises and Assorted Brainstorms

If this book is going to be a best seller, it needs either sex or controversy. I'm sure you've noticed how sexy the first few sections are, so let's try for controversy. How about this: **in a strong club system, the limit raise in a major suit is one of the most useless bids in bridge**, **at least in terms of accurate evaluation of game prospects**.(only my opinion, of course)

How do I reach this conclusion, which is obviously not in line with the common wisdom? Let's look at some typical 1-spade openers, all limited to no more than 16 HCP.

A.	♠ AQxxx	B.	♠ KQxxx	C.	♠ AKQxx
	♥ Kxx		♥ x		♥ xx
	♦ xxx		♦ AQxx		♦ Jx
	♣ Ax		♣ Qxx		♣ Kxxx

All of these hands have 13 HCP. All are perfectly good 1-spade openings. All have one thing in common:it is a pure guess whether they will make 4 spades opposite a limit raise to 3S.

If the responding hand has a singleton diamond, hand A is likely to make game. If it has key honors in clubs and not much in hearts, hand B will probably take 10 tricks. Shortness in either red suit or a good fit in clubs would be nice on hand C. In practice, the average aggressive player will probably close his eyes, rub his rabbit's foot, and bid game on all three. On a good day, he may make all of them. On a bad day, he can blame three minus scores on his partner's lousy limit raises. Unfortunately, once partner bids 3 spades, it's a little late to get a detailed description of his hand.

Which brings me to the point of this discussion. There is a much better way to raise partner's major suit opener. It is especially useful when opener's hand is specifically limited to a range of 11–16 HCP, but it could also be adapted to any standard system.

Some of the raises I'm about to outline are basically modifications of the Jacoby 2NT and standard jump shifts. My contribution is merely to alter them so that they can cover hands with limit raise values. Along with the 2/1 responses already outlined in a previous section, they form a cohesive, if slightly offbeat, response scheme for major-suit openings.

I needed a snappy label for these bids, and for some reason, the names Sartor 2/1, Sartor Raises, and Sartor Jump Shifts seem to roll off the tongue.(Heck, if Marty Bergen and Oswald Jacoby can get their names on bids, why can't I?) So henceforth, I will refer to our set of major suit responses by those names. We will combine them with a forcing 1NT, constructive single raises, and splinter bids to form a comprehensive set of responses to major suit openings.

To be even more specific,, a Sartor Raise is a jump in the denomination just above opener's major. That is, a jump to 2NT in response to a 1S opening bid is a Sartor Raise, just as with a Jacoby 2NT. But the Sartor Raise over 1H is 2S. This seemingly minor difference allows for one more descriptive bid than would be possible in a 1H-2NT auction. The 2NT jump in response to 1H is simply switched to mean a jump shift in spades.

The Sartor Raise, unlike the Jacoby 2NT, promises only limit raise values (11+HCP). But it can be a very strong hand with slam ambitions. It allows both responder and opener to take part in the decision to go to game or slam. First, opener describes his hand. Responder can then bid game, sign off at 3 of opener's suit, or make a descriptive bid of his own. If game is bid, it will not be based solely on guesswork as with a standard limit raise. Here is the scheme:

Opener	Responder
1S	2NT (Sartor Raise)

Opener's rebid options:
- 3C-minimum, balanced, or minimum with a second 5-card suit.
- 3D-singleton diamond
- 3H-singleton heart
- 3S-singleton club (because 3C conventionally shows minimum hands)
- 3NT-maximum, balanced
- 4C- a 5-card club suit, 14+ to 16 HCP (a non-minimum hand)
- 4D- a 5-card diamond suit, 14+ to 16 HCP (a non-minimum hand)
- 4H-a 5-card heart suit, 14+ to 16 HCP (a non-minimum hand)
- 4S- a minimum hand with a very long spade suit

After a 3C rebid by opener, responder can sign off at 3S or probe further by bidding 3D or 3H, showing side strength in one of those suits. With the balanced minimum hand, opener will bid 3S—or 4S if responder's probe has helped his hand. With the 5-5 hand, opener can bid his second suit at the 4 level over any 3-level bid by responder.

An alternative would be for opener to simply show his singleton when holding a minimum hand with a second 5-card suit. With only 11–13 HCP, it may not be wise to go to the 4-level unless the responder likes the singleton response. After a singleton response, responder can bid 3S to show a non-fitting minimum, bid game, or show a feature, still probing for game or slam. The rebids after a 1H-2S auction are basically the same, with 2NT bids showing the balanced hands.

Opener	Responder
1H	2S (Sartor Raise)

Opener's rebid options:
- 2NT-minimum, balanced, or a minimum with a second 5-card suit
- 3C-singleton club
- 3D-singleton diamond
- 3H-singleton spade (because 2S and 3S are not available to show short spades)
- 3S-maximum, balanced
- 3NT- an extra bid, since a 5-card spade suit is unlikely (possibly best used for a solid heart suit)
- 4C- a 5-card club suit, 14+ to 16 HCP (a non-minimum hand)
- 4D- a 5-card diamond suit, 14+ to 16 HCP (a non-minimum hand)
- 4H- a minimum hand with a very long heart suit

Follow-up bids after opener's 2NT and singleton rebids follow the same pattern as those following the 1S-2NT options. Don't forget the two big differences:

- 1H-2S= a heart raise
  2NT= a minimum balanced hand or a minimum with a 5-card side suit
- 1H-2NT= a jump shift in spades (the 2S and 2NT bids just switch meanings)

Cue Bidding After a Sartor Raise

After responder has made a Sartor Raise, he can initiate a cue-bidding sequence in search of a possible slam. This can occur whether opener shows a singleton, a balanced minimum, or a balanced maximum.

In order to facilitate these sequences, we will adopt a modified version of Marty Bergen's "moving along" 3NT bid. We will only use the bid to initiate a search for aces, rather than cue bidding both aces and kings. We will use the "moving along" 3NT bid over 1S-2NT sequences. When the bidding goes 1H-2S, 3 spades will be the bid if it is available. Essentially, we will use the cheapest available bid above 3 of the trump suit.

For example, on the sequence 1S-2NT-3D (singleton), 3NT would indicate slam interest and ask opener to cue bid his cheapest ace. A cue bid of the singleton could be used to ask for controls or aces, depending on partnership agreement. On the sequence 1H-2S-2NT (minimum balanced), 3S would serve as the slam invitation. Opener's 3NT would then show the spade ace.

Should opener show a balanced maximum, one alteration is necessary. Over 1H-2S-3S (balanced maximum), 3NT is still available. However, over 1S-2N-3N, responder will simply have to bid his cheapest ace at the 4 level.

In Bergen's original version, the 3NT bid was not only a slam signal but also denied club control. Otherwise, 4C showed club control and 4D showed both diamond and club control. Since we are showing only aces, not kings, this may not be necessary. Each partnership can develop its own variations.

Here are some sample auctions:

	Opener	Responder		
A.	♠AQxxx	♠ Kxxx	1S	2NT (Sartor Raise)
	♥Kx	♥Axx	3C (balanced minimum)	3H (feature)
	♦Kxxx	♦ xx	4S (not ironclad,	
	♣xx	♣ KJxx	but reasonable)	
B.	♠ KQxxx	♠ Jxxx	1S	2NT
	♥ x	♥ AKxxx	3H (singleton)	4S (responder might
	♦ AQxx	♦ Kxx		have bid an immediate
	♣ Kxx	♣ x		4S, but had mild slam
				hopes)
C.	♠ AQxxx	♠ Kxxx	1S	2NT
	♥ x	♥ xx	3H	4C
	♦ AQxx	♦ Kxxxx	4D	4NT (RKCB)
	♣ Kxx	♣ Ax	5S (2 KC+Q)	6S

D.	♠Jx	♠ Qx	1H	2S (Sartor Raise)
	♥AQxxx	♥ xxxx	2NT (balanced minimum)	3C (feature)
	♦Jxx	♦ KQxx	3H (no D feature)	P
	♣KQJ	♣ Axx		

E.	♠ xxx	♠ Axx	1H	2S
	♥ AJxxx	♥ KQxxx	3C (0-1 C)	3S (cue)
	♦ AQxxx	♦ Kx	4C (void)	4NT (RKCB)
	♣	♣ xxx	5H	5NT
			6C	6H

F.	♠ KQx	♠ x	1H	2S (3S could work))
	♥ AJ10xxx	♥ Kxxx	3S (balanced maximum)	3NT (bid cheapest ace)
	♦ Kx	♦ Axx	4H	5C
	♣ Kx	♣ Axxxx	5D	6H

With the Sartor Raise covering everything from a limit raise to a slam try, the raise to three of a major can be used as a preempt. For example, this annoying hand can be bid intelligently:

G.	♠AQxxx	♠ KJxxx	1S	3S
	♥xx	♥ Jx	P	
	♦Kxxx	♦ xx		
	♣Kx	♣ xxxx		

With luck, the opponents may never enter the auction with 4 hearts cold for their side.

Sartor Three-Way Jump Shifts

For those who like to play Bergen Raises, I have come up with a diabolically clever way to have all the benefits of strong jump shifts and be able to make use of a quasi-Bergen raise. In conjunction with the already explained Sartor Raises, it covers all of the 4-card-limit raise hands that a Bergen 3D bid would encompass. The weaker 4-card raises can be handled by the jump to 3 of opener's major or the constructive raise to 2H or 2S.

As a bonus, this scheme can even cover a big splinter bid without unduly straining the structure or your partner's memory. We thus gain the benefit of being able to describe standard splinters of two different strengths: 12–14 and 15+HCP.

The idea is simple: a jump shift in response to a major suit opening shows either a strong jump shift, a strong splinter bid (15+ HCP), or a mini-splinter (the type of hand that would be shown by a Bergen 3D bid), but with a specific singleton. (Good 4-card raises without singletons are shown by a Sartor raise.) To clarify, if the jump is in spades, it will either show a raise with short spades or a strong hand with long, strong spades. If the jump is is in clubs, diamonds, or hearts, the same principle applies It will either show shortness or a strong jump shift in the bid suit. Opener asks which hand responder holds with the cheapest practical suit or NT bid. If the cheapest bid is the trump suit, then it is the asking bid only with a minimum hand. If the opener is willing to accept game opposite a mini-splinter, he asks with the next higher bid.

The answers follow a few simple rules, as follows:

1. The cheapest bid of opener's major at responder's second turn sets that suit as trump and shows the mini-splinter (9–11 HCP and 4+ trump).
2. If the asking bid is too high to allow an answer of 3 opener's suit, then bidding 4 of the agreed-upon major shows the mini-splinter.
3. A jump in the agreed-upon trump suit at the 4-level or a bid of 4 of the suit in which responder first jumped shows the 15+ HCP splinter bid. The rebid in the splinter suit is used only when lack of bidding room forces responder to use 4 of the opener's major to show the mini-splinter (see rule 2).
4. The bid of the cheapest side suit or 3NT in response to opener's inquiry shows the strong jump shift.
5. If the opening bid is 1H, then 2NT is the jump shift in spades. 2S would be a Sartor raise.

One further mandate applies: the jump shift will only be a single-suited hand with at least a semi-solid 6+-card suit (such as AKJ10xx or KQJ10xxx).Other types- big balanced hands or those with a fit with opener's suit—will be described in other ways. We'll discuss those in the section on "Other Routes to Slam."

The following is the three-way jump shift scheme:

1H-   **2NT** (singleton spade, 9–11 or 15+HCP, OR 17+HCP and a strong spade suit)

3C (asking) **3D=(17+HCP,** spade jump shift)

3H (a return to the trump suit) = singleton spade,4+ hearts,9–11 HCP

4H = singleton spade, 4+ hearts, 15+HCP

1H   **3C** (singleton club, 9–11 or 15+HCP, or 17+HCP, strong club suit)

3D (asking) **3H** = singleton club, 4+hearts, 9–11 HCP

3S= strong jump shift in clubs, 17+HCP

4H = singleton club, 4+ hearts, 15+ HCP

1H   **3D** (singleton diamond, 9–11 or 15+ HCP, or 17+ HCP, strong diamond suit

3H (asking, minimum) (willing to be passed opposite a mini-splinter)

Pass = singleton diamond, 4+hearts, 9–11 HCP

3S= strong jump shift in diamonds, 17+HCP

4H = singleton diamond, 4+ hearts, 15+ HCP

1S   **3C** (singleton club, 9–11 or 15+ HCP, strong jump shift in clubs)

3D asking) **3H** –strong jump shift in clubs, 17+ HCP

3S – singleton club, 4+ spades, 9-11 HCP

4S- singleton club, 4+ spades, 15+ HCP

1S   **3D** (singleton diamond, 9–11 or 15+ HCP, or 17+ HCP, diamond suit)

3H (asking) **3S** =singleton diamond, 4+ spades, 9–11 HCP

3NT= 17+ HCP, strong jump shift in diamonds

4S =singleton diamond, 4+ spades, 15+ HCP

1S   **3H**

3S (asking-willing to be passed if responder has mini-splinter)

P =singleton heart, 4+ spades, 9–11 HCP

3NT=17+HCP, strong jump shift in hearts

4S =singleton heart, 4+ spades, 15+ HCP

3NT (asking-will accept game even if responder has a mini-splinter)
        4C= 17+ HCP, strong jump shift in hearts*
        4H=singleton heart, 4+ spades, 15+ HCP*
        4S=singleton heart, 4+ spades, 9-11 HCP*

Here are some example hands:

A.   ♠AKxxx   ♠Qxxx   1S   3H*
     ♥xxx   ♥x3   3NT (good ask)   4C (9-11 HCP, 4-1-4-4)
     ♦Axx   ♦K10xx   4D (cue-ace)   5C (cue-ace)
     ♣Kx   ♣ AQxx   6S

B.   ♠AKx   ♠x   1H   2NT*
     ♥K10xxx ♥AQxx   3C (ask)   4H (15+HCP, 1-4-4-4)
     ♦xx   ♦KQxx   4NT   5S (2KC+Q)
     ♣Kxx   ♣AQxx   6H

C.   ♠ Kxx   ♠Ax   1H   3D*
     ♥ AQxxx ♥ x   3H (weak ask)   3S (ace, diamond suit, 17+)
     ♦ Kxx   ♦ AQJ10xx 4D (fit, keycard) 4NT (RKCB)
     ♣ xx   ♣ AKxx   5H   5NT
                    6D (Kof D already shown) 7D

D.   ♠ AJ10xxx ♠ Qxxx 1S   3C*
     ♥ Qxx   ♥ KJxx   3D (ask)   3S (9–11, Singleton club)
     ♦ Qxx   ♦ KJxx   4S (a coin flip)
     ♣ Qx   ♣ x

Though all of my 9–11 HCP examples show 4-4-4-1 distribution, there might be some 5-4-3-1 hands that could be bid with this convention, especially if the 5-card suit is the suit partner opened.

Direct Splinter Bids

As we have seen, responder can describe hands with 4-card trump support, a singleton, and 9–11 HCP or 15+HCP by using the three-way jump shift. Hands between those two ranges (12+ to 14 HCP) are shown by direct splinter bids. These hands are all good direct splinter responses to a 1S or 1H opener:

A. ♠ Kxxx (1S-4D)   B. ♠ AJxx (1S-4H)   C. ♠ QJxxx (1S-4C)
   ♥ AQxx   ♥ x   ♥ AKx
   ♦ x   ♦ KJ10xx   ♦ Axxx
   ♣KJxx   ♣ AQx   ♣ x

D. ♠ KQx (1H-4D)   E. ♠ x (1H-3S)   F. ♠ AJxxx (1H-4C)
   ♥ KQxx   ♥ J10xxx   ♥ KQxx
   ♦ x   ♦ AKJ   ♦ QJx
   ♣ A109xx   ♣ KQxx   ♣ x

Other Routes to Slam

Delayed Splinters/Jumps to Game

Besides the strong jump shift, dual-level splinter bids, and standard splinters outlined in the last section, responder has several other ways to explore for slam after an opening 1H or 1S. These include extensions of auctions using a Sartor Raise; forcing new-suit rebids after a Sartor 2/1; delayed splinters and same-suit jumps to the 4-level; and one specific jump to 4 of opener's major. Remember that in many cases where a trump fit has been found and responder sees no reasonable prospect of slam opposite a limited opening bid, he may simply jump to game. When he decides to go through a more complicated description of his hand and then winds up bidding game in opener's suit, it implies at least some interest in bigger things.

One method is simply to bid out his shape. If responder makes a 2/1 response, bids a new suit, and then bids 4 of opener's major, he is making a mild slam try and implying 5-4-3-1 distribution with 3-card trump support. With the same distribution and 4-card support, he can make a 2/1 response and jump to a new suit at the 3 or 4-level-a delayed splinter bid. With 5-4-2-2 distribution, he can make a 2/1 bid and jump to game in the major. This is a picture bid, showing excellent values in the side suit and 4 good trumps but no outside controls.

Similarly, with 6-3-3-1 or 6-3-2-2 distribution and a very good minor suit, responder can bid his suit, bid a feature, and then splinter or bid 4 of opener's suit. He can also make a jump rebid in his own suit, showing 6-3-2-2 or 7-2-2-2 distribution, good trump, and no outside controls—another picture bid. Opener can evaluate his hand after one of these auctions and either cue bid a control or sign off in game.

Here are some possible auctions:

A.	♠ AQ10xx	♠ KJx	1S	2D (either real diamonds or)
	♥ xxx	♥ x		6+hearts
	♦ Kxx	♦ AQxxx	2H (accept if hearts)	3C (5+ diamonds/4+clubs)
	♣ KQ	♣ Axxx	3D (natural.)	3S (3 spades, thus short
				hearts)
			4C (control)	4D (control)
			4S	4NT (RKCB)
			5C (if 1430)	5D (Q ask)
			6D (Q of S, K of D)	6S

B.	♠ Kx	♠ AJxx	1H	2C
	♥ KQxxxx	♥ Axx	2D (accepting	
			diamonds)	2S
	♦ AJx	♦ x	2NT	4H (4-3-1-5)
	♣ Jx	♣ KQ10xx	4NT	5H
			6H	

(Another possibility, if responder is the aggressive type:1H- 4NT-5S-6H)

C.	♠ x	♠ Qxx	1H	2D
	♥AQxxxx	♥ Kxx	2H (forced)	3C (GF)
	♦ Kxx	♦ AQJxxx	3H	4H
	♣ Axx	♣ x	4NT	5H
			6H	

D. ♠ QJ10xx   ♠ AKxx   1S   2D
    ♥ Ax   ♥ xx   2H (accepting hearts)   4S ("picture"-5D,4S,2C,2H)
    ♦ Qx   ♦ AKJ10x   4NT   5D (if 1430)
    ♣ KJx   ♣ xx   6S

E. ♠ KJxxx   ♠ AQxx   1S   2C
    ♥ Qxx   ♥ x   2D (accepting diamonds) 4H (delayed splinter)
    ♦ AQx   ♦ Kx   4NT   5S
    ♣ Kx   ♣ AQxxxx   6S

F. ♠ x   ♠ Jxx   1H   2S (Sartor Raise)
    ♥ Axxxxx   ♥ KJxx   3H (singleton spade)   3NT (slam try)
    ♦ KQx   ♦ Ax   4C   4D
    ♣ Axx   ♣ KQxx   4NT   5H
                           6H

G. ♠ xx   ♠ AKJxxx   1H   1S
    ♥ AQxxx   ♥ KJxx   1NT   4D (delayed splinter)
    ♦ Axx   ♦ x   4NT   5H
    ♣ Axx   ♣ xx   6H

H. ♠ AKxxx   ♠ QJx   1S   2D
    ♥ x   ♥ xx   2H (accepting hearts)   3S (forcing 3-card raise)
    ♦ Qx   ♦ AKJ10xx   4C   4D
    ♣ Axxx   ♣ xx   4NT (if aggressive)   5H
                           6S (more likely auction
                           will end in 4S)

I. ♠ x   ♠ xxx   1H   2C
    ♥ AQ10xx   ♥ KJx   2D (accepting diams.)   3H
    ♦ Kx   ♦ Ax   4NT   5D
    ♣ Kxxxx   ♣ AQxxx   6C   P or 6H

Passed Hand Responses to a 1H or 1S Opening

There is nothing extraordinary about passed hand bidding in this system. Any approach a partnership feels comfortable with should work fine. Playing Sartor 2/1, the system actually provides a built-in form of Drury without having to use the convention. Responder merely bids his best minor and then rebids 2 of opener's major. This would show the same 11 HCP raise even if responder were not a passed hand. With a subpar hand, opener just passes. With a decent opening bid, he can invite or just bid game. For those opting to use more standard responses to a major, I would just use simple Reverse Drury.

Raises in Competition

The Sartor 2/1 responses also provide a good continuation scheme when our side opens one of a major and the opener's LHO doubles. Responder can use the transfer responses (1NT=clubs, 2C=diamonds, 2D=hearts) to escape into a 6+ card suit. He can also use the same bids to make lead-directing raises of opener's suit.

A bid of 1NT followed by 2 of opener's major would suggest a club lead, 2C followed by 2 of opener's suit would suggest a diamond lead, and 2D followed by 2S would suggest a heart lead. A transfer into opener's suit (1H-Dbl-2D or 1S-Dbl-2H) could be a raise with a high spade honor, while a direct raise (1H-Dbl-2H or 1S-Dbl-2S) would deny the ace, king, or queen.

With stronger hands, fit-showing jumps could be used to invite game and give partner the information needed to decide whether to bid on or defend.

Alternatives for the Less Adventurous

As I promised before I started trotting out some of my more unusual (some would say harebrained) ideas, I have some alternate suggestions for those who might wish to play this system but without some of its offbeat aspects. It is perfectly possible to play the system using either a standard or a 2/1 bidding structure in the major suits (with obvious adjustments for the fact that opening 1H and 1S bids are limited to 16 HCP).It will not affect the other opening bids.

In fact, since there is a limited supply of mad scientists willing to take on the entire system, I usually wind up playing a fairly standard major suit scheme with many of my partners at the local club. You will find an outline of that scheme in Appendix D if you are actually interested.

Other Possible Improvements for the Slightly More Adventurous

A slight tweak to the major suit structure that could be useful is a variant of Eddie Kantar's interchange of the 1S and 1NT responses to a 1H opening. Though you might not be able to use it in many events due to the ACBL's classification of it, I think it is a sensible convention. A discussion of how it would fit the system is in Appendix C.

Changing 3-way jump shifts to 2-way jump shifts would simplify that convention. The strong single-suited hand could be handled another way. The jump shift could be modified to show only the mini-splinter (9-11 HCP) or the maxi-splinter hands (15+ HCP). Direct jumps to 3S, 4C,4D, or 4H would still show standard splinter bids with 12-14 HCP .This would keep the advantage gained by having narrow ranges for our splinter bids, making it possible to better judge whether to push aggressively for games or slams.

CHAPTER 3

The 1 No-Trump Opening

The 1NT opening bid in this system shows 14–16 HCP. It is probably best described as intermediate. It allows you to start with a 1NT bid a little more often than standard bidders, but still looks and feels like a real 1NT opener. The range is slightly offbeat, but it is logical. Any balanced hand with 17-19 or 20-21 HCP is opened 1C, so a 15–17 1NT would create an unnecessary overlap in range.

What sets this NT scheme apart from standard practice are some unusual response treatments. The structure is a little complex (surprise!), but not radically so. Before I go into detail, let me digress briefly to state that, just as with the major suit structure, almost any NT structure will work quite well with this system. I'd like to think, however, that some of my slightly unorthodox ideas may actually offer some advantages over what is commonly used. Actually, I should admit up front that many of "my" ideas are modifications or thinly disguised thefts of ideas I've found in books or magazines. Some are completely original. I've tried to take them and form them into a coherent system.

Let me start by trying to describe some of the nonstandard treatments and give at least a brief rationale for their use. First, 2C is Stayman, but it does not guarantee a 4-card major. Since 2NT is a transfer, the only way to make an invitational raise is to first bid 2C. While we're on the subject of invitations, we might as well discuss a second major non-standard treatment: 2C also begins invitational sequences in clubs, diamonds, and spades.

The delayed transfer invitation in spades is probably the most off-the-wall treatment in the entire system. I'll explain it after the reader has had time to prepare for it. The only standard invitational sequence is in hearts. Since all invitational hands are covered by those bids, transfers to the minors are always either weak or very strong—never in-between.

The seemingly bizarre method of making invitations in the majors allows the use of the cheapest call after a major suit transfer to be used as an artificial game-forcing bid. This allows leisurely game and slam exploration. It also allows the responder to make non-forcing direct rebids at the 3-level with weakish 2-suited hands. Finally, all direct bids from 2S to 3S are conventional and cover specific types of hands.

The system was not created simply for novelty. It was designed to allow and facilitate the following:

- the 1NT bidder declaring a large majority of contracts by the use of various transfers
- the description of weak, invitational, and game-forcing hands in all suits
- the description of 5-4 and 5-5 hands
- the description of 4-4-4-1 hands
- the exploration for slam when both hands are balanced, with ability to find 4-4 fits in all suits
- the avoidance of 3NT when both partners are weak in one major, and a route to a 4-3 fit in the other major or to a minor suit game
- slam bidding in one-suited hands

In order to meet all of these goals, it was necessary to make some bids do double duty, with their meaning not fully defined until responder's second bid. Here is a brief overview:

1. Transfers are used in all 4 suits, with those in the minors either weak or game-forcing.
2. 2C is Stayman, but also begins many invitational sequences.
3. 2S is game-forcing and starts slam exploration on many balanced and semi-balanced hands. It also serves as a slam invitation on 4-4-4-1 hands.
4. 2NT is a transfer to clubs, either weak or game-forcing. If strong, it shows either a 1-suited slam try in clubs or a game-forcing 6-4-2-1, 5-4-2-2, or 5-4-3-1 hand with 3-1 distribution in the majors.
5. 3C is a transfer to diamonds, either weak or game-forcing. If strong, it shows a 1-suited slam try in diamonds or a game-forcing hand with 3-1 distribution in the majors.
6. 3D shows 5-5+ distribution in the majors with at least game-invitational values. Smolen is used for 5-4 hands with game-forcing values.

7. 3H and 3S show singletons with 5-5+ distribution in the minors and at least game values.
8. 4C is Gerber.
9. 4D and 4H are Texas Transfers, usually indicating no slam ambitions. However, a "transfer and pull" shows slam interest and key cards.
10. 4 spades is a delayed raise to 6NT. It asks for point count and any good 5-card suit that might provide an extra trick for a grand slam.
11. Since slam invitations can begin with an artificial 2S or 2NT after a transfer, 4NT after a transfer is Roman keycard Blackwood, and jumps to 3S,4C,4D, or 4H are splinter bids.

"Rube Goldberg" Stayman

Most of the system responses to a 1NT opening are logical and consistent, but there is one area that admittedly looks like it was designed by Rube Goldberg.(For those too young to get the reference, he was a character famous for impractical, complicated, and often comical inventions.) That is the area of invitational and forcing rebids with 5-card majors. I wanted a way to show an invitational hand with a 5-card major at the 2-level while adding the ability to make a low-level game-forcing bid. I also wanted to be able to make a non-forcing bid in a second 5-card suit at the 3-level. Yet I still wanted to preserve a transfer into both majors. Sound impossible? That's where the Rube Goldberg in me came to the fore.

After sifting through several old versions of Stayman, I decided the solution lay in returning to an idea that was part of the earliest versions of the convention. That idea was that bidding Stayman showed at least invitational values. When that was the understanding, Stayman followed by 2 of a major was invitational, not weak. Since I was already using Stayman to invite in NT and both minors, this seemed to work into my scheme very well. But combining that idea with transfers into the majors seemed like an insurmountable hurdle. It worked well in spades but failed miserably in hearts.

Finally, the solution hit me. I could use the Stayman sequence in spades but use a standard transfer in hearts. Obviously, using a different bidding plan for each major may initially cause a few memory problems, but I think any competent pair can handle them.

There is one bidding habit that a lot of players will have to overcome. With a weak hand and 5/4 distribution in the majors, responder can no longer bid Stayman and then sign off in his 5-card suit when opener bids 2D. He simply has to transfer into his long suit and pass. Occasionally missing a 4-4 fit and playing in a 5-2 fit is admittedly a downside of this treatment, butI think it is a small price to pay.

The Rube Goldberg approach only applies to invitational hands with 5-card suits. When responder has a 5-card suit with either weak or game-forcing values or a 6+ card suit, standard transfers are used. Continuations after the transfer may be nonstandard, however.

Oops! There is one last exception. Responder can still use Stayman with a weak 4-4-4-1 hand, planning to pass whatever opener bids. Should opener bid 2D, 2H, or 2S, all will be well. If opener bids 3C, showing both majors and a maximum, there is still no problem. Should he bid 2NT, however, showing both majors and a minimum, we may get too high. But in that case, there is a good chance the opponents can make 3C, so we may not get a bad score for going down at the 3-level anyway. At any rate the combination of the weak 4-4-4-1 opposite a 1NT with both majors will probably occur with roughly the same frequency as the arrival of Halley's Comet, so I wouldn't spend much time fretting over it.

Let's look at all the responses in logical progression, beginning with Stayman and going right on up to 4-level bids. I'll explain the more unusual bids as we come to them.

1NT-2C: The Gory Details

Our Stayman 2C response differs from the standard version in several ways. For one thing, it does not guarantee a 4-card major. Because a direct 2NT is used as a transfer, starting with a 2C bid is the only way to make an invitational raise to 2NT. For another, it may be used to begin an invitational raise to 3C or 3D. These treatments may be slightly outside the box, but they don't qualify us for a trip to the funny farm.

What may lead to a visit from little men in white coats carrying butterfly nets is my next brainstorm. Stayman is also used to make an invitational transfer bid in spades. With 5 spades and a good 9 to a bad 11 HCP, responder bids 2C. If opener replies 2D, responder now bids 2H—a delayed transfer.

Why go to all this trouble? Because now we can use a standard 2H transfer to spades followed by 2NT (the cheapest continuation) as an artificial game-forcing bid. We don't have to go through all this nonsense in hearts because we have two follow-up bids available after a standard transfer (2S as the artificial force and 2NT as the standard invitation).

An obvious question occurs. What if our uncooperative partner bids something other than 2D in reply to 2C? If he shows a 4-card spade suit, there is obviously no problem. Responder invites or bids game. The only response that fouls up our carefully laid plans is a bid of 2H. This tends to preclude using 2H yourself for a transfer. Since we still want to maintain the transfer, we have to switch the meaning of responder's next bid. So 2S becomes the equivalent of a 2NT bid, while 2NT shows exactly 5 spades and invitational values. This shouldn't cause excessive brain overload. Responder simply has to remember that once he sets out to transfer into spades, he should never be the first to bid the suit.

Once you get past learning these invitational spade sequences, the rest of the NT setup is relatively straightforward. Having said that, there are still several departures from standard bidding.

Responses to 2C are only semi-standard. Opener bids a 4-card major if he has one or bids 2D to deny holding one. However, if he has *two* 4-card majors, he has two bids to show exactly that holding. With both majors, he bids 2NT (minimum) or 3C (maximum).Responder then transfers into hearts by bidding 3D or into spades by bidding 3H. Since 3S is not needed at this point, it can serve as an artificial slam try. In addition, since 2NT and 3C show both majors, a 2H or 2S answer to Stayman denies a second major. A cue bid of the other major can be used as an artificial force, either as a relay to 2NT or a slam invitation.

Because responder is almost always promising at least invitational values by bidding Stayman, there is generally no problem with gettingtoo high. The sole exception, as previously mentioned, will be if responder has the 4-4-4-1 hand with a singleton club and wants to pass opener's next bid. If opener has both majors, he will have to play 3H or 3S instead of 2H or 2S.

1NT-2C-2D-2S

This set of bids leaves the sequence 1NT-2C-2D-2S unused. It can be put to use as follows: In every response scheme to 1NT, there is a problem hand—one with which you would like to explore for a 4/4 major fit, but it's just short of the values for an invitational 2NT if a fit is not found. In this system, that is a hand with 8+/9 HCP. After 1NT-2C-2D, the rebid of 2S can be used for a special purpose. It says, "Bid 2NT. I have a subpar (8–9 HCP) hand for a raise to 2NT and want to sign off."

The sequence 1NT-2C-2D-2NT shows an actual invitational raise to 2NT. It does not promise a 4-card major. This makes exploring for a major fit on a slightly subpar hand a little safer. If opener fits responder's major, he can pass or raise to 3. If he bids 2D, he can sign off at 2NT by bidding 2S. The worst case is when opener bids the wrong major. Responder has to rebid 2S over 2H or 2NT over 2S, risking being raised to 3NT.

If opener tends to open 1D with exactly 14 HCP and a 4-card major (recommended), the risk is less.

Note one special case: If opener responds 2H to 2C, then 2S is the invitational bid in NT, while 2NT shows 5 spades and invitational values, thus preserving the transfer. However, 2S still shows 10–11 HCP here, not 8–9.

There's an extension to this. The 2S "please sign off in 2NT" bid can also be part of the solution to another special problem: what should responder do with 11–12 HCP and 5-4-3-1 distribution with 3 cards in one major and 1 card in the other? He can certainly just blast to 3NT and hope his short suit won't prove fatal. This at least has the virtue of not tipping off opponents about his weakness. If he wishes to go the scientific route, however, our NT structure can supply some useful information upon which to decide on a final contract.

Since we often go through Stayman without a 4-card major, he can start with a 2C bid. One of the following things will happen as a result:

- Opener can show 4 cards in a major. If the suit is hearts, responder can use the 2S relay to force the opener to bid 2NT. Instead of passing, however, he can now bid 3H, showing 3 hearts and a singleton spade. Opener may then steer the contract into 3NT, 4H, or 4 or 5 of a minor. If the suit is spades, responder can just bid a direct "impossible" 3H over 2S, showing 3 spades and 1 heart. Again, opener should have a good idea about the best contract.
- Opener can bid 2D, denying a four-card major. Responder can just use 2S to relay to 2NT then bid an "impossible" 3H or 3S, showing a singleton and 3 cards in the opposite major. This may allow us to avoid a hopeless 3NT.

Smolen

Smolen is used for game-going hands with 5-4 or 6-4 distribution in the majors. With 5 hearts and 4 spades, responder bids 2C and jumps to 3S, his 4-card suit, if opener shows no major. With 5 spades and 4 hearts, he jumps to 3 hearts. Opener chooses between 3NT and 4 of the major. With 6-4 in the majors, responder can retransfer into the 6-card suit at the 4-level. It is also possible to use a direct jump to 4D or 4H after 1NT-2C-2D to show a 6-4 hand. Since there are two ways to show the same distribution, some pairs may choose to use one sequence as a slam try and use the other to simply set the final contract in game.

Example Auctions (1NT-2C)

Here are some sample auctions involving responder's 2C response:

	Opener	*Responder*		
A.	♠ Qxx	♠ Kx	1NT	2C
	♥ A10x	♥ Kxx	2D	2NT
	♦ KQxx	♦ xx	P	
	♣ QJx	♣ Axxxx		
B.	♠ KJx	♠ Qxxx	1NT	2C
	♥ A10xx	♥ Qx	2H	3NT
	♦ Kxx	♦ AJ109x	P	
	♣ KJx	♣ Qx		
C.	♠ Kxxx	♠ A10xx	1NT	2C
	♥ QJxx	♥ Kx	2NT (both majors, minimum)	3H (transfer)
	♦ Axx	♦ Q109x	3S	P
	♣ Ax	♣ Jx		
D.	♠ KQxx	♠ A10xx	1NT	2C
	♥ QJxx	♥ Kx	3C (both majors, maximum)	3H (transfer)
	♦ Axx	♦ Q109x	3S	4S
	♣ AQ	♣ Jx		
E.	♠ KQx	♠ A10xx	1NT	2C? P?
	♥ QJx	♥ Kxxx	2D	2S (relay to 2NT)
	♦ Axxx	♦ Jxx	2NT	P (subpar raise)
	♣ AQx	♣ xx		
F.	♠ xxx	♠x	1NT	2C
	♥ AKJ	♥ Q10xx	2D	2S (relay to 2NT)
	♦ KJxxx	♦ Qx	2NT	3C (natural, forcing)
	♣ Kx	♣ AQJxxx	3H	4H
			5C	

G.	♠ KQx	♠ J10xxx	1NT	2C
	♥ QJx	♥ Axx	2D	2H (transfer, 5 spades)
	♦ KJxxx	♦ Ax	3S	3NT
	♣ Ax	♣ Jxx	4S	

H.	♠ KQx	♠ J10xxx	1NT	2C
	♥ QJxx	♥ Axx	2H	2NT (5 spades, invit.)
	♦ KJxx	♦ Ax	4S	
	♣ Ax	♣ Jxx		

I.	♠ KQx	♠ J10xxx	1NT	2C
	♥ QJx	♥ Axxx	2D	3H (Smolen-5S,4H)
	♦ Kxxxx	♦ Ax	4S	
	♣ Ax	♣ Qx		

Semi-Standard Transfers

Except for the specific invitational spade hands already discussed, standard transfers (2D = 5+ hearts, 2H = 5+ spades) are used. With a weak hand with no second 5-card suit, responder will transfer and pass. With a 6+-card suit, he can transfer and pass, raise to 3 as a game invitation, or raise to game. With likely slam hands he can transfer at the 2-level and raise to game or splinter at the 4-level (more about this shortly). But in addition to the usual choices, we have two additional tools at our disposal. They are available because of all the complicated folderol surrounding the spade suit.

First, we now have an artificial bid to create a game-forcing auction and indicate slam interest. After a transfer is accepted, the responder's cheapest bid (2S over 2H or 2NT over 2S) is now game-forcing and artificial. After the force, each partner can bid new suits at the 3-level, make later cue bids at the 4-level, and generally explore for slam pretty thoroughly before bidding one or signing off.

Secondly, we can now describe weakish 2-suited hands. A transfer and a bid of a second suit at the 3-level is now non-forcing. It shows at least 5-5 distribution and a possibility of either finding a better partscore fit or reaching a hard-to-bid game based on fit. There are occasional cases where a double fit may allow 10 tricks to be taken in a hand where it is "impossible" to bid game. This treatment may allow us to bid some of them.

Transfer Slam Tries

As mentioned earlier, one way to invite slam is to transfer to 2 of a major and then bid 4. The general idea is widely used, but I think it can be more useful if given a specific meaning. I'd like to suggest a useful definition for this sequence and coordinate the bid with what I call "West Of Texas Transfers."I also have a suggestion for the use of asking bids after a 2-level transfer and a splinter bid.

Let's start with the simple 1NT-(2-level transfer)-(jump-to-4) auction. We will treat this as the weakest of our slam invitations. It will show a specific holding-exactly 2 keycards without the queen of trump. This is the invitation least likely to excite opener. We can now coordinate this with direct 4-level transfers. West of Texas Transfers will start with the next strongest hand and proceed in logical steps.

I realize that most people only use Texas Transfers to sign off in game, but there is no logical reason for this. After a direct jump to 4D (6+hearts) or 4H (6+spades), responder can simply pass opener's acceptance of the transfer if he has no slam ambitions. If his hand warrants further action, however, he just makes another bid. This is essentially an answer to an "Invisible RKCB" query. His first step starts where our mild slam try left off. It shows 2 keycards *with* the queen of trump. The second step shows *3* keycards *without* the queen. The third step shows 3 *with* the lady, etc.

These responses will also turn up in many other slam auctions beginning with a 1NT opening. They are appropriate because it is almost impossible to have the 15+HCP required to make a slam try opposite our 14–16 HCP 1NT without at least 2 keycards. To save space, I will use the label "Texas" whenever this type of keycard ask is used.

After a transfer and a splinter, 4 of the trump suit denies slam interest. The cheapest non-trump bid asks for keycards and the answers follow the same pattern: 2 keycards without the queen, 2 with, 3 without, 3 with, etc. If my prose description isn't 100 percent clear, here is a chart: (M, of course, stands for Major; KC stands for Keycard)

- 1NT-transfer to 4M, then pass = no slam ambition
- 1NT-transfer to 2M, then 4M = 2KC, no Q of trump
- 1NT-transfer to 4M, then 4M+1 = 2 KC + Q of trump
- 1NT-transfer to 4M, then 4M+2 = 3 KC, no Q of trump
- 1NT-transfer to 4M, then 4M+3 = 3 KC + Q of trump
- 1NT-transfer to 4M, then 4M+4 = 4KC, no Q of trump (unlikely to occur)
- 1NT-transfer to 4M, then 4M+5 = 4 KC + Q of trump (unlikely to occur)

Similarly, after a transfer and a splinter bid, 1NT-transfer to 2M, then splinter-4M= no slam interest (responder takes full responsibility if he goes on). Cheapest non-4M bid asks for keycards; responder bids in steps in either case:

- first step = 2 KC, no Q
- second step = 2 KC +Q
- third step = 3 KC, no Q
- fourth step = 3 KC + Q, and so forth.

1NT-2D

The use of the 2D transfer to 2H is at least partly standard. Rebids of 2NT and 3H are invitational with 5- and 6-card suits. Jumps to 3S, 4C, and 4D are splinters. After a splinter, the cheapest non-trump bid can ask for keycards, with the same Texas responses as before.(Those who prefer 1430 may decide to use those responses to the cheapest suit or just use 4NT.)

Jumps to 3NT or 4H are standard, with 4H being a mild slam try. A direct 4D is either to play or a West of Texas slam try, as discussed above.

Nonstandard bids begin with the rebid of 2S. This is artificial and game-forcing, and usually shows at least some interest in slam. Direct bids of 3C or 3D after the original transfer bid show a second 5+-card suit and are non-forcing. Here are some sample auctions:

	Opener	Responder		
A.	♠ Ax	♠ KQ	1NT	2D
	♥ Kxxx	♥ Axxxxx	2H	4H (mild slam try-2 KC, no Q)
	♦ Kxx	♦ A	P (probably 2 losers)	
	♣ KQxx	♣ Jxx		
B.	♠ Ax	♠ Kxx	1NT	2D
	♥ Kxx	♥ AQxxxx	2H	4C (splinter)
	♦ Kxxx	♦ AQx	4H	4S (Texas ask)
	♣ KQxx	♣ x	4NT (2 KC, no Q)	6H

C. ♠ Kxx	♠ Jxx	1NT	2D
♥ Ax	♥KJxxx	2H	2NT (standard, invitational)
♦ Axxx	♦Kx	P	
♣ Kxxx	♣ Qxx		
D. ♠ Axx	♠ Qx	1NT	2D
♥ Qx	♥ Kxxxxx	2H	3H (invitational,6-card suit)
♦AQxx	♦ x	P	
♣ Qxxx	♣ KJxx		
E. ♠ Axxx	♠ x	1NT	2D
♥ AJxx	♥ Kxxxx	2H	3D (5-5+ distribution,
♦KQx	♦ Axxxx	4H (great fit,	non-forcing)
♣ Jx	♣ xx	no wasted values)	
F. ♠ AJxx	♠ Qx	1NT	4D (West of Texas transfer)
♥ Kx	♥ AQ10xxx	4H	5C (transfer and pull-
♦ Kxx	♦ Axx	6H	3 steps=3 KC + Q of trump)
♣ K10xx	♣ Ax		
G. ♠ QJx	♠ x	1NT	2D
♥ Kxxx	♥ AQJxx	2H	2S (artificial, GF)
♦ Ax	♦ KJxx	3C	3D
♣ KQxx	♣ AJx	3H	3NT ("Baby RKCB")
		4H (2KC, no Q)	6H

If the responder bids 2S as a game force, either partner can use 3NT as "Baby Blackwood" and drive to slam. Of course, the partners may decide that 3NT is more useful as a natural bid. Then 4NT would be used for ace-asking. It might also be noted that using a splinter jump to 3S rather than the game forcing 2S would be a sensible alternative route to the slam.

1NT-2H

The 2H transfer to 2S is also at least partially standard. With a weak hand, responder transfers and passes 2S. With an invitational hand and a 6-card suit, he still transfers and raises to 3S. With game-going values and no slam interest, he can transfer and then bid 3NT or just use a direct 4H to transfer to 4S, like any standard bidder. Using the 4H transfer and then bidding again shows keycards and slam interest, as previously discussed. A bid of 2NT after 1NT-2H-2S is artificial and game-forcing. Bids of 3C, 3D, or 3H after 1NT-2H-2S are non-forcing, showing a second 5+ card suit. Here are some example hands:

	Opener	Responder		
A.	♠ Axxx	♠ Kxxxxx	1NT	2H
	♥ Kx	♥ Axx	2S	4C (splinter)
	♦ Kxx	♦ Axx	4D (key cards?)	5D (4 KC, no Q)
	♣ KQxx	♣ A	7NT	(13 top tricks)
B.	♠ Ax	♠ J10xxx	1NT	2H
	♥ KQx	♥ xx	2S	P or 3D (non-forcing)
	♦ QJx♦	Axxxx		
	♣ KJxxx	♣ Q		
C.	♠ KQx	♠ J10xxx	1NT	2H
	♥ Axxx	♥ xx	2S	3C (non-forcing)
	♦ Jxx	♦ A	4S (nice double fit-an almost "unbiddable" game)	
	♣ AJx	♣ Qxxxx		
D.	♠ Kx	♠ J10xxx	1NT	2H
	♥ KQ10x	♥ x	2S	3D (non-forcing)
	♦ J10xx	♦ Qxxxxx	P	
	♣ KQJ	♣ x		
E.	♠ AQx	♠KJxxx	1NT	2C
	♥ Kx	♥ xxx	2D	2H (invitational, 5 spades)
	♦ AJxxx	♦ x	4S	P
	♣ Qx	♣ AJ10x		
F.	♠ AQx	♠ J10xxx	1NT	2C
	♥ Kx	♥ AQJx	2D	3H (Smolen=4H,5S)
	♦ AJxxx	♦ Kxx	4S	
	♣ Qx	♣ x		

G.	♠ Ax	♠ Q109xx	1NT	2C
	♥ KQxx	♥ Jx	2H	2NT (invitational, 5S)
	♦ Qx	♦ Axxx	3C	3NT
	♣ AJxx	♣ Kx	(Responder planned to bid 2H to invite with 5 spades.

(Responder planned to bid 2H to invite with 5 spades. When opener bids 2H, 2S = NT, 2NT = spades)

Sartor Slam Try

The 2S response to a 1NT opening bid is a slam try. It shows at least 15 HCP and either 4-4-3-2, 5-4-2-2, or 4-4-4-1 distribution. This bid combines the common 4-4-4-1 try with CONFI, invented by George Rosencranz. My contribution is concocting a way to combine the asking bids to cover all those possible distributions.

The idea is to find 4-4 fits that may allow slam to be made with slightly less than the ideal 33 HCP. With our range for 1NT (14–16 HCP), that translates into needing 15+ HCP in a balanced hand or 14 HCP outside the singleton in a 4-4-4-1 hand in order to justify making this bid, which I'll abbreviate as SST from now on. If the decision is close, the quality of responder's spot cards should be an important factor in the decision.

When making a SST, responder starts by bidding 2S. The 2S bid is a relay to 2NT and is the first step in a two-step process. It announces that the partnership may have enough strength to bid a slam but does not specify responder's exact hand type. After opener's forced 2NT bid, responder moves on to the second step. His next bid describes his hand type and enlists opener's cooperation.

If responder rebids 3C, he announces a balanced or semi-balanced hand and asks for the number of controls in opener's hand (A=2, K=1). Opener answers in steps. With a 14–16 HCP NT opening, the number of controls will generally range from 3 to 8. So his first-step answer will show 0–3 controls. His second step shows 4, his third, 5, etc. There are 12 controls possible (4 aces and 4 kings) in the deck. If the total number of controls in the two hands is less than 10, responder signs off in 3NT.

At this point, partnerships will have to establish an agreement. They can decide to always play 3NT, even if it means missing an occasional 4-4 major fit. Or they can allow opener to bid his cheapest major, with 4NT as the fall-back contract if no fit is found in 4H or 4S. Since the partnership will always have at least 30 HCP, 4NT should be safe. Of course, if they always stop in 3NT, their extra strength may provide a top score when the same number of tricks are available in both 3NT and 4 of a major. At any rate, without 10 controls, the pair must give up on slam.

If the partnership has at least 10 controls, they bid suits up the line at the 4 level. The minimum requirement for a biddable suit is QJxx, Kxxx, or Axxx. Partner must have at least that to raise. This ensures that there will never be more than 1 trump loser if the opponents' trumps split no worse than 3-2. If no decent 4-4 fit is found at the 4-level, the bidding ends at 4NT. If a fit is found, opener can bid 5 of the suit with a minimum or bid slam with a maximum. The opponents can't have more than 1 ace or 2 kings when our side has 10 controls, so we should be in a reasonable spot.

What if responder has the 4-4-4-1 hand? Simple. Instead of rebidding 3C, he rebids his singleton. A 3D bid shows a singleton diamond; 3H a singleton heart; 3S a singleton spade; and 3NT a singleton club. Opener then has several options: He can sign off at 3NT, 4H, 4S, 5C, or 5D. He can make a forcing bid in a suit below game, showing some slam interest, setting trump, and asking for controls. If the singleton is in spades, he can bid an artificial 4C, also asking for controls (same answers as the West of Texas bid) or an artificial 4D, asking for aces (simple Blackwood). A cue bid of the singleton can be used as simple Blackwood when the singleton is in a suit other than spades. After controls or aces are shown, 4NT or any game bid is a sign-off.

Once again, a chart may make things clearer.

After 1NT-2S-2NT:

- **3C** = shows a balanced (4-4-3-2 or 5-4-2-2) hand and asks for controls (A=2,K=1)
  Answers: 3D = 0–3;   3H = 4;   3S = 5;   3NT = 6;   4C = 7
  Opener's non-game rebids then ask for controls or aces.
- **3D** = 4-4-1-4 hand (singleton diamond)
- **3H** = 4-1-4-4 hand (singleton heart)
- **3S** = 1-4-4-4 hand (singleton spade)
- **3NT** = 4-4-4-1 hand (singleton club)

Opener's non-game rebids now ask for controls or aces—3NT, 4H, 4S are sign-offs.
Here are some example auctions:

	Opener	Responder		
A.	♠ Kxx	♠ AQxx	1NT	2S (SST-says bid 2NT)
	♥ KQxx	♥ xx	2NT (forced)	3C (balanced, asking controls)
	♦ Axxx	♦ KQxx	3S (5 controls)	4D (we have 10+ controls)
	♣ Kx	♣ AJx	4H	4S
			5D	6D (a good 31 HCP slam)

B. ♠ Kxx   ♠ AQxx   1NT   2S (SST)
    ♥ KQxx   ♥ xx   2NT   3C (asking)
    ♦ Axxx   ♦ QJxx   3S (5 controls) 3NT (too few controls)
    ♣ Kx   ♣ AQx   4H (4-4 fit?)   4S (no—how about here?)
                           4NT (no—here's
                           where we stop)

C. ♠ Kxx   ♠ AQxx   1NT   2S (SST)
    ♥ KQxx   ♥ AJxx   2NT   3D (4-4-1-4, singleton D)
    ♦ Axxx   ♦ x   3H (sets trump, 4C (4 controls outside
    ♣ Kx   ♣ QJxx   asks controls)   of diamonds)
                           6H

D. ♠ Kxx   ♠ AQxx   1NT   2S (SST)
    ♥ KQxx   ♥ x   2 NT   3H (4-1-4-4, singleton H)
    ♦ Axxx   ♦ Kxxx   3NT (poor fit;
    ♣ Kx   ♣ AQxx   sign-off)

E. ♠ Axxx   ♠ x   1NT   2S (SST)
    ♥ QJxx   ♥ A10xx   2NT   3S (1-4-4-4, singleton S)
    ♦ Kx   ♦ AQJx   4C (asking-4H   4S (5 controls)
    ♣ A10x   ♣ KJxx   would be a sign-off)
                           6H

F. ♠ xxx   ♠ x   1NT   2S (SST)
    ♥KJ   ♥ AQxx   2NT   3S (1-4-4-4, singleton S)
    ♦KQJx   ♦ Axxx   4D (ace asking) 5C (3 aces)
    ♣ KQxx   ♣ Axxx   6D

Special Extension

It may be desirable to add one special treatment to the Sartor Slam Try. As we shall see in the next section, rebids after transfers from 1NT into long minor suits followed by bids showing second suits take up more space than is readily available. Some 5-4-4-0 hands can't be easily described below the 5 level. Since the SST already covers 4-4-4-1 hands and the entire 4 level is completely unused, the bids I am about to suggest are a sensible way to describe this other type of 3-suited hand. It could apply to either minor, but here is one set of bids for diamonds only:

1NT	2S (SST)
2NT	4C = club void (5 diamonds,4 hearts, 4 spades)
	4D = heart void (5 diamonds, 4 clubs, 4 spades)
	4H = spade void (5 diamonds, 4 clubs, 4 hearts)

A convenient bid of the next suit now serves as an exclusion keycard ask, while bids in the other suits or 4NT are to play. This is much more efficient than trying to figure out the right contract at the 5 level. A more complete discussion of this addition to the SST will be presented in the next section.

Transfers into the Minors

Basic System

In this system, transfers into the minors after a 1NT opening are either weak and intended to be passed or game-forcing with at least mild slam interest. Hands with invitational values go through Stayman, while many hands in the 11–15 HCP range simply jump to 3NT or look for a major suit fit and then bid 3NT or the appropriate game in a suit. The transfers are only used for single-suited hands with a 6+(occasionally a very good 5) card minor suit or for hands with 5 or 6 cards in the long minor and a 4-card second suit.

When a responder transfers into 3C or 3D and then takes a second bid, he is suggesting that his long minor offers a chance to bid and make a slam, or possibly that his unbalanced distribution makes 5C or 5D the most tenable game available. In the process, the partnership may veer off into a game in a secondary suit or wind up settling for a 4NT or 5NT contract when slam exploration produces discouraging results.

The continuation scheme proposed here allows the description of many different distributions with an emphasis on pinpointing short suits and 3-or 4-card holdings in the side suits. I've tried to make the club and diamond responses as similar as possible to minimize memory strain, though it is impossible to make them identical.

Both sets of bids follow a few basic precepts.

- With a 1-suited hand, responder transfers into 3C or 3D and then rebids either 3NT (showing no shortness in a side suit) or a suit at the 4 level or above (showing a specific short suit).

- With a long minor and a 4-card side suit, responder transfers into 3C or 3D, then relays into the side suit, using a second transfer or conventional continuation. He then shows his complete distribution at the next level. Some variations do occur requiring the second transfer to serve as a relay to the next higher suit rather than a true transfer. This is caused by the constricted space at the 3 level after a transfer to 3D.

- All singletons are shown at the 4 level. The singleton-showing bids are often in a suit just below the short suit, allowing a cue bid of the short suit to be used for key card or control asking.

- The major difference between the structures for clubs and diamonds is in the treatment of 5-4-4-0 hands. In clubs, the continuations after the initial transfer follow patterns that are similar to those seen in other parts of the system. Voids can be shown below the 5 level. Unfortunately, the lack of bidding space after a transfer to 3D makes using exactly the same continuation structure impossible. Void showing would require 5-level bids, something I want to avoid. The high level would make showing controls or aces difficult. So I have devised one deviation from the basic structure that applies only to diamonds. It was described in the last chapter under "Special Extension" (See page 73-74) and will be reviewed in the section on diamond transfers.

I've tried to make the methods seem as natural as possible (assuming most modern players are so used to transfers that they almost regard them as natural), though some may regard that effort to be an abject failure. As previously mentioned, secondary transfer sequences and conventional singleton and void-showing bids are involved. Compared to some of my early hyper-scientific versions, though, the final suggested scheme is downright simple.

In the next two sections, I will go through the transfers to clubs and diamonds separately.

1NT-2NT (Transfer to 3C)

The 2NT response to a 1NT opening bid commands opener to bid 3C. It is either a weak hand with 6+ clubs, which will be passed in 3C, or it is a strong hand (usually 15/16+ HCP) with 5+ clubs that will be explored for game or slam. Any second bid by responder after opener's bid of 3C is forcing to game. With 11–13/14 HCP, you invite through Stayman or just bid game.

In general, responder should have a minimum of 15–16 HCP to use either minor suit transfer (2NT for clubs, 3C for diamonds) as a slam try. With little in the way of distributional values (say a 5-4-2-2-suiter), I'd recommend 17 HCP. With a very long suit, less may be adequate.

Here is a description of responder's possible continuations after 1NT-2NT-3C:

When responder is single-suited with no side shortness
- 3NT = natural, 5-6+ clubs, no side shortness, no 4-card side suit.
- Opener can now use 4C to ask for keycards (1430 or Texas steps) or use 4D to ask for controls (first step = 0-3, second= 4, third= 5, fourth = 6, etc.)

When responder is single-suited with a singleton or void
Direct 4-level bids after 1NT-2NT-3C are used to show shortness.
- 4C = 6+ clubs with no 4-card side and a singleton diamond (likely 6-3-3-1 or 7-3-2-1 distribution)
  4D asks for key cards—1430 or Texas answers (first step= 2 KC, no Q of clubs; second step= 2 KC + Q, etc.)
- 4D = 6+ clubs with no 4-card side suit and a singleton heart (likely 6-3-3-1 or 7-3-2-1 distribution). The cheapest bid (4H) can serve as 1430 or a Texas keycard ask.
- 4H = 6+ clubs with no 4-card side suit and singleton spade (likely 6-3-3-1 or 7-3-2-1 distribution); 4S asks for key cards
- 4S,4NT, 5C = 7+ clubs, no side suit, 7-3-3-0 or better distribution with voids shown in ascending order (4S = diamond void, 4NT = heart void, 5C= spade void). This allows key-card asking and escapes at the 5 level. Bids in the voids can ask for key cards. Cheapest NT or 5C is to play, as are 5-level bids in real suits.

At the risk of being completely redundant, here is a simple recap of hands with no 4-card side suits:

1NT	2NT
3C	3NT= 5-6+ clubs, no short suit
	4C = 6+ clubs, singleton diamond
	4D = 6+ clubs, singleton heart
	4H = 6+ clubs, singleton spade
	4S = 7+ clubs, diamond void
	4NT = 7+ clubs, heart void
	5C = 7+ clubs, spade void

When responder has 5+ clubs and a second 4-card suit

- He bids a new suit at the 3 level (all secondary transfers)
- 3D= forces opener to bid 3H (usually shows four hearts)
- 3H= forces opener to bid 3S (guarantees four spades)
- 3S=asks opener to bid 3NT (guarantees four diamonds); see special exception below

After opener's rebid, responder completes a description of his distribution. He bids 3NT over opener's 3H or 3S rebid or 4C over his 3NT rebid to show 5-4-2-2 distribution. He makes the cheapest available suit follow-up bid at the 4 level to show the lowest possible singleton and the second cheapest suit rebid to show the higher possible singleton.(I specify at the 4 level because rebidding 3S after a transfer to 3H has a special conventional meaning which I'll discuss in a moment.) Therefore, if he has shown 5+ clubs and 4 hearts, the cheapest follow-up is 4C, which would show a singleton diamond. The next cheapest bid (4D) would show a spade singleton. If he has to use 4C to show a 2-2-4-5 hand, then, 4D shows the singleton heart and 4H shows a stiff spade.

He can also use the third and fourth cheapest rebids (4H and 4S or 4S and 4NT) to show voids in either of the same two side suits. By inference, if he shows a singleton, he will usually have 5-4-3-1 or 6-4-2-1 distribution, with 2 or 3 cards in the fourth suit. If he shows a void, he is probably 6-4-3-0 or 7-4-2-0.This is because of the special meaning of the 3S rebid I mentioned.

All 5-4-4-0 hands must first rebid 3D (supposedly showing 4 hearts) and then bid 3S over opener's forced 3H, rather than bidding a genuine second suit and then showing shortness at the 4 or 5 level. Opener then bids 3NT and responder shows his void. I'll go through that sequence in detail later. This is why opener *must* accept the 3D transfer to 3H.

Special Exception

Opener may bid 4C or 4D instead of 3NT over responder's 3S (5+ C,4D). If responder shows 9+ cards in the minors by bidding 3S and opener has no stopper in one major, he may be understandably nervous about the safety of a NT contract. He may disregard the relay to 3NT and bid the minor he feels offers the best trump fit. This asks responder to bid 4H or 4S to show a solid stopper or 4NT to show that both majors are stopped. If a wide-open major is discovered, he may then set the final contract at 5C or 5D.

Here is a chart which may give a clearer picture of the whole scheme:

1NT	2NT
3C	3D (usually 4 hearts)
3H (forced)	3S-artificial= any 5-4-4-0 hand
	(3NT follow-up=asks for void)
	3NT = 5-4-2-2 distribution (5C,4H, 2D,2S)
	4C = 5/6 clubs, 4 hearts, 2/3 spades, 1 diamond
	4D= 5/6 clubs, 4 hearts, 2/3 diamonds, 1 spade
1NT	2NT
3C	3H (4 spades)
3S (forced)	3NT=5-4-2-2 distribution (5C,4S,2D,2H)
	4C = 5/6 clubs, 4 spades, 2/3 hearts, 1 diamond
	4D = 5/6 clubs, 4 spades, 2/3 diamonds, 1 heart
1NT	2NT
3C	3S (4 diamonds)
3NT (suggested,	4C=5-4-2-2 distribution (5C,4D,2H,2S)
but not forced	4D = 5/6 clubs, 4 diamonds, 2/3 spades, 1 heart
**see text above	4H= 5/6 clubs, 4 diamonds, 2/3 hearts, and 1 spade

Going past the two cheapest denominations would show voids. To wit:

1NT	2NT
3C	3D (4 hearts)
3H (forced)	

4C and 4D would show diamond/spade singletons
So: 4H = void in diamonds (probably 4-3-0-6)
4S = void in spades (probably 4-0-3-6)

1NT	2NT
3C	3H (4 spades)
3S (forced)	

4C and 4D would show diamond/heart singletons
So: 4H = void in diamonds (probably 4-3-0-6)
4S = void in hearts (probably 4-0-3-6)

1NT	2NT
3C	3S (4 diamonds)
3NT (expected relay	4C = 5-4-2-2
to ask responder's	4D = singleton heart / 4S-heart void
exact distribution)	4H= singleton spade/ 4NT-spade void
OR:	

4C (bypassing normal 3NT)-asks for major stopper (s) for NT
4D (bypassing normal 3NT)- asks for major stopper (s) for NT

Once responder has described his distribution, opener can now ask for aces if interested in slam. Ace-asking requires some clear agreements. If at all possible, we want to ask with some bid at the four level other than 4NT. This allows us to use 4NT as a natural suggested sign-off.

Here is my suggestion: After responder has made a shortness-showing bid, any bid in a suit in which responder has less than 4 cards can be used to ask for key cards, while the cheapest bid in NT or one of responder's long suits is to play. Pairs may decide to use 1430 or Texas responses, with clubs as the assumed trump. Texas would be my choice, since the pair possesses at least 30 HCP and a 0 or 1 key-card response is almost impossible. I would make the first step show 0-2 keycards without the queen of clubs. The second step would show 2 *with* the queen; the third, 3 without; the fourth, 3 with, etc.

For further clarity, let's go through some auctions which would show 5+ clubs and a second suit.

Opener	Responder
Opener	*Responder*
1NT	2NT
3C	3D - responder has 5+clubs and 4 hearts
3H (forced)	3NT- responder is 2-4-2-5
4C (asking)	(X) (#of key cards or controls)

1NT	2NT
3C	3H- responder has 5+clubs and 4 spades
3S (forced)	4C** singleton diamond (lower side suit)
4D (asking)	(X) (#of key cards or controls)

1NT	2NT
3C	3D- responder has 5+clubs and 4 hearts
3H (forced)	4H- responder is 3-4-0-6 or 2-4-0-7
4S (asking)	(X) (#of key cards or controls)

(*4H shows the lower side void; 4S is the cheapest of the two remaining suits available for asking purposes—"exclusion" when a void is shown.)

1NT	2NT
3C	3S- responder has 5+clubs and 4 diamonds
3NT (relay-asks)	4C** responder is 2-2-4-5
4D (asking)	(X) (#of key cards or controls)

(After a 3NT relay, 4C=no singleton,4D= heart singleton, 4H= spade singleton, 4S= heart void,5C=spade void)

*He *might* have a 5-4-4-0 hand. Here he really has 4 hearts.
**One would assume that the king of clubs is a key card after any transfer to clubs, but it would certainly be possible to use 4D as KC for clubs and4H as KC for diamonds, or some variation thereof.

Special Sequence For 5-4-4-0 Hands

As promised, I will now give a more detailed discussion of the 1NT-2NT 3C-3D-3H-3S bidding sequence. On rare occasions, responder may have a 5-4-4-0 shape. To avoid 5-level void-showing bids, a special sequence is required. As already noted, a transfer to 3C followed by an immediate jump to 4S, 4NT, or 5C is used to show specific voids in 1-suited hands with 6+clubs. And, to be further redundant, with long clubs and one 4-card side suit, we transfer to 3C, retransfer to the second suit, and then bid 4S or 4NT to show a void in the lower or higher of the two remaining suits. What we lack is a way to show three specific suits and a void while not going past 5C. Unfortunately, all of the obvious ways of asking at the 4 level are already taken.

Luckily, the mad scientist in me has come up with a solution. I already explained part of it earlier when I outlined a useful extension to the SST—the Sartor Slam Try. We'll return to that in the next section when we discuss transfers into diamonds. For the moment, what is needed is a way describe a hand with 5 clubs and 2 side suits that allows us to pinpoint specific voids at the 4 level.

To differentiate a 5-4-4-0 hand from a 1-suited or 2-suited hand with a void, we will use the following meandering (but brilliant) sequence. We will first transfer into 3C, make a secondary transfer to 3H, and then make a completely artificial bid of 3S. This will show any 3-suited (5-4-4-0) hand with 5 clubs. If we don't get completely lost, the fact that we bid 3 suits at the 3 level may be a useful memory aid to remind us that it shows a 3-suited hand.

Opener, assuming he is not totally confused, can now bid 3NT to find responder's void. This may seem overly complicated, but it allows responder to give an exact description of his hand and allows opener to ask for keycards or controls and get an answer at the 4 level.

Over 3NT, responder shows his void in ascending suit order, using a familiar pattern:4C shows a diamond void, 4D a heart void, and 4H a spade void. You'll notice each bid is directly below the void. It is now a simple matter to cuebid the void suit to ask for keycards or controls. This double transfer and delayed 3S bid works well when the long minor is clubs but isn't possible if the long suit is diamonds. That brings us back to the special treatment we will use to bid 5-4-4-0 hands when the long minor is diamonds. It was briefly described on p.73-74 and will be discussed again as part of the 1NT-3C section (transfers to diamonds) on p.85-86.

Here are some example hands involving the 1NT-2NT sequence:

	Opener	Responder		
A.	♠ AQx	♠ xx	1NT	2NT
	♥ xxx	♥ xx	3C	P
	♦ KQxx	♦ Jxx		
	♣ KJx	♣ Qxxxxx		
B.	♠ AQx	♠ Kxxx	1NT	2NT
	♥ xxx	♥ x	3C	3H (relay-shows 4S)
	♦ KQxx	♦ AJx	3S (forced)	4D (4 spades, singleton heart)
	♣ KJx	♣ AQxxx	4H (keycards?)	4NT (2 KC + Q of clubs-Texas)
			6C	(5D, if 1430)
C.	♠ AQx	♠ Kxx	1NT	2NT
	♥ xxx	♥ x	3C	4D (6+ clubs, singleton heart)
	♦ KQxx	♦ Axx	4H	4NT (2KC + Q of clubs-Texas)
	♣ KJx	♣ AQxxxx	6C (5D if 1430)	
D.	♠ AQxx	♠ Kx	1NT	2NT
	♥ Jx	♥ xx	3C (forced)	3S (5+C, 4D)
	♦ KJxx	♦ AQxx	4D (afraid of hearts)	4S (stopper—no heart stopper)
	♣ KJx	♣ AQxxx	5D (most likely game)	

D is an example of a hand that might bypass the normal relay to 3NT. Bidding 3NT and then having responder show his 2-2-4-5 distribution with 4C finds the 4-4 diamond fit and lets us ask for key cards but doesn't provide a way to find major suit stoppers and to diagnose the lack of a heart control. With both minors, a semi-balanced hand, and one open major, it is better to let opener use his judgment and ignore the suggested 3NT relay. Bidding 4D sets that suit as an alternative to a hopeless 4NT contract if no heart stopper is found. In this case, either 5C or 5D are makeable.

	Opener	Responder		
E.	♠ AQx	♠ xx	1NT	2NT
	♥ xxx	♥ Ax	3C	3NT (6+ clubs, no shortness)
	♦ KQxx	♦ Axx	4D (keycards?)	5C (3 KC +Q)
	♣ KJx	♣ AQxxxx	6C (or 6 NT if very greedy at MP)	

F.	♠ AQx	♠ x	1NT	2NT
	♥ xx	♥ AKx	3C	3S (4 diamonds, relay to 3NT)
	♦ Kxxx	♦ AJxx	3NT (relay)	4H (5-6 C, 4D, 2-3H, 1S)
	♣ AQxx	♣ K10xxx	4S (keycards?)	5D (3 KC, no Q or 5C if 1430)
			6C	

G.	♠ Ax	♠ KJxx	1NT	2C (not enough for 2NT)
	♥ J10xx	♥ Q	2H	3NT
	♦ Kx	♦ AJxx		
	♣ AQxx	♣ Kxxxx		

H.	♠ AQxx	♠ KJxx	1NT	2NT
	♥ Kxx	♥ AQJx	3C	3D (forces 3H)
	♦ Qxxx	♦ void	3H	3S (any 5-4-4-0 hand)
	♣ Ax	♣ KQxxx	3NT (asking)	4C (4-4-0-5,diamond void)
			4D (asking)	4S (2 KC, + Q of C)
			5C (kings ?)	5H (1 king)
			7S (Our roundabout sequence worked!)	

As already noted (perhaps ad nauseum) a different solution for 5-4-4-0 hands with 5 diamonds will be outlined in the next section. Despite extensive experimentation, I couldn't devise any sensible set of void-showing bids that didn't involve the 5-level. By the time one asks for keycards, the answer is often past the last makeable contract. We will address that problem on pages 85-86.

1NT-3C (Transfer to 3D)

Just as the 1NT-2NT sequence shows long clubs, 1NT-3C is a transfer into a long diamond suit. The 3C bid demands that opener bid 3D. It shows either a weak hand with 6+ diamonds, which will be passed in 3D, or a strong hand (usually 15–16+ HCP),which will explore for game or slam. Any second bid by responder after opener bids 3D is forcing to game. With only 11–14 HCP, you invite through Stayman or bid 3NT.

The continuations that follow the transfer to 3D are similar, but not identical, to those used after the transfer to 3C. In the case of hands with long diamonds and no second suit, they are almost identical. After that, complications ensue.

When Responder Has 5/6+ Diamonds and No Side Suit

Direct 4-level rebids after the initial 3C transfer to 3D show single-suited hands and specific distribution. They are designed to allow easy 4-level key-card-asking bids for responder at his next turn as well as giving him the ability to show voids below the 5-level of the void suit. After opener accepts his transfer to 3D, responder can show a hand with no side shortness by bidding 3NT. He can then ask for key cards by bidding 4C.

Side suit shortness is also shown rather simply. After opener's 3D rebid, a direct 4C shows a singleton in that suit, while 4D shows a singleton heart, and 4H shows a singleton spade. A bid of the next higher suit can now ask for key cards (1430 or Texas responses).

It is harder to keep the void-showing rebids at a convenient level. Holding them to 5D or below is the best I could do. Direct jumps to 4S, 5C, and 5D can show voids in ascending order (4S=club void, 5C=heart void, 5D= spade void). The fact that those bids are below 5 of the void suit at least allows a bid of the void to serve as an exclusion key-card-asking bid, possibly indicating grand slam interest, without driving the auction past a small slam.

The two minor suit schemes begin to diverge when 2 or 3 biddable suits are involved. The diamond scheme involves complications that aren't present in the club structure.

When Responder Has 5/6+ Diamonds and a 4-Card Side Suit

The first difference occurs when responder has 5 or more diamonds and a 4-card side suit. A small problem pops up immediately. The 3NT rebid for hands with no side shortness is taken, and the whole 4-level must be used for extended descriptions of 1-suited hands with singletons or voids.

That leaves responder with a dilemma. If he wants to show a second suit, he must do it at the 3 level. He must use the remaining 3-level bids (3H and 3S) to make secondary transfers into 3 side suits. It sounds impossible, but it can be done. The trick is to make one bid do double duty. That bid is 3H.

By using a simple relay, we can use 3H to show either black suit. A 3S bid shows 4 cards in the one remaining suit: hearts.

With 5/6+ Diamonds and 4 Spades

After a 1NT-3C-3D auction, responder bids 3H, a relay to 3S. If he next makes a bid at the 4 level he is showinga real 4-card spade suit and completing the description of his distribution. The continuations are almost the same as those used for 1-suited hands. A bid of 4C shows a singleton in diamonds. 4D shows a singleton heart. Voids are shown in ascending suit order by bidding the next two suits (4H=club void; 4S=diamond void). A bid of 4NT is reserved for hands with no side shortness. This single deviation from the club structure is caused by our need to use 3NT for a special purpose, which I will now describe.

If responder's side suit is clubs, he makes a relay bid to 3NT, cancelling the message that he has 4 spades before describing his shape. Opener must then bid 4C (the real side suit) to get more information. The answers are familiar. For efficiency, singletons are shown by bidding the suit below the short suit, just as in the club transfer scheme; 4D shows a heart singleton (hence 3-1-5-4 or 2-1-6-4 distribution); 4H shows spade shortness (1-3-5-4 or 1-2-6-4); 4S and 5C show heart and spade voids; and 4NT shows a semi-balanced 2-2-5-4.

This scheme does not completely eliminate all 5-level responses, but it does confine them to hand types that are relatively rare. Hands with 6-4-3-0 or 7-3-3-0 distribution are unusual enough that a system user may never have to use a 5C or 5D bid to show this shape.

When responder has specifically 2-2-5-4 (5D,4C) distribution, though, opener faces the same problem we saw in the 1NT-2NT structure. When responder is forced to show his 2-2-5-4 shape by bidding 4NT, it is still possible for both hands to be completely open in the same major.

Opener is left with at least three choices. With a maximum, he may simply assume that responder must have the ace or king in the weak suit in order to be strong enough to justify his bidding. He may then try for slam with a 5C (the first short suit available) key-card inquiry. With a minimum, he may take a chance and pass 4NT (especially at matchpoints) or bid a much safer minor suit game (more attractive at international matchpoints).

Actually, there is another option. Just like the situation when responder was 2-2-4-5 (see page 78-79), opener may choose to refuse to make the expected 4C inquiry. Instead, he may bid 4D, asking responder to show any solid major suit stopper (A, KQ, QJx) that he may possess. If the answer indicates opponents may be able to run 5 or 6 tricks in an open suit, he can retreat to 5D.

When Responder Has 5-4-4-0 Distribution

Finally, we come to the handling of 5-4-4-0 hands with 5 diamonds. The other hand types already occupy all of the void-showing slots through 5C or 5D. Unfortunately, this leaves no space below the 5 level to show voids. A bid of 5H, 5S, or 5NT will tend to commit us to slam even when we find the void is not an asset. So I have devised a special sequence to allow us to show 5-4-4-0 hands with 5 diamonds at the 4 level: modified 5-4-4-0 transfers.

To avoid going to the 5 level to show a 5-4-4-0 hand, we will make use of a bid that is already used to show 3-suited hands with 4-4-4-1 distribution: the 2S (Sartor Slam Try) response to 1NT. We will extend it to cover one specific type of 5-4-4-0 hand—a hand with 5 diamonds and two 4-card side suits. This simple addition will allow us to pinpoint the void efficiently at the 4 level, thus allowing us more room to assess game and slam prospects.

The 5-4-4-0 hands with 5 clubs can be handled fairly well by our regular 1NT-2NT structure, first transferring to 3C and then going through our 3-level dance routine. We will leave that as it is.

Here is SST extension for hands containing 5 diamonds:

1NT	2S (SST)
2NT (forced)	4C= club void (5 diamonds,4 hearts, 4 spades)
	4D = heart void (5 diamonds, 4 clubs, 4 spades)
	4H = spade void (5 diamonds, 4 clubs, 4 hearts)

A convenient bid of the next suit now serves as an exclusion key-card ask, while bids in the other suits or 4NT are to play.

Summary: 1NT-3C Auctions

One-suited hands (5, usually 6+ diamonds)

1NT	3C (forces 3D)
3D	3NT= no shortness (6-3-2-2, 7-2-2-2, 5-3-3-2)
	4C= singleton club (6-3-3-1, 7-3-2-1)
	4D= singleton heart (6-3-3-1, 7-3-2-1)
	4H = singleton spade (6-3-3-1, 7-3-2-1)
	4S = club void
	4NT =heart void, then cheapest non-game or void bid asks for keycards or controls (4NT and 5D are sign-offs)
	5C= spade void, then cheapest non-game or void bid asks for keycards or controls (4NT and 5D are sign-offs)

Two-suited hands (5-6+ diamonds, 4-card side suit)

1NT   3C (forces 3D) -any rebid but pass = GF
3D   3H=forces 3S (shows 4 spades or 4 clubs)
               3S follow-ups:

Direct 4-level bids show 4 spades

       4C= 5-6+D, 4S, 2-3H, 1C
       4D= 5-6+D, 4S, 2-3 C, 1H
       4H= 6-7D, 4S, 2-3H, 0C
       4S= 6-7D, 4S, 2-3C, 0H
       4NT= 5D, 4S, 2C, 2H

Relay to 3NT shows 4 clubs/opener bids 4C (asking)

Then:	OR
4D= 5-6+D, 4C, 2-3S, 1H,	opener ignores 4C relay, and
4H= 5-6+D, 4C, 2-3H, 1S	bids 4D (asking for major stopper/s)
4S= 6-7 D, 4C, 2-3C, 0 H	
4NT= 5D, 4S, 2C, 2H	
5C= 6-7D, 4C, 2-3H, 0 S	

1NT   3C
3D   3S= shows 4 hearts, forces 3NT
3NT (forced) then:

       4C= 5-6+D, 4H, 2-3S, 1C
       4D= 5-6+D, 4H, 2-3C, 1S
       4H= 6-7D, 4H, 2-3S, 0C
       4S= 6-7D, 4H, 2-3C, 0S
       4NT= 5D, 4H, 2C, 2S

Special case

5-4-4-0 hands (5 diamonds, two 4-card side suits)
Responder uses SST instead of 3C transfer

1NT   2S (SST) (forces 2NT)
2NT (forced) 4C = club void (5 diamonds,4 hearts, 4 spades)
               4D = heart void (5 diamonds, 4 clubs, 4 spades)
               4H = spade void (5 diamonds, 4 clubs, 4 hearts)

A convenient bid of the next suit now serves as an exclusion key-card ask, while bids in the other suits or 4NT are to play. This is much more efficient than trying to figure out the right contract at the 5 level

Here are some example hands involving the 1NT-3C-3D sequence (and a couple involving the SST:

	Opener	*Responder*		
A.	♠ Kx	♠ Qxx	1NT	3C
	♥ AJxx	♥ x	3D	P
	♦ AJxx	♦ Qxxxxxx		
	♣ Qxx	♣ xx		
B.	♠ Kx	♠ Qxx	1NT	3C
	♥ AJxx	♥ x	3D	3H (4 spades or 4 clubs)
	♦ AJxx	♦ KQxxx	3S (ask)	4D (5+D, 4S, 2/3 C, 1H)
	♣ Q10x	♣ AKxx	4H (keycards?)	5C (2 KC + Q-Texas)
			6D	
C.	♠ Kx	♠ Ax	1NT	3C
	♥ AJxx	♥ Kx	3D	3NT (6+D, no shortness)
	♦ AJxx	♦ KQxxxx	4C (key cards?)	4S (2 KC + Q-Texas)
	♣ Qxx	♣ Kxx	5C (kings?)	5S (2)
			6D (a good partner	
			will have a club control)	

D.	♠ Kxxx	♠	1NT	3C
	♥ AJ	♥ Kxx	3D	5C (one-suiter, spade void)
	♦ AJxx	♦ KQxxxxx	5S (key cards?)	6C (2 KC + Q-Texas)
	♣ Q10x	♣ AJx	6D	
E.	♠ Qxxx	♠ x	1NT	3C
	♥ AJ	♥ KQx	3D	4H (6+D, 1S)
	♦ AQJx	♦ Kxxxxx	4S (key cards?)	4NT (2 KC, no Q)
	♣ Qxx	♣ AKx	6D	
F.	♠ Qx	♠ AKxx	1NT	2S (SST)
	♥ Q10x	♥	2NT (forced)	4D (4-0-5-4 shape)
	♦ Kxxx	♦ AQxxx	4H (asking)	4NT (2 KC+ Q)
	♣ AQJx	♣ Kxxx	5H (kings?)	6C (2)
			7C or 7D	
G.	♠ Qx	♠ AKxx	1NT	2S (SST)
	♥ Q10x	♥ Kxxx	2NT (forced)	4C (4-4-5-0 shape)
	♦ Kxxx	♦ AQxxx	5D (asking)	4NT (2 KC+ Q)
	♣ AQJx	♣	P	

1NT-3D (5/5 in the Majors)

The 3D response to 1NT is relatively simple. It shows at least 5/5 distribution in the majors and allows the opener to play all major suit contracts from his side. The bid only promises game-invitational values (9–10 HCP) but may be much stronger. With a bare minimum NT or a hand with wasted values in the minors, opener may bid 3H or 3S, allowing responder to pass if he also has a minimum. With a solid opener (15–16 HCP) or with minor suit aces and a good fit in one or both majors, opener can force to game by bidding 3NT.

In response to 3NT, responder bids his short suit, completing a fairly precise description of his distribution. Opener now establishes trump by bidding 4H or 4S. At this point, responder is in a good position to decide whether to pass and settle for game or try for slam. If he thinks slam prospects are good, he continues by showing his key-card holding, just as if opener's 4H or 4S bid were a key-card ask. This "invisible Blackwood" continuation is essentially the same as that used after a"West of Texas" transfer (see page 67).The steps are slightly compressed to make sure it is possible to stop in 5 of the trump suit when there are inadequate key cards for slam. The first step—the cheapest bid—shows 1 keycard. Opener can use the next step to ask about the queen of trump or just sign off at 5 of the trump suit. The second step shows 2 keycards without the queen of trump. The third step shows 2 keycards plus the queen; the fourth, 3 without, etc.

Opener can then sign off at the 5 level, bid 6, or try for a grand slam by bidding 5NT if the bidding establishes the fact that our side possesses all of the important controls. Responder may show a specific king at the 6 level or just jump to 7 if he can count 13 tricks (this often involves bidding 7 of a solid 6-or 7-card side suit).

It might be a good idea give responder the option of asking about opener's keycards instead of showing his own in certain situations. This can be done by not counting 4NT as a step in the answer scheme but rather letting it be a query about opener's keycards.

Here are some example auctions:

	Opener	Responder		
A.	♠ Qxxx	♠ KJxxx	1NT	3D (5-5+ in majors)
	♥ Kx	♥ QJxxx	3NT (ideal fit,4 spades	4D (shortness)
	♦ AJx	♦ x	(two minor aces)	
	♣ Axxx	♣ Jx	4S	P
B.	♠ Qxxx	♠ KJxxx	1NT	3D
	♥ Kx	♥ Axxxx	3NT	4D (shortness)
	♦ AJx	♦ x	4S	5C (2 KC, no Q)
	♣ Axxx	♣ KQ	5D (responder	6S (accepting the slam try)
			must have extra	
			strength to show his keycards-	
			last train slam try)	
C.	♠ Kx	♠ Axxxx	1NT	3D
	♥ Axx	♥ Qxxxx	3H	P (but 4H not that bad)
	♦ QJxx	♦ K		
	♣ KJxx	♣xx		

D. ♠ Kx   ♠ QJxxx   1NT   3D
    ♥ Axx   ♥ QJxxx   3H   3NT (slow tricks, help in C, D)
    ♦ QJxx   ♦ K   P
    ♣ KJxx   ♣ Qx

E. ♠ Kx   ♠ Axxxx   1NT   3D
    ♥ Axx   ♥ Kxxxx   3H (minimum)   4NT (if responder can ask)
    ♦ QJxx   ♦ Ax   5C (if 1430)   5D (Q ask)
    ♣ KJxx   ♣ A   5H (no Q)   P or 6H

F. ♠ Kx   ♠ AQxxx   1NT   3D
    ♥ Axx   ♥ KQxxxx   3H (minimum)   3S (ace-slam barely possible)
    ♦ QJxx   ♦ x   3NT   4H (could have just bid 4H)
    ♣ KJxx   ♣ x   P

The 3H and 3S responses to 1NT are very much like the 3D response. They also show specific 5/5+ distributions and shortnesses.

1NT-3H (Heart Shortness, 5/5+ in the Minors)

When responder jumps to 3H in response to 1NT, he shows a very specific hand. The hand contains at least 5 cards in each minor and a singleton or void in hearts. It is game-forcing. Thus when opener chooses a minor by bidding 4C or 4D, that bid serves as RKCB (or Texas if preferred) for that suit. He may choose to bid 3NT (to play) with sufficient strength in the majors. Here are some typical examples:

	Opener	Responder		
A.	♠ AQx	♠ Kx	1NT	3H
	♥ xxx	♥ x	4D (keycards?)	4H (2 KC, no Q-if Texas)
	♦ KQxx	♦ AJxxx	6D	
	♣ KJx	♣ AQxxx		
B.	♠ AQx	♠ Jx	1NT	3H
	♥KQxx	♥ x	4C (keycards?)	4H (2KC+ Q- if Texas)
	♦Qx	♦ AKJxx	4NT	P
	♣Jxxx	♣ KQ10xx		
C.	♠ Axxx	♠ x	1NT	3H
	♥ AJx	♥ x	4C (keycards?)	4H (2 KC + Q- if Texas)
	♦ Kx	♦ AJxxxx	6C	
	♣ Kxxx	♣ AQ10xx		

1NT-3S (Spade Shortness, 5/5+ in the Minors)

The 3S response to 1NT promises the same 5/5+ minor suit distribution as the 3H bid, but with a singleton or void in spades. It also is game-forcing. A 3NT rebid is to play, and 4C and 4D are key-card-asking (Texas) for those suits.

A.	♠ Axxx	♠ x	1NT	3S
	♥AJx	♥ xx	4C (keycards?)	4S (3 KC, no Q of C)
	♦Kx	♦ AQJxx	5H (any extras?)	6D (yes, good diamonds)
	♣Qxxx	♣ AKxxx	7C	
B.	♠ AQxx	♠ x	1NT	3S
	♥ Kxx	♥ Qx	4C (keycards?)	4S (3 KC, no Q)
	♦ Kx	♦ AJ9xx	6C	
	♣ QJxx	♣ AKxxx		
C.	♠ xxxx	♠ x	1NT	3S
	♥ AKxx	♥ QJ	4D (keycards?)	4H (2 KC, no Q)
	♦ Axx	♦ KJ10xx	5D	
	♣ KJ	♣ AQ10xx		

Throughout the last two sections, I have sometimes used 1430 and sometimes what I have labeled "Texas" responses in answer to key-card inquiries. Either set of answers will work. For that matter, so would 0314 responses. Partnerships will just have to pick a structure they prefer and then use it consistently. Varying the systems will probably be too big a strain on most players' memories.

Summary of the 1NT Response System

2C = Stayman (may not have a 4-card major). 2C starts invitational sequences in spades, NT, clubs, and diamonds—heart invitations start with a transfer. Smolen is used with 5-4 or 6-4 distribution in the majors and game-going values.

2D =Transfer (5+hearts). After opener bids 2H, 2S= artificial and GF, 2NT= invitational,   3C/3D show 5/5+, non-forcing.

2H = Transfer (5+spades). After opener bids 2S, 2NT= artificial and GF, 3C/3D/3H= 5/5+, non-forcing.

To invite with 5S, responder bids 2C. After 2D by opener, 2H= transfer (5 spades, invitational values). After a standard transfer in either major (1NT-2D/ 1NT-2H), raises to 3H or 3S, 3NT, and 4H or 4S are normal. After transfers, double jumps in new suits (3S,4C,4D, or 4H) are splinter bids.

Other Invitational Sequences

1NT-2C-2X-3C   1NT-2C-2X-3D (natural,5+ cards in bid minor)

2NT response to Stayman = 4/4 in majors, **minimum. After 2NT, responder either passes 2NT, raises to 3NT, or TRANSFERS into a major at the 3-level 1NT-2C-2NT-3H is a transfer to 3S. Responder can then pass, raise to game, or cue bid in search of slam.

3C response to Stayman = 4/4 in majors, **maximum. 3D=transfer to 3H, 3H=transfer to 3S

2S-artificial GF/slam try (SST)

1NT-2S (SST)-2NT (forced)-3C= CONFI (asks controls) then:

- 3D = 0-3 controls (A, K or K, K, K)
- 3H = 4 controls (A, A or A, K, K or K, K, K, K)
- 3S = 5 controls (A, A, K or A, K, K, K)
- 3NT = 6 controls (A, A, A or A, A, K, K)

If responder sees the partnership does not have 10 controls, he signs off at 3NT. Bidding a new suit guarantees 10 controls and starts the search for a 4/4 fit. Note: Bidding a suit after first bypassing it shows a 5-card suit withoutat least the QJ.

4-4-4-1 hands—responder bids 2S, then 3D,3H,3S,3NT
So: 1NT-2S (SST) forces 2NT; then
    3D = 4-4-1-4 (diamond singleton, GF)
    3H = 4-1-4-4 (heart singleton, GF)
    3S = 1-4-4-4 (spade singleton, GF)
    3NT= 4-4-4-1 (club singleton, GF)

Then: 4C = asks for controls (Texas responses)
        4D = Blackwood (just aces)
        4H,4S,5C,5D = sign-offs in game

***possible extension—see Modified Minor Transfers (5-4-4-0 hands with 5 diamonds))

Minor suit transfers after 1NT-2NT (clubs)/3C (diamonds) may be weak, planning to pass, or slam invitational.

After 1NT-2NT-3C, responder bids as follows:
- Pass = weak,6+ clubs

Any other bid is slam invitational

- 3D = 5+ clubs+ 4 hearts or any 5-4-4-0 hand with 5 clubs
- 3D forces 3H; then 3S= artificial relay to 3NT showing a 5-4-4-0 hand
- direct 4-bids show 5+D,4H
- 3H = 5+ clubs+ 4 spades, forces 3S
- 3S = 5+ clubs+4 diamonds, forces 3NT; responder can now show a short suit or bid 3NT/4C with no singleton
- 3NT = 6+ clubs, no side suit or shortness
- 4C = 6+ clubs, 1 diamond
- 4D = 6+ clubs, 1 heart
- 4H = 6+ clubs, 1 spade
- 4S =6+ clubs, diamond void
- 4NT = 6+ clubs, heart void
- 5C =6+ clubs, spade void

After 1NT-3C-3D, responder bids as follows:

- Pass = weak, 6+ diamonds

Any other bid is slam invitational

- 3H = 5+ diamonds, 4 spades, or 4 clubs
- 3H forces 3S, then 3NT shows 4 clubs
- 4C=asks; 4D = singleton heart
- 4H = singleton spade
- 4S= heart void
- 4NT = 5 diamonds, 4 clubs, 2-2 in majors
- 5C =spade void
- Direct 4-level bids over 3S confirm 4 spades
- 4C=singleton club
- 4D=singleton heart
- 4H = club void
- 4S = heart void
- 3S = 5+ diamonds, 4 hearts (1NT-3C-3D-3S auction)
- 3NT = 6+ diamonds, no side suit or shortness

1NT-3C General Rules

With diamonds and a 4-card side suit: Transfer to 3D,3H/3S rebid (forcing 3S or 3NT) then show lower/higher side suit singleton with first two available 4-level bids/show voids with next two available suit bids. Transfer to 3D, show second suit, then bid 4NT to show 5-4-2-2 hand

With 1-suited hand, transfer to 3D, then bid 3NT (no shortness) or make a direct 4-level bid:

- 4C = 6+ diamonds, singleton club
- 4D = 6+ diamonds, singleton heart
- 4H = 6+ diamonds, singleton spade
- 4S = 6+ diamonds, club void
- 4NT = 6+ diamonds, heart void
- 5C = 6+ diamonds, spade void

Use Extension of SST (1NT-2S) for All 5-4-4-0 Hands with 5 Diamonds

Using SST instead of transfer to 3D:

- 1NT 2S 2NT Then-
- 4C = club void (4-4-5-0)
- 4D = heart void (4-0-5-4)
- 4H = spade void (0-4-5-4)

Partnerships may choose to simplify or modify the continuation sequences.

3D response to 1NT =5/5 in majors, invitational to game or slam

After 1NT-3D, responder bids as follows:

- 3H or 3S = minimum, willing to play in 3 opposite invitational-to-game values.
- 4H or 4S = minimum with 4-card fit or maximum with 3
- 3NT =maximum, game-forcing
  Responder bids his short suit.
  Opener now bids 4H or 4S, setting trump.

If responder wishes to make a slam try, he shows his keycards, just as if the bid of 4H or 4S were key-card-asking.

Partnerships may choose 1430, 0-3-1-4, or "Texas" answers (see "jumps to 4D/4H" steps below)

Jumps to 3H/3S in response to 1NT = singleton in bid suit, 5/5+in minors, game-forcing, slam invitational—opener can bid 3NT with good major stoppers, or 4C or 4D with slam interest. Responder starts cue bidding at second turn.

Jump to 4C = Gerber

Stayman, followed by jump to 4C = Gerber if no major shown by opener/RKC Gerber for opener's bid major

Transfers to 2H or 2S, followed by jump to game

Mild slam try—shows 2 key cards, no queen of trump

Jumps to 4D/4H = modified Texas Transfers—after opener bids 4H or 4S, responder may try for slam as follows:

- Bid of next highest suit (first step) = 2 key cards + queen of trump
- second step = 3 key cards, no queen of trump
- third step = 3 KC + Q
- fourth step = 4 KC, no Q
- fifth step = 4 KC + Q etc.

Note:The responses are slightly different when the 2-level transfers and jumps to 4 can't be used for 2KC with no Q (i. e. transfers to minor-suit sequences). Then first step = 2 KC, second= 2 KC + Q, third= 3 KC, fourth= 3 KC + Q, fifth=4 KC, sixth = 4 KC

After Interference Over 1NT

Over a double

When our opening 1NT bid is doubled (whether naturally or conventionally), I prefer the following system of responses and continuations:

1. Responder can pass. This bid forces opener to redouble. Responder will do this with one of the following three types of hands:
    *   He may have a good balanced hand (at least 8–9 HCP) and want to either play 1NT redoubled or double the opponents when they run.
    *   He may have a weakish hand with 2 suits in which to play. After opener redoubles, he will bid the lower of his 2 suits, à la DONT (a convention used against opponents' 1NT opening).Opener may pass or bid a higher suit, looking for a better fit. This sequence is used instead of Stayman.
    *   He may have 4-3-3-3 distribution but be too weak to risk a pass of their double. In this case, he will have to escape to 2C even if this is one of his 3-card suits. His object will be to simply avoid playing a doubled contract. He hopes to find at least a 4-3 fit. If he's lucky, he may even have opener scramble into his 4-card suit. (A bold alternative might be an immediate transfer into the 4-card suit.)
2. Responder can redouble. This bid forces opener to bid 2C. This is a two-way bid. It serves as a transfer into a 5+ card club suit. With clubs responder will simply pass. It may also (rarely) show two 5-card majors.*With that hand, he pulls 2C to 2D. Opener then chooses his best major. (actually, you could also do it with two 4-card majors. It wouldn't make any difference to the opener. He'll still choose his best major.)
3. Responder can make an immediate transfer into a 5+ card diamond, heart, or spade suit. A bid of 2C is *not* Stayman. It is a transfer to 2D; 2D and 2H are normal transfers into the majors. With a hand that might normally use Stayman, responder passes and then tries to find a fit, as described above.
4. Responder can bid 2S or 2NT (partnership preference) with at least 5-5 in the minors. This system may not be perfect, but it allows you to escape from 1NT, transfer into all four suits, and put the doubler on opening lead in many cases.

Alternate treatment

Redouble = weak hand with 5+ clubs or diamonds,
2C = Garbage Stayman
2D = transfer to hearts
2H = transfer to spades
2S = 5/5 in minors

Over Opponents' Overcalls of Our 1NT

As much as I really want to keep the traditional penalty double to punish the opponents when they have the audacity to overcall our 1NT opening, I have reluctantly come to the conclusion that the negative double is probably more frequently useful. Therefore, when opponents make a 2-level overcall, our doubles will be primarily takeout.

Over a 2C overcall, double is essentially Stayman. All transfers still apply. Over 2D, 2H, or 2S, the double is negative, tending to deny a higher 5-card suit. Lebensohl 2NT is used for non-forcing or invitational bids of 5+ card suits at the 3 level. Direct 3-level bids are either forcing or highly encouraging, depending on partnership preference. With a stack in the opponent's suit, one can only pass and pray to the bridge gods for a reopening double.

Simple Summary

Over 2C- double =Stayman, 2-bids = transfers
    2NT=Lebensohl
Over 2D/2H/2S—2-bids = natural, NF 2NT= Lebensohl
    3-bids = forcing or highly invitational
Over double—pass forces redouble
(shows willingness to pass 1NT redoubled or 2 suits to run to)
(will also double opponents' run out with the good hand)
Over double redouble forces 2C-(5+card club suit) or
    (pull to 2D = 5/5{or 4/4}in majors)
Over double-transfers into D, H,and S
    (2C= 5+D, 2D=5+H, 2H=5+S)

CHAPTER 4
The 2-Club Opening Bid

The 2C opening bid is defined as a hand with 11–16 HCP and at least a good 5-card club suit. If the club suit is only 5 long, the hand will always have a 4-card major. Otherwise, it will have a 6+ card club suit.

Responder bids 2D on most hands with enough values to rebid at the 2NT or 3C level. All game-forcing responding hands begin with 2 diamonds, with subsequent new suit bids forcing. Direct responses of 2H and 2S are non-forcing, usually showing 6-card suits. Jumps to 3D, 3H, and 3S are invitational, with semi-solid 6+ card suits. A direct 2NT is invitational.

There are many hands containing 5 clubs that should not be opened 2C. With a bad 5-card suit, opener should almost always try to find a better alternative. This is usually either a 1D or a 1NT opening. With 4 diamonds and 5 clubs and 11–13 HCP, 1D is the proper system opening. With 5-4 2-2 distribution, 14–16 HCP, and decent stoppers in the 2-card suits, 1NT may be best. A bid of 1D is the other reasonable choice.

My prejudice against 2C opening bids with bad 5-card club suits includes almost all 5-4-3-1 hands, even to those with only 1 diamond and 4-3 distribution in the majors. With those hands, I always open 1D. There are two reasons for this. First, the 2C bid is the most awkward bid in a strong club system. Responder often is forced to pass with a weakish hand when a much better fit is available in another suit. Second, if responder does manage to check for a better spot, he may still be forced to return the contract to 3C when the combined trump holding is very poor. He will often be a level higher than anyone else in the room and down an extra trick. If the opening bid decision is not clear-cut, my advice is to look for a bid other than 2C*.

When the partnership assets are minimal or only slightly better, the 1D opening almost always gives us the best opportunity to find a major suit fit. It also gives us a chance to get to a 1NT contract, which is obviously impossible if you open 2C. Here are some very common minimum openers:

A. ♠ x ♥ AQx ♦ KQxx ♣ Jxxxx   B. ♠ KJx ♥ x ♦ AKxx ♣ Qxxxx
C. ♠ KQJ ♥ AQxx ♦ J ♣ 10xxxx

I wouldn't open any of them 2C. I would open hands A and B with 1D, with no second choice. A 1H bid would be conceivable on hand C, but I would probably open it 1D. With a 1D opening, all three hands give you good rebid options and the chance to find a decent 2H, 2S, or 1NT contract opposite a minimum responding hand. The 1D opening will also give you a chance to duplicate (sort of) the way the bidding will go at most other tables. Non-strong clubbers will open 1C on many of the hands in question, of course, but a major suit response will put them in almost exactly our position.

With hand A, you raise 1H to 2H, bid 1NT over 1S, bid 2C over 1NT, and raise two of either minor. With B, you bid 1NT over 1H, raise 1S to 2S, and treat 1NT, 2C, and 2D just as before. On C, you raise partner's 1H, 1S, and 2C bids. You pull 1NT to 2C, since responder is almost certain to have 3+ clubs. A forcing 2D bid is a little annoying, but you just bid 2NT.

These hands bring us to a little system rule which covers 1D-1NT auctions. **When a 1D opener pulls a 1NT response to 2C, he does not promise both minors. Responder is absolutely prohibited (by common sense, not law) from correcting the contract to 2D without at least 5 good (preferably 6) diamonds.** Hand C is a perfect example of why.

Now that we've gone over reasons to avoid a 2C opener, let's discuss hands that we want to open 2C. If it sounds like I think the 2C opening is a big liability, that is not really true. While it may have some awkward aspects, it also has some distinct advantages. Responder never has to worry about a short club suit in competitive auctions. It

---

* In the spirit of full disclosure, I must admit that those who use a more traditional Precision Club structure actually have an even better solution for this type of hand. They play an opening 2D bid shows a 3-suited hand short in diamonds. I would be happy to make that part of this system, but it runs into a minor problem—the 2D opening bid is already earmarked for a different purpose (see chapter 11). Since the hand can be handled quite well by our 1D bid, we will make that our default treatment.

often allows easy bidding to club games and slams that would be harder to reach with a vague 1C opening bid. It helps responder picture a good source of tricks for a 3NT contract. It is even mildly preemptive. A good response scheme can make it an effective bidding tool.

Here is the response scheme:

- Pass = not strong enough to try to improve the contract or search for game via a forcing 2D, an invitational 2NT, or a 3-level jump. Also not able to bid a non-forcing 2H or 2S (weak hand, 5/6+ card suit).
- 2D = artificial; enough values to force at least to 3C, and the start to most invitational and game-forcing auctions. A 2D bid followed by a new suit shows a 5+ card suit and is forcing. A 2D bid followed by a raise of opener's 2H or 2S rebid to 3H or 3S is invitational. With game-forcing values, responder can bid an artificial 2NT over a 2H or 2S rebid, letting opener define his hand more exactly. An immediate raise of opener's 2H or 2S rebid requires 5-card support. This is because the bid may just show a feature, not a 4-card suit. This will be explained in the next section.
- 2H or 2S = non-forcing, resembling a weak 2-bid. It shows a 6+ card suit, although 5 may do if responder is desperate to escape a 2C contract. Opener is expected to pass, although he may raise with a maximum and a great fit.
- 2NT = balanced or semi-balanced, 11–12 HCP, invitational to 3NT
- 3C = 6–9 HCP, 3+ clubs
- 3D, 3H, 3S = good 6+card suit, invitational
- 4C = RKCB 1430
- 4D, 4H, 4S = splinter bids, 4+ clubs, singleton or void, 13+ HCP

Opener's Rebids After 2C-2D

Opener's rebids after 2C-2D are unique to the system. In most strong club systems (unless they use 2C only for 6+-card 1-suiters), a 2H or 2S rebid is strictly natural, showing 5+ clubs and a 4-card second suit. A 2NT bid is usually natural, showing a better-than-minimum semi-balanced hand with stoppers in the side suits. A 3C rebid merely shows 6+ clubs. The common bidding schemes do not allow opener to differentiate between a maximum and a minimum hand when he does not have no trump distribution.

The solution? I'm glad you asked. The solution is to make a 2H or 2S rebid by opener a two-way bid. When the auction goes 2C-2D-2 of a major, it shows one of two hands. Opener either has 5+ clubs and 4 of the bid major, or he has 6+ clubs, a maximum hand (15–16 HCP), and a feature in the bid major. This allows him to show a good unbalanced hand not suitable for a 2NT rebid. The 2NT rebid now guarantees a maximum with 6+ clubs and semi-balanced distribution. A simple 3C rebid after 2C-2D shows 6+ clubs and a minimum (11–14 HCP) hand.

"How does responder know which hand opener has?" I hear someone ask. As I usually answer questions of that sort, "Simple!" Responder bids 2NT to inquire. If opener has the unbalanced maximum with 6+clubs, he raises responder to 3NT. Since responder will usually have values in the suits opener didn't bid, this will generally right-side the 3NT contract.

If opener actually has 4 cards in his bid major, he has a choice of rebids. All guarantee 5+ clubs and 4 of the bid major. With minimum values, he bids 3C. With maximum values, he can bid 3 of a side suit (showing a singleton or void) or rebid 3 of his major (showing exactly 5-4-2-2 distribution. Responder can then sign off in game or try for slam. When neither partner has much in a particular side suit, it may steer them to a good 5C contract. The pair may also be able to find a good 5-3, 5-2, or even a 4-3 fit in opener's feature suit. Of course, if opener shows a 4-card major and a 4-4 fit is found, responder can simply invite or bid game in the major.

Here are some sample auctions featuring a 2C opening bid:

	Opener	Responder		
A.	♠ Kx	♠Jxxx	2C	2D(artificial/forcing)
	♥ xxx	♥xx	3C (6+ clubs, minimum)	P
	♦ Ax	♦KJxx		
	♣ AQ10xxx	♣Kx		
B.	♠ QJxx	♠Axxx	2C (1D also possible)	2D
	♥ Kx	♥ Qxxx	2S (2-way)	2NT (asking)
	♦ xx	♦xxx	3C (5+C,4S-minimum)	3S (invitational)
	♣ AKxxx	♣Qx	P	
C.	♠ KQx	♠ xxx	1D (not 2C!)	1H
	♥ AQxx	♥K10xx	2H	P
	♦x	♦Kxxx		
	♣ Qxxxx	♣10x		

Don't open 2C with a bad suit and/or a weak hand. If you do, you play Hand C in 2C.

D.	♠ Qx	♠A10xx	2C	2D
	♥ AJx	♥xx	2NT (maximum,	3NT
	♦Kx	♦Qxxx	semi-balanced)	
	♣ KQ10xxx	♣Ax		

E. ♠ Kxx   ♠ J10xx   2C   2D
    ♥ x   ♥AJxx   2S!   2NT (forcing, asking)
    ♦KQx   ♦Jx   3NT (maximum,   P
    ♣ AKJ10xx ♣Qx   (unbalanced, 6+ clubs)

F. ♠ AJx   ♠KQ10xxx 2C   2S (NF/with Q of C, could bid 3S
    ♥ xx   ♥xx   3S   4S or P (coin flip)
    ♦ Kx   ♦Qx   NF=non-forcing
    ♣ AKxxxx xxx

G. ♠Qxx   ♠ KJ10xx 2C   2D
    ♥ J   ♥Axx   3C   3S (5+ spades, forcing)
    ♦KQx   ♦Jx   4S
    ♣ AJ10xxx ♣Kx

H. ♠ AJxx   ♠ Q10x   2C   2D
    ♥ x   ♥ xxx   2S (2-way)   3D (5+ diamonds, forcing)
    ♦ Axx   ♦KJxxx   3S (4 spades)   4C
    ♣ KQxxx ♣Axxx   4D (cue)   5C (no side ace to cue)
                        P

I. ♠x   ♠AKxxx   2C   2D
    ♥AKxx   ♥QJx   2H   2S
    ♦ xx   ♦x   3H (confirms 4 hearts) 4H (Sonny Moyse lives!*)
    ♣ KQxxxx ♣Jxx

Responder could bid 4C instead of 4H. The final contract would then be 5C.

---

*Sonny Moyse was a longtime editor of *Bridge World* magazine. He was an ardent advocate of 4-3 fits. The 4-3 fit is widely known as the Moysian Fit.

Interference Over a 2C Opening

It is important to have good agreements to handle opponents' competition over our opening bid of 2C. We especially don't want to miss 4-4 major suit fits that may be easier to reach after a standard 1C opening. Direct overcalls and doubles offer no special problems. They are treated essentially the same way standard bidders treat them (negative doubles, etc.), though at a higher bidding level.

If opener's LHO doubles, responder can redouble to show strength. He may be laying the groundwork for a subsequent penalty double. He may also be planning to make a later bid in a new suit (forcing), showing a good hand and at least a good 5-card suit. A third possibility is a good (better than a direct 3C) raise of clubs. Opener will generally pass the redouble around to the doubler with a decent opener and no unusual distribution.

He may occasionally pull it to his side major or 3C with a 6- or 7-card club suit or a really atrocious defensive hand. Any immediate suit bid over the double is non-forcing and shows length in the suit without much interest in defense or belief that our side can make a game. It is essentially the same bid responder would make without the double, taking into account the fact that the doubler may have 4 or 5 of the suit.

When the opponents bid and the auction gets back to responder, a double should be for penalty. A bid of 2NT could be natural and invitational, but I think it might be more useful to use it as a conventional takeout bid, guaranteeing 4 cards in the opposite major (assuming the opponents have bid 2H or 2S) and at least a partial fit for clubs. Opener could then revert to 3C or bid 3 or 4 of the major. If the opponents have run out to 2D, I would suggest a special treatment. A double should still be penalty, but a bid of 2H or 2S should show only a 4-card suit. With a 5-card suit, responder can bid 3D (transfer with 5+ hearts) or 3 hearts (transfer with 5+ spades). Alternatively, responder could just bid and rebid the major with 5, and use the transfer with 6. Any reasonable agreement should work. Opener is free to bid 3 with a minimum or jump to game with a maximum.

Two-level overcalls of the 2C opening pose no special problems. Over a 2D overcall, a double by responder just asks opener to continue his description of his hand. Responder simply makes a standard negative double over 2H or 2S. That guarantees 4 cards in the opposite major, but it should also show at least 2 (3 would be nice) clubs, in case opener has to retreat to 3C.

With a 5-card or longer suit, he has two options: he can make a free bid in his suit (2H, 2S, 3D), which is forcing for one round; this may be a hand strong enough to force to game. With a 6+ card suit worth no more than a competitive bid at the 3 level, he may make a negative double and then bid his suit (probably bidding 3H or 3S). Opener is expected to pass. The bid is non-forcing. A jump to 3D, 3H, or 3S directly over the opponent's double can be treated as preemptive or invitational.

Fourth-seat competition by the opponents requires slightly different treatment. Actions after 2C-P-P-double simply involve common sense. Opener may redouble to show a maximum with good defensive values. If the opponents then get too high, the responder might find a double with modest values. Opener might also bid 3C with exceptional length, simply to get in the way and annoy the opposing pair. The passed hand responder is unlikely to get involved with his limited strength, but he could conceivably toss in a bid with a very long suit that he couldn't bid earlier—especially if he wouldn't mind a lead of his suit.

When the auction goes 2C-P-2D-(action by opponent), however, the situation is different. The responder has to have some values for his 2D bid and will often have a 4-card major for which he was seeking a fit. Game is often feasible.

Let's start when RHO sticks in a double. This action is rather easy to handle. The opener can make his first rebid almost exactly as he would without the double, with two extra options— he can redouble to show a maximum with solid defensive values and pass to show a minimum without a 4-card major. With 4 hearts or 4 spades, he can bid his major. With extra length or especially good offensive values (partners might even want to specify a solid or semi-solid suit) he can bid 3C. If opener passes or bids, responder can basically continue as he would have in an uninterrupted auction. He can bid a new suit (forcing), raise a 4-card major, bid NT, or raise clubs. If opener redoubles, he may decide to sit for that contract or to play for penalty and begin doubling any escape bids made by the opponents.

Finally, we come to the situation which is most likely to lead to confusion. When the auction goes 2C-P-2D-(2H or 2S), what does a double by opener mean? Does it show that the opponent has bid his 4-card major? Is it for takeout? As in other areas of the system, more than one scheme will work. What's really important is that both partners are on the same page. The official system is as follows: Since the 2C bid shows, by definition, either 6+ clubs or 5 clubs, and a 4-card major, we can show a hand that might want to double the overcall for penalty by a process of elimination. We don't need to use an immediate double by opener for penalty. When partner bids 2D and RHO overcalls 2H or 2S, opener has the following choices:

- double = 4 cards in the opposite major
- 2NT = maximum with 6+ good clubs and a stopper in the opponent's suit
- 3C = minimum with 6+ clubs

Here's where the process of elimination comes in. If the 2C bid does not contain a 6+ card club suit he wishes to bid or 4 cards in the other major, there are only two possibilities. He either has 4 of the overcaller's major or he has a maximum with a high honor in the suit. The overcaller has stolen his planned rebid. Therefore, a pass shows that hand. Responder can now do one of the following:

- double = giving opener the chance to pass for penalty
- bid a new suit = forcing
- cue bid = suggesting opener bid 3NT
- raise opener to 3C = stronger than an immediate 3C

In general, we can say that once responder has bid 2D, showing values, the partnership is committed to some action over 2-level overcalls. They must either compete to at least the 3 level or double the opponents.

SECTION 2

Big Hands

The Big Club

We now come to the anchor bid of the system: the strong 1C opening bid. This bid shows a minimum of 17 HCP (occasionally an exceptional 16) and defines the limits for the 1D, 1H, 1S, 1NT, and 2C opening bids. All of those bids are limited to a maximum of 16 HCP by definition. The "1D with muscles"(17–20 HCP.) and two big NT openings (2NT, 3NT) are the sole exceptions. The 1C opener handles a vast majority of the big hands.

The negative response to a 1C opening bid is 1D. The 1D bid usually shows 0–8 HCP. The only exception, which will occur less than 10 percent of the time, is a modified version of the old Precision "Impossible Negative" bid. We will go over that bid in a separate section of this chapter.

The most common positive suit responses (1H, 1S, 2C) show 9+ HCP. I am tempted to qualify that by saying a positive response can be made with a "good" 7-8 point hand, but I really don't want to encourage the current fad of upgrading hands that don't really meet supposed system standards. It has become common for strong clubbers to open good 15 HCP or even 14 HCP hands with 1C and to give positive responses on lousy hands simply because they have decent distribution. I think this undermines the usefulness of the whole system.

There is really no need to upgrade a 15–16 HCP opener. It is easy to open one of a suit and make a strength-showing jump if you think it necessary. It is also not a crime to have a maximum for your opening bid. Upgrading a 7–8 HCP hand to a positive response is even worse. Not only will it sometimes encourage opener to push to a bad marginal contract based on an extra queen that you "have to" have for your bid, it also often wrong-sides the contract while gaining no significant advantage.

The most common 1C auction in this system is 1C-1D-1NT, showing a balanced hand with 17–19 HCP. When this occurs, responder can easily describe a 5+ card suit with near-positive values with a transfer bid and invitation. If, however, he decides to be a genius and makes a bad 1H or 1S response, the same contract will probably be reached with the weak hand as declarer. The advantage of having the opening lead coming into the strong hand is lost. So too is the advantage of having the strong hand concealed. So **upgrading a responding hand is not just misleading. It is also dumb**.

The 1NT response and all 2-and 3-level responses have non-conventional meanings and will be discussed in individual sections. Several have more than one meaning or serve as relays.

One major difference between this system and most other strong club systems is the fact that **an opening 1C and rebid of 1H or 1S is forcing** for at least one round. Opener does not need jump rebids in the majors to create a game force. As we shall see when we discuss big suit-oriented hands, game forces are only created after an exchange of information at the 1-level.

A major advantage of this approach is that those jumps to 2H, 2S, and 2NT can be used for other purposes. In the "Big Balanced Hands" section, we will see one of them. The jump rebid of 2H will take the place of a standard 2NT opening bid. We will discuss that bid as part of our discussion of big balanced hands.

In addition, the jump rebids to 2S and 2NT are now used to describe traditional "strong 2-bids" in the minors. Those sequences will also be discussed thoroughly in separate sections. But first we will examine how the system handles big balanced hands.

CHAPTER 5

Big Balanced Hands

1C-1D-1NT (17–19 HCP)

Our first range for a powerful balanced hand is 17–19 HCP. Assuming responder gives a negative (0–8 HCP) response to the 1C opening bid, this hand is described by the simple rebid of 1NT. Should responder start with a positive 1-level response, the 1NT rebid is made with any 17+ hand. There is no need to jump around to show extra strength. Opener will let the responder show his strength and then decide whether to make any move toward slam.

By far the most common auction is 1C-1D-1NT. This bid handles all the hands that would be shown by a jump to 2NT if one were playing a standard system. A couple of advantages are obvious. If the auction stops at 1NT, we are a level lower than the field and no suits have been mentioned by either partner. The opening leader is making a blind lead. It may not make any difference, but it can't hurt.

Although this is just like opening a very big 1NT, at this point there are several differences in responder's continuations. Simple Stayman (no longer guaranteeing invitational or better values) and standard transfers now apply. The 2NT and 3C answers to Stayman can still be used, but the sequences involving transfers to 2S are now just identical to those surrounding transfers to 2H.

Opener will still bid 2NT over 2C to show both majors and a minimum, and will bid 3C to show both majors and a maximum. This should not be a problem. If responder has a NT invitation, he passes 2NT or raises 3C to 3NT. If he has the weakish hand with one or both majors, he simply transfers into 3H or 3S. With a better hand (7–8 HCP), he just bids the appropriate game after the transfer.

Slam is probably out of the question (unless responder has an "impossible negative"), so the meanings of the 2S and 2NT continuations are altered. Jumps to 3C,3D,

3H, and 3S are "impossible negatives". They usually show 9+ HCP, a singleton in the bid suit, and 4-4-4-1 distribution. However, I have added 7+/8 HCP limit raises with 4 trump and a singleton to the convention. At any rate, this eliminates the 3D, 3H, and 3S bids used in response to an opening 1NT. It will probably be useful to go through the entire response scheme one bid at a time.

Assuming a 1D response, these hands would all be opened 1C and rebid 1NT.

A.	♠ AKxx	B.	♠ Ax	C.	♠ AQx
	♥ Kx		♥ Kxx		♥ KQx
	♦ Qxx		♦ AQxxx		♦ KQx
	♣ AKxx		♣ KQJ		♣ Jxxxx

Our definition is fairly simple. The hand contains 17–19 HCP and (almost always) no 5-card major. It may contain a 5-card minor. The following responses apply:

2C-Stayman

Stayman is no longer used as a convoluted way to make an invitational bid in a 5-card spade suit. It is a simple request for opener to show a 4-card major. It does not guarantee that responder has a 4-card major. It may be the beginning of a 2-step invitational raise in NT, shown by rebidding 2NT over opener's 2D, 2H, or 2S reply to 2C. It may also be the start of a Smolen rebid at both the 2 and 3 levels.

With 5-4 in the majors and 5 to a bad 7 HCP, responder bids 2C. If opener bids 2D, responder bids his 4-card suit at the two level. Opener can sign off at 2S or 3H or make a game try in another suit. If responder has 8 HCP (or a good 7), he bids his 4-card suit at the 3 level. Opener will choose the appropriate game—either 3NT or 4 of responder's long major.

What if responder has 5-4 in the majors but 0-4 (or a bad 5) HCP? He should simply transfer into his long major and pass. Similarly, with 5-5 in the majors and a very weak hand, transfer and pass is my choice of actions. (I would transfer into spades. If the opponents balance, you can compete with a 3H bid.)

With 5-5 in the majors and better (mildly invitational) values, we have a slight problem. The "impossible negative" jump to 3D after 1C-1D-1NT has taken away the 3D bid we use to show both majors after a 1NT opener. If we still want to make the strong hand the declarer in any heart or spade contract, we have to use some ingenuity. Fortunately, we mad scientists are just full of it (you may interpret that any way you wish). Here is the solution: With two 5-card majors and 5–8 HCP, we bid 2D to transfer into 2H and then rebid 3D as a completely artificial bid showing that hand. The loss of 3D as a natural bid here is not a big deal. Opener can then bid 3H or 3S to play or jump to 4H or 4S with the right hand.

What if we have a maximum (good 7+-8 HCP) negative response and 5-5+ in the majors? We should be willing to force to game in one of our suits. When opener shows a minimum by bidding 3H or 3S, just raise him to 4 anyway and hope he makes it. What can he do? Revoke your bidding privileges?

2D and 2H—Standard Transfers to Majors

As previously mentioned, the 2D and 2H transfers to the major suits after 1C-1D-1NT are fairly standard. Responder transfers and invites with 2NT or a new suit when holding only 5 of his major. With a 6+ card suit, he can invite with a simple raise to 3H or 3S. New suits after a transfer are now simply help-suit game tries. Since opener has 17–19 HCP, invitations show about 6-7 points. With a decent 8 HCP, it's best to just jump to 3NT or 4 of the major in most cases.

The Two-Way 2S Response (Invitational)

Since slam is not usually in the picture, 2 spades is no longer needed for a slam try. It is more useful as a bid to show a long minor which may run in 3NT or to show a two-suited hand with 5/5+ in the minors and 7-8 HCP. In the first case, it shows a 6+ card suit headed by AQ, KQ, or AJ10 and suggests opener bid 3NT with the ace, king, or a good 3-card fit in the suit. It implies the complete lack of an outside entry. In the second case it may show the way to a minor suit game when 3NT has a fatal weakness in one of the majors.

After 1C-1D-1NT, responder bids 2S. Opener is required to bid 2NT. If responder now bids 3C or 3D, he is showing the one-suited invitational hand. If he instead bids 3H or 3S, he is showing a singleton or void in the bid suit, 7-8 HCP, and 5/5+ distribution in clubs and diamonds. Opposite the long suit, opener can either bid 3NT with the right fit or pass. If facing the minor 2-suiter, he can bid 3NT with solid major suit stoppers. He can sign off in 4C or 4D. If he likes his fit, he can bid 4H (RKC for clubs) or 4S (RKC for diamonds), or just jump to 5C or 5D.

The Multi-Minor 2NT Response:"1-Suit Weak or 2-Suit Freak"

The 2NT bid after 1C-1D-1NT is a multipurpose call. Primarily it serves as a way to stop in 3 of a minor with a very weak hand (0-5 HCP) and a long suit. Opener is forced to bid 3C. Responder can then pass or correct to 3D.

However, by pulling 3C to bids other than 3D, responder can describe several other types of hands. It is tempting to overload the bid with too many additional meanings, but some are useful. Basically, they are all two-suited "freaks" in the minors. They should show about 6–8 HCP—strong enough to feel safe playing at the 4 level and offering a reasonable chance for a minor suit game if a good fit is found. With fewer points, responder will either sign off in his best suit or pass 1NT.

The invitational 2S response already covers hands with 5-5 in the minors. The 2NT response can be used to handle even more freakish hands. One nice feature is that the exact same set of responses can be used after a 1C-1D-2H auction (20–21 HCP, balanced), which will be discussed in the next section.

These bids follow a logical pattern, which should help with memory strain. The lower of any touching pair of bids shows longer clubs (the lower minor), while the higher shows longer diamonds (the higher minor). Lower level bids (3H,3S) show slightly less extreme distribution (6-5-1-1). Higher (4-level) bids show voids and more freakish (6-5-2-0 or 7-5-1-0) shape. At the 4 level, the lower bids (4C,4D) show voids in hearts (the lower major) and the higher bids (4H,4S) show voids in spades (the higher major). Hands with 6-6-1-0 shape are shown by bidding 3NT. The void suit can be found by a 4H asking bid if opener thinks game or slam is possible.

Since all of this is probably as clear as mud, let me explain with a chart:

After a 1C-1D-1NT-2NT auction, these are to play
Pass = 0–5 HCP, 5-6+ clubs   3D = 0-5 HCP, 5-6+ diamonds

Any other bid is a two-suited "freak" with 6–8 HCP.
3H = 6C, 5D, 1H, 1S   3S = 6D, 5C, 1H, 1S
4C = 6C+, 5+D, H void   4D = 6+D, 5+C, H void
4H = 6+C, 5+D, S void   4S = 6+D, 5+C, S void

Finally, one can describe a minor 6-6 two-suiter with a void.
3NT= 6C+, 6D+, void. Opener can sign off in 4C or 4D or use a 4H bid to ask
for the void if planning to try for game or slam.

If all of this is too complicated, one could simply bid 3H with any 6+-5+ hand with
longer clubs, 3S with any 6+-5+ hand with longer diamonds, and 3NT with any 6-6
hand. Meanwhile, 4H or 4S continuations could ask about distribution.

The following is a group of hands held by a 1D responder. Assume that in every case,
the auction has proceeded 1C-1D (by you)-1NT. What bid or sequence of bids would
you use to describe your hand? Cover the right side of the page to hide the answers until
you decide on an action on each hand.

A.	♠Kxxxx ♥10xxx ♦xxx ♣x	A.	2H - with 0-5 HCP, just transfer and pass.
B.	♠xx ♥QJxxx ♦Kx ♣Jxxx	B.	2D, followed by 2NT. With 5+-7 HCP, you can invite game.
C.	♠x ♥J10x ♦Q10xxxx ♣xxx	C.	2NT, followed by 3D. 2NT forces 3C; the correction to 3D is "drop dead."

D. ♠xxx
   ♥xx
   ♦xx
   ♣KQxxxx

D. 2S, followed by 3C.
2S forces 2NT, then
3C (or 3D) is
invitational to 3NT

E. ♠AQxx
   ♥ x
   ♦Kxxx
   ♣Qxxx

E. 3H—impossible negative.
3H shows a singleton
heart, 4-1-4-4, 9+ HCP.

F. ♠ x
   ♥xx
   ♦A10xxx
   ♣KJxxx

F. 2S, followed by 3S.
This sequence shows a
singleton spade,7-8 HCP,
and 5/5+ in the minors

G. ♠K10xxx
   ♥QJxxx
   ♦x
   ♣xx

G. 2D, followed by 3D, then P
3D is artificial, showing
5-5+ in H, S, and 5+-8 HCP.
(This sequence makes the 1C
declarer in either major.)

H. ♠Qxxxx
   ♥AQxxx
   ♦xx
   ♣x

H. 2D, followedby 3D, then
raise 3H or 3S to 4.
This shows 5/5+ in the
majors with 7–8 HCP

I. ♠ x
   ♥x
   ♦A10xxxx
   ♣QJxxx

I. 2NT, followed by 3S.
This sequence shows 1-1-6-5
distribution, 6–8 HCP.

J. ♠ x
   ♥x
   ♦A10xxx
   ♣Kxxxxx

J. 2NT, followed by 3H.
This sequence shows 1-1-5-6
distribution, 6–8 HCP.

K. ♠ x
    ♥
    ♦ Q10xxxx
    ♣ KQxxxx

K. 2NT, followed by 3NT.
    This sequence shows 1-0-6-6
    or 0-1-6-6 distribution,
    6–8 HCP.

L. ♠
    ♥ xx
    ♦ A10xxxx
    ♣ KJxxx

L. 2NT, followed by 4S.
    This sequence shows 0-2-6-5
    or 0-1-7-5 distribution,
    a spade void, 5–8 HCP.

M. ♠ xx
    ♥
    ♦ A10xxx
    ♣ KJxxxx

M. 2NT, followed by 4C.
    This sequence shows 2-0-5-6
    or 1-0-5-7 distribution,
    a heart void, 5-8 HCP.

N. ♠
    ♥ x
    ♦ A10xxxx
    ♣ Qxxxxx

N. 2NT, followed by 3NT.
    This sequence shows 0-1-6-6
    or 1-0-6-6 distribution,
    5-8 HCP.

1C-1D-2H (a Standard 2NT Opening—20–21 HCP)

We now come to the 20–21 HCP balanced hand. "What's to discuss?"you may ask. "Everyone bids 2NT and plays Stayman and transfers, don't they?"No, not everyone. Many other mad scientists have come up with suggestions for ways to handle this hand more efficiently, but none of the ideas has caught on. We'll have to see whether my brainstorm will have any more success.

The standard 2NT opener is often as much of a problem for the opening side as it is for the opponents. It is known in some circles as "the slam killer." It also frequently winds up as the final contract opposite very weak hands, with declarer having to play the contract entirely out of his own hand and going down 2 or 3 tricks. It makes it almost impossible to escape into a minor suit partscore. You would obviously not choose to throw it in and ask for a redeal, but you have to recognize that this holding has possible pitfalls.

The California Club version of a standard 2NT opener begins with an opening bid of 1C. This gives us an immediate advantage whenever responder has a positive response or one of the holdings covered by a special 2-or 3-level response. Responder may be able to give a good description of his hand while opener just listens and sets the contract. When responder has a 1D response and opener has to show his exact strength, though, our nonstandard bidding scheme is still a major improvement on ordinary methods.

As previously mentioned, a 1H rebid by a 1C opener is forcing and can include very strong hands. That frees a jump to 2H for a special purpose—it takes the place of a 2NT opening bid. It shows a balanced hand with 20–21 HCP.

Starting two denominations below the standard 2NT gives us a couple of major advantages. By differentiating between bids made directly at the 3 level and bids that start with a 2S relay, it doubles the number of responder's possible descriptive bids. It also creates the ability to make both invitational and sign-off bids in clubs and diamonds. Anyone who has ever gone down in 2NT when dummy's entryless 6-card minor would have produced an easy +110 or +130 at 3C or 3D will appreciate this last feature.

The standard 2NT opening does have one major positive feature: ordinary Stayman and transfer sequences automatically make the big hand the declarer in all major suit and NT contracts. It took a bit of ingenuity to make that happen in the new scheme, but eventually it was accomplished. An underlying principle was established. **Hands with less than 4 spades use 2S as** a **relay to 2NT. Hands that have 4 or more spades bypass the 2S relay to 2NT and are bid directly at the 3 level**. The weak hand never bids spades or NT first if those are possible final contracts. The strong hand declares all major suit and NT contracts, just as in standard bidding.

For clarity, it might be helpful to look at a summary of the possible continuations after an auction which begins 1C - 1D -2H. Here they are:

Bids That Deny a 4-Card Spade Suit (Must First Use the 2S Relay)

2S requires opener to bid 2NT. It begins several descriptive sequences. The continuations are:

- 3NT=5–8 HCP, balanced or semi-balanced
- 3C or 3D= 5–6 HCP, 5/6+ card suit, needing fit for 3NT
- 3H= 5–8 HCP, 4-card heart suit
- 3S= 5–8 HCP, 5+card heart suit (2S denies spades)

[Memory aid: **with a heart suit, responder must go through the 2S relay** to bid the suit.]

- 4C =This shows 6+ clubs and 5+ diamonds with 5-8 HCP.
- 4D =This shows 6+diamonds and 5+ clubs with 5-8 HCP.
- 4H =This shows 6+ hearts and 5-8 HCP.

Direct 3/4-Level Bids (Not Using the 2S Relay)

2NT requires opener to bid 3C. He will usually pass or correct to 3D, making that the final contract. An additional option is to use a pull of 3C to any denomination other than 3D to describe hands that will never play in NT because of freakish distribution (see later discussion.)

3C is Smolen. (5H/4S or 5S/4H). Because responder's first bid was 1D, he is limited to 8 HCP. If opener shows a 4-card major, responder raises it to game. With no 4-card major, opener bids 3D. Responder then bids his 4-card major, allowing opener to bid 3NT or the other major. Thus the contract is always declared by the big hand.

3D is modified Stayman. It guarantees 4 spades. It may also show 4 hearts. If opener has both majors he bids spades. If he bids 3H, responder raises to 4H or uses 3S as a relay to 3NT.

3H is a transfer to spades. With only 2 spades, opener bids 3NT. With 6+ spades, responder can retransfer by bidding 4H.

3S shows a singleton spade, 9+ HCP, and 1-4-4-4 distribution.
Improved version—see pages 127 ("Two-Tiered impossible negative")

4C shows a singleton club, 9+ HCP, and 4-4-4-1 distribution.
Improved version—see pages 127 ("Two-Tiered impossible negative")

4D shows a singleton diamond, 9+ HCP, and 4-4-1-4 distribution.
Improved version—see pages 127 ("Two-Tiered impossible negative")

4H shows a singleton heart, 9+ HCP, and 4-1-4-4 distribution.
Improved version—see pages 127 ("Two-Tiered impossible negative")

The best way to get a handle on the "Not Your Standard 2NT" 2H bid is to think in terms of the following general principles rather than trying to memorize a list of bids:

- Whenever your object is to place the contract in NT, you use the 2S relay. This makes the strong hand declarer. You only use the 2S relay when you have no interest in spades as a possible contract. The 2S relay almost always denies 4 spades. There are two exceptions:
  o a very weak hand that responder plans to pass in 2NT after using the 2S relay
  o a 4-3-3-3 hand that responder plans to raise to 3NT over opener's forced 2NT without bothering to look for a 4-4 spade fit
- Whenever you plan to show a 4-card or longer heart suit and you hold less than 4 spades, you use the 2S relay. This again makes the strong hand declarer should you wind up in NT instead of hearts.
- The weak hand tries to never bid NT first when there is any possibility that the contract will wind up in that denomination. Therefore. the 2NT response (after 1C-1D-2H) is used in only two circumstances:
  o responder plans to sign off in 3C or 3D
  o responder has a freak hand with at least 6-5 distribution in the minors.
- Whenever responder has 4 or more spades (including when he also has 4 or more hearts), he avoids the 2S relay and bids directly at the 3 level or higher. The 3-level bids have been carefully designed to make the strong hand declarer

in spades, hearts, and NT. Again, the guiding rule is that a responding hand with a spade suit never bids that suit first.

Keeping those principles in mind should make it much simpler to remember what to do when you are responder and your partner has jumped to 2H after opening 1C. Let's go over some specific instances.

1C-1D-2H-2S

- You have a balanced hand and will place the contract in 2NT or 3NT.
- You have a long minor with no sure side entry, and you plan to bid an invitational 3C or 3D over opener's forced 2NT bid.
- You have 4+ hearts. With exactly 4, you will bid 3H over opener's 2NT. With 5, you will bid 3S. Opener can bid 4H or 3NT. With 6 hearts, you can now correct to 4H if you wish. Note that there are two ways to bid the 6-card heart suit. You may want to establish a partnership agreement that the slow route (1C-1D-2H-2S-2NT-3S-3NT-4H) is simply to play, while the more direct 1C-1D-2H-2S-2NT-4H indicates at least mild slam interest, perhaps guaranteeing 2 keycards. Remember, we can't use a simple jump to 4D as a transfer because that's an impossible negative with a singleton diamond.

The auction begins 1C-1D- 2H (20–21 HCP, balanced). How would you follow up with the following hands?

A.	♠ Jxx	B.	♠ xx	C.	♠ x	D.	♠ xx	E.	♠ x
	♥ Qxx		♥ xxx		♥ xxxx		♥ QJxxx		♥ Axxx
	♦ J10xx		♦ KQ10xxx		♦ K10x		♦ K10x		♦ QJxx
	♣ Qxx		♣ xx		♣ KJxxx		♣ xxx		♣ Kxxx

A. Bid 2S, then 3NT
B. Bid 2S, then 3D (invitational)
C. Bid 2S, then 3H (4hearts)
D. Bid 2S, then 3S (5 hearts)
E. Jump to 3S (1-4-4-4, 9+ HCP)

1C-1D-2H-2NT

- You have a very weak (0–4 HCP) hand with a long minor. Opener is forced to bid 3C. You will pass or bid 3D, which opener must pass.
- You have a freak two-suiter with at least 6-5 in the minors. You have 4–8 HCP. Instead of passing opener's 3C or correcting to 3D, you may make an unexpected higher bid. With 6-5-1-1 distribution, you may bid an invitational 3H (6C/5D) or 3S (6D/5C). Opener can bid 3NT, 4C, 4D, or force with 4 of a major. With 6-6-1-0 shape, you bid 3NT (6C/6D).If you assume that 5 of a minor will always have decent play opposite a 6-6 hand, you can treat 4C as an asking bid. Opener's 4C bid then asks for the void (4D= a heart void, 4H= a spade void; a bid of the void can then ask for keycards).If responder is allowed to pass a 4C or 4D bid, then 4H would be the void inquiry.
- You can also show 6-5-0-2 or 7-5-0-1 hands with void by bidding directly at the 4 level with game-forcing hands. Direct 4C and 4D bids would show at least 6 of that suit and a heart void. A bid of 4H (longer clubs) or 4S (longer diamonds) would show 6-5 or 7-5 and a spade void. Since the auction started with 1C-1D, transferring the contract to the strong hand is moot. Opener will play all the club contracts and responder will declare in diamonds.

If all of the possibilities in that second option give you a headache, just use the first. After 1C-1D-2H, what do you bid with the following hands?

A.	♠ x	B.	♠ xx	C.	♠ x	D.	♠ x	E.	♠
	♥ xx		♥ xxx		♥ x		♥		♥ x
	♦ Jxx		♦ Qxxxxx		♦ Kxxxxx		♦ QJxxxx		♦ KQxxx
	♣ 109xxxxx		♣ xx		♣ Q10xxx		♣ Q10xxxx		♣ QJxxxxx

A. 2NT, then pass 3C
B. 2NT, then correct 3C to 3D
C. 2NT, then 3S (1-1-6-5)
D. 2NT, then 3NT (1-0-6-6)
E. 2NT, then 4H (longer clubs, spade void).

With a very weak hand, responder would simply sign off at 3C or 3D, despite extreme distribution.

1C-1D-2H-3C

This is **modified Smolen.**

- You have 5-4 in the majors. If opener bids a major, you will raise to game. Occasionally, you may bid 3NT as a mild slam try. If opener bids 3D, denying a 4-card major, you bid your 4-card suit. Opener can then bid game in your 5-card suit or bid 3NT.
- You have 6-4 in the majors. You may choose to ignore the 4-card suit and just relay or transfer into the 6-carder. However, should you decide to bid your shape, you start with 3C. If opener bids a major, you may raise to 4 or make the 3NT slam suggestion. If he bids 3D, you show the 6-4 by indirectly showing the 6-card suit. First, you bid your 4-card major, showing 5 in the other major. If opener shows a 3-card fit, you can make a slam try by bidding a short minor or just settle for game. If he denies the 5-3 fit by bidding 3NT, you show 6 of your long suit by taking 3NT out to your short minor.
- You have 5-5 in the majors. You first bid 3C. If opener bids 3H or 3S, you can raise to game or even bid a singleton in a minor with a maximum. If opener bids 3D, a 4C or 4D bid shows the 5H/5S hand and shortness in the bid suit.

After 1C-1D-2H, what do you do with the following?(Opener bids 3D over 3C.)

A.	B.	C.	D.	E.
♠ Qxxx	♠ A10xxx	♠ J10xx	♠ QJxxxx	♠ K109xx
♥ KJxxx	♥ J10xx	♥ A10xxxx	♥ Kxxx	♥ KQxxx
♦ x	♦ Qx	♦ Q	♦ J10	♦ x
♣ xxx	♣ xx	♣ xx	♣ x	♣ xx

A. Bid 3C, then 3S.
B. Bid 3C, then 3H.
C. Bid 3C, then3S. If opener bids 3NT, bid 4D (6 hearts, short diamonds).
D. Bid 3C, then 3S. If opener bids 3NT, bid 4C (6 spades, short clubs)
E. Bid 3C. Over 3D, bid 4D (5-5 in the majors).

1C-1D-2H-3D

This is **"Telling Stayman."** It always guarantees 4 spades. Responder may also have 4 hearts. If opener has no major, he can just bid 3NT. If he has both majors, he always bids 3S, the known fit. If he has 4 hearts but not 4 spades, he bids 3H. Responder can then raise him to 4H or bid 3S, which is now just a relay to 3NT. As always, this maneuver makes the strong hand the declarer.

After 1C-1D-2H-3D, what do you bid with these hands?

A.	♠ KQxx	B.	♠ AQx	A.	Bid 3S; responder promises 4 spades.
	♥ A109x		♥ K10x		
	♦ AJ		♦ AJ10x	B.	Bid 3NT.
	♣ AQx		♣KQJ		

1C-1D-2H-3H

Believe it or not, this is a standard **Jacoby Transfer**. Opener's bids are not quite standard, however. With 3 or more spades, he accepts the transfer and bids 3S (or 4S). With only 2, he bids 3NT. The reason for this is, as usual, to make the 1C opener the declarer. If responder now bids 4H, a retransfer, responder shows 6+ spades. He can also bid 4C or 4D to show a second 5+card suit.

- After 1C-1D-2H-3H, what does a 3S bid show? 3NT? 3S= opener has 3+spades 3NT= opener has only 2 spades
- After 1C-1D-2H-3H-3NT what does a 4C bid show? 4D? 4H? 4C= 5 spades, 5+ clubs 4D= 5 spades, 5+diamonds, 4H=6+ spades

1C-1D-2H-3S,4C,4D,4H

These bids are all "impossible negatives".They show 4-4-4-1 distribution, 9+ HCP, and a singleton in the bid suit. This is fine, but it may not be enough for opener to accurately judge prospects for slam.

Opposite a 20–21 HCP hand, it might be prudent to separate the impossible negatives into two groups. Those with only 9–10 HCP might best be handled by "Telling Stayman" (if the hand has 4 spades) and the regular sequence showing a 4-card heart suit (if spades is the singleton). That way, any of these jumps would be in at least marginal slam territory. This would allow more confident exploration, which might take us up to the 5 level. This would have to be a matter for partnership agreement.

Here is a better, although slightly more complex, approach:

Two-Tiered "Impossible Negatives"

After 1C- 1D- 2H (20-21 HCP, balanced), do the following:

1. Use the 3D ("Telling Stayman") bid for all minimum (9-11 HCP) 4-4-4-1's except those with singleton spades. (Since the 3D bid guarantees a 4-card spade suit, the direct 3S bid will have to cover all hands with singleton spades.)
2. Use the direct 3S bid for both minimum and maximum 1444 hands. Use opener's subsequent 3NT bid to ask for clarification.
3. Use the 4C, 4D, and 4H bids for maximum 4441 (12+ HCP) hands. These are the hands that are most likely to produce makeable slams.

Here is a simple review of the 1C-1D-2H scheme:

Opener	Responder
1C	1D
2H	3S (9+, 1-4-4-4)
3NT (rightsides NT, asks	4C= 9-10 HCP
for HCP range)	4D=11-12 HCP
	4H=13+ HCP

Over a 4C or 4D answer, 4H or 4NT would be a sign-off; 4S would be RKCB or 1430.

1C	1D
2H	3D ("Telling Stayman")
3H,3S, or 3NT	4C,4D,4H = 9-11 HCP, 4-4-4-1
	(singleton, in bid suit)

Any game bid in opener's bid major would now be a sign-off. A bid of 4D or of the opposite major would be RKCB or 1430.

1C	1D
2H	4C, 4D, or 4H (12+ HCP,4-4-4-1, singleton in bid suit)

Any suit bid at this point should set trump and serve as RKCB or 1430. The only 4-level sign-off should be 4NT, since there is a minimum of 32 HCP between the hands.

Although I included the very simple version of the "impossible negative" as the basic method of showing 4-4-4-1 hands opposite the 20-21 HCP opener, I think the two-tiered scheme is far superior. It can help find good slams and keep us out of bad ones. I would treat it as our default choice for the system.

The Opening 2NT Bid (22-24 HCP)

The opening 2NT is remarkably mundane. It shows a balanced 22-24 HCP hand. The responses are equally unexciting:

- 3C is standard Stayman with Smolen rebids.
- 3D and 3H are standard Jacoby Transfers.
- 3S serves as a signal of slam interest in one of the minors.
- 4C may be Gerber—either directly or after a Stayman or transfer reply (an alternative is to have the responder give his keycard holding using our "Texas" continuations)
- 4D and 4H are Texas Transfers, either to be passed in 4H or 4S or to be followed by a slam try.

Responder is able to use the "invisible Blackwood" continuations that we discussed in "Little Bit West of Texas" over both major and minor suit transfer sequences.

It is not practical to use exactly the same set of slam tries over 2NT as we use over a 1NT opening. We would have to use jumps to the 5 level to duplicate the complete response scheme. The responses of 4C, 4D, and 4H are already in use as Gerber and transfers to the majors. They necessarily take up bidding space that we must use to investigate possible major suit and NT slams. We do, however, have the bids of 3S, 4S, and 4NT available for non-major suit slam exploration. We can use each of these bids to cover a different type of responding hand—one that has minor suit slam potential or one that is semi-balanced with enough strength to invite 6NT. We'll look at those sequences first.

The 3S response will show a long (6+) card minor. By using it as a relay to 3NT, we can arrange to have all minor suit contracts played by the 2NT opener. After opener accepts the relay, responder will use 4C as a transfer to 4D, showing a slam try in that suit. After opener accepts the transfer, he can then use a rebid of 4H, 4S, 4NT,5C, etc. to give his number of keycards (4H = 1 KC, 4S =1 KC + the Q of diamonds, 4NT = 2 KC, 5C = 2KC + the Q, etc.). With 3 KC, he skips 5D and continues the pattern with 5H.

When responder's suit is clubs, he merely avoids bidding that suit. After 2NT-3S-3NT, he bids his keycards directly, as if he had already bid 4C (4D = 6+ clubs, 1 KC, 4H = 6+ clubs, 1 KC +Q of clubs, 4S = 6+ clubs, 2 KC, 4NT = 6+clubs, 2 KC + Q of clubs, etc.).Should he have 3 key cards, he skips over 5C and continues the pattern with 5D or 5H. This preserves the transfer to clubs. Any bid higher than 5H is most unlikely but should mean we belong in 7C or 7NT, so there's no danger of getting too high.

With 3S taking care of one-suited hands, 4S and 4NT can be used to cover invitational balanced and semi-balanced hands. Several continuation schemes are possible: A bid of 4S might show 2 possible biddable suits, asking the opener to bid suits up the line if he accepts the slam invitation; 4NT might show 4-3-3-3 distribution or 4-4-2-2 shape with weak 4-card suits, simply asking opener to pass with a minimum or bid 6NT with a maximum. Alternatively, both could ask for suit exploration, with 4S being invitational and 4NT forcing. Partnership preference should decide what scheme is chosen. Here is a slightly more complex scheme:

Opener	Responder
2NT	4NT = invitational, balanced or semi-balanced
Can pass 4NT or bid (with no Stayman, a 4-card major is less likely) suits if accepting	
2NT	4S = minor oriented- either 4/4+ in minors or one 5-card minor
4NT = to play	
5C = 4+ clubs	5D = 4C/4+D
	5H = 2C/5D
	5S = 3C/5D
	6C = 5C
5D = 4+ diamonds	
	5H = 4C/4D
	5S = 2D/5clubs
	5NT = 3D/5clubs
	6D = 5D

Finding a 4/4, 5/4, 5/3, or 5/5 minor fit may help him decide between a minor slam and 6 NT.

Major suit exploration after a 2NT opening is much closer to the bidding after an opening 1NT. The obvious difference is that there is very little room for jump rebids to show such things as Smolen rebids, two-suited hands, and splinter bids.

A bid of 3C is Stayman, with non-jump Smolen rebids at the 3 level. That is, after 2NT-3C-3D, 3H shows 4 hearts and 5+ spades, while 3S shows 4 spades and 5+ hearts. Should opener rebid 3NT to deny interest in either major, a bid of 4D or 4H is a re-transfer, showing 6 of the longer major. Since an immediate jump to 4D cannot be used to show a major two-suiter, that hand is also shown by starting with Stayman. After 2NT-3C-3D, responder bids 4D to show 5/5+ in hearts and spades. After opener bids 4H or 4S, responder can try for slam by using the Texas key-card continuations.

Responder has several other major suit slam tries available. If he uses Stayman and

opener bids a 4-card suit that fits his hand, a new suit is now a slam try. I would recommend using our Texas key-card scheme (cheapest new suit =1 KC, next = 1KC+Q,
third= 2 KC, etc.) but other methods (Gerber, cuebids, controls, natural second suits)
are certainly possible.

With exactly 5 cards in a major, responder can transfer into 3H or 3S and then
jump to a denomination above 4 of the suit. The first step above 4H or 4S would show
1 keycard with no queen; the second, 1KC with the queen; etc. For those still unsure of
what I'm saying, here are Two examples:

2NT-3D-3H-4NT=1KC + Q of H

2NT-3H-3S-5D=2 KC, no Q of S.

Opener would be able to sign off in 4NT, 5NT, or 5 of the major.

With a 6+ card major one-suiter, responder has a couple of choices. A simple 3-level
transfer followed by a raise to game is a mild slam try. Opener could ask for keycards if
interested. A 4-level (Texas) transfer is either to play or the start of a stronger slam try,
with responder showing his key card holding.

The Opening 3NT Bid and Variations (25-27 HCP)

The opening bid of 3NT is probably the clumsiest instrument in our entire bidding arsenal. Luckily, it only rears its head about once a decade. The worst aspect of a 3NT opening is that you may belong in a 4-4 major suit fit, but you will wind up in 4NT if you try to find one and fail. In the process, you may go down when you have exactly 9 tricks.

It is probably not worth designing an extremely sophisticated scheme to deal with this type of hand. However, this system actually allows a pretty fair way to solve the problem described above. Because a 1C-1D-1H sequence is forcing, we actually have three ways to show a balanced 25-27 HCP:

1. Opening 3NT= balanced 25-27 HCP, no 4-card major
2. Opening 1C-1D-jump to 3NT= same hand, 4-card spade suit
3. Opening 1C-1D-1H (forcing)-any rebid-jump to 3NT = same hand, 4-card heart suit

With 25–27 and both majors, you're out of luck. Try #2 or #3.

There is one caveat which must be attached to the previous paragraph. It is based on the assumption that a 1C-1D-3H or 1C-1D-3S auction has not been assigned another meaning—i. e. as an asking bid (see Appendix G). Partners will have to decide which treatment they prefer.

CHAPTER 6

Big Suit-Oriented Hands (Majors)

There is nothing extraordinary about the California Club's initial treatment of strong suit-oriented hands. In most cases, they are opened 1C. The 1C is somewhat stronger than that of most other strong club systems. It shows 17+ HCP, though judgment is allowed with a very good 16. In my opinion, most 15-16-point hands don't really qualify as "strong." They are just nice solid openers.

Be that as it may, when a California Club user opens 1C, he has a strong hand. And when responder makes a positive (9+ HCP) response, the auction is almost (maybe 99.9 percent) forcing to game. Fudging—or as it is now popularly known, upgrading—is not encouraged. If a player is not quite strong enough for a strong action at his first turn, he can show a maximum limited hand at his second turn. This avoids a lot of overbidding.

The first major diversion from more conventional systems comes with opener's initial rebid. As previously noted, **a rebid of 1H or 1S after a 1C-1D sequence is forcing** for one round. This means that the 1-level major suit rebid may include hands that standard bidders would open 2C.(We have already seen how a 2H rebid shows a balanced 20–21 HCP). When opener has a really huge hand, he shows it by jumping at his second turn. This delayed sequence allows the weak responder a second chance to define how weak his negative response actually is before opener shows his full strength.

This is important because the 1D bidder could have anywhere from 0 to 8 points. He could even have 9 or more and an "impossible negative". He can have a raise or a suit of his own. He gets a chance to describe his hand at a low level. When opener makes his second bid, he at least knows whether he's facing a hand with some value or a complete bust.

This is partly accomplished by an artificial "warning bid" response that responder can use to curb an overly optimistic 1C bidder's enthusiasm for his strong hand. This bid works with narrowly defined raises and new suit bids to give opener a good idea of responder's hand. Let's look at how the responder defines his hand.

Raises of Opener's Major

If the responder has a true negative response, he has three possible raises of opener's major. With 0–3 HCP, he will make a "warning bid" (discussed in a subsequent section) and then make the cheapest possible bid of opener's suit. With 4–6 HCP, he will raise directly to 2 of the suit. With 7–8 HCP, he will raise to 3.

There is a fourth possibility. With 4-card support, 7–8 HCP, and a singleton in a side suit, he can make an "impossible negative" jump in his short suit. The entire impossible negative bidding scheme is described in the next section.

The Impossible Negative (Slightly Improved) The original Precision Club "impossible negative" was very specific. Responder bid 1D, promising a weak hand, and then made a later jump that showed values it was "impossible" for him to have. Specifically, it showed 4-4-4-1 distribution and a positive response. The jump is made in responder's singleton. If the singleton is in opener's suit, the jump is in NT. The California Club uses the basic Precision idea but with a couple of significant adjustments.

I have added one additional type of hand to the convention. That is the 4+-card limit raise (7–8 HCP) with a side singleton mentioned in the last section. It may have any distribution as long as it has at least 4 trump and a singleton.

The second change is the mechanism that allows opener to get additional information about responder's hand. After the jump, opener makes the cheapest possible bid to ask about responder's exact strength. Responder answers in steps, as follows:

- First step = 7–8 HCP, 4 trump
- second step = 4-4-4-1, 9–10 HCP
- third step = 4-4-4-1, 11–12 HCP
- fourth step = 4-4-4-1, 13–14 HCP
- fifth step = 4-4-4-1, 15-16 HCP
- sixth step = unlikely, but….

Opener can ask for aces by bidding the singleton or the cheapest NT. He should be able to set the contract accurately at that point, but he can ask for kings if a grand slam is possible.

New Suit Responses

If the responder does not have a fit for opener's major, he has two options. With 5–8 HCP and a 5-card suit, he can bid a new suit. With 0–4 HCP, he must first make a warning bid (1S over 1H or 1NT over 1S—see the next section). In that case, he may not ever bid his suit. He may just pass opener's rebid or take him back to his major on a doubleton. Since 1S is the warning bid over 1H, a 1NT bid substitutes for the 5-card spade suit with 5–8 HCP.

The Warning Bid

After a forcing rebid of 1H or 1S, the cheapest next bid is the warning bid. This bid warns the opener that responder has one of four types of hands:

1. A very weak hand (0–3 HCP) with at least 3-card support for opener's major. Responder's next call will be the cheapest possible bid of opener's suit.
2. A very weak hand (0–4 HCP) with no fit for opener's suit but support for any other suit (4-4-4-1 or 4-4-3-2 with shortness in opener's suit).Responder may pass any new suit bid by opener.
3. A non-fitting (4-4-4-1 or 4-4-3-2) hand with 5–8 HCP. Responder will raise any new suit bid by opener or bid 2NT.
4. A very weak (0–4 HCP) hand with a long (6+) suit and 0 or 1 cards in opener's major. A later bid of the long suit is optional.

In cases 1, 2, and 4, this warning bid serves essentially as a second negative, similar to those used by some standard bidders after a strong 2C opening.

To repeat, the warning bid is the cheapest bid available after the auction goes 1C-1D-1H or 1S. If the 1C opener rebids 1H, the warning bid is 1S. Over a 1S rebid, the warning bid is 1NT. Opener, having been warned that his partner may have a very unhelpful hand, should now proceed cautiously. Unless he actually can guarantee a play for game opposite a possibly trickless dummy, he simply rebids 1NT, bids a second suit at the 2 level, or bids his major again with 6 cards in the suit. These bids can be passed. If responder happens to hold the type 3 hand, he may give a simple raise in the second suit. He may also bid 2NT or raise the major to 3 if the rebid shows a 6-card major.

The use of the warning bid usually ensures that the bidding will not get past the 2 level when responder has a really miserable hand. It allows the partnership to find a secondary 4-4 fit at the 2 level or to stop at 2 of opener's major.

At the risk of being redundant, here is a review of responder's bids when he doesn't make a warning bid. Bids of 2C, 2D, and 2H (over 1S) show 5–8 HCP. Single raises show 4–6 HCP and double raises show 7–8. Jumps to 2NT, 3C, or 3H over 1S are the "impossible negative", usually showing 4-4-4-1 distribution and 9+ HCP. However, I have modified this bid to include 7–8 point hands with 4 trumps and a side singleton, even with 5-4-3-1 shape. The next bid asks responder for clarification.

After the auction 1C-1D-1S, 2-level bids in a new suit show 5 cards in that suit and from 0–2 spades. With 3 or more spades, responder would give an immediate raise of some sort. After 1C-1D-1H, bids of 2C and 2D are the same. However, since 1S is the second negative response to 1H, 1NT is used to show a 5-card spade suit and 5–8 HCP. After responder's first rebid, bidding is essentially natural.

Non-fitting 4-4-4-1 or 4-4-3-2 hands are started with the second negative bid. With 5–8 HCP, a rebid of 2NT or a raise of a second suit is made to deny a 0–4 HCP bust. Very weak (0–4 HCP) hands with long suits are also shown by bidding the second negative first. Responder later bids his suit, if convenient.

On the pages that follow, there are extensive examples that illustrate all these bids. They may clarify some things that are still unclear.

Getting back to the 1C bidder, he can still show a monster hand and force the weak hand to bid again. He does this by jumping in a second suit or his own suit. If he knows that responder is not going to be of much help, he can also just jump to game.

If opener makes any simple rebid, he knows it can be passed. Responder has already warned that he either has a non-fitting hand or a very weak raise. With shortness in opener's major, he very likely has 3-or 4-card support for a second suit. He will pass with 0–4 HCP or raise with 5–8. Otherwise, with 0–3/4 HCP, he will return to opener's major with 3 or more trump or bid a long suit of his own.

Here are some examples to illustrate the scheme.

The following is an average 1C opening with 5 hearts: ♠ Ax♥AKJxx♦ Kxx♣ KJxx.
How will the auction go when responder has a heart fit? Let's see.

	Responder's Hand	Opener	Responder
A.	♠xx	1C	1D
	♥Qxxx	1H	1S (warning bid)
	♦Jxxx	2C	2H (heart raise, 0-3 HCP)
	♣xxx	P	

Repeating opener's hand: ♠ Ax ♥AKJxx ♦ Kxx ♣ KJxx

	Responder's Hand	Opener	Responder
B.	♠x	1C	1D
	♥Qxxx	1H	2H (heart raise, 4-6 HCP)
	♦Qxxxx		
	♣Qxx		
C.	♠x	1C	1D
	♥Qxxx	1H	2S (impossible negative)
	♦Qxxxx	2NT (asking bid)	3C (in this case,7–8 HCP limit raise)
	♣Axx	etc.	
D.	♠ x	1C	1D
	♥ Qxxx	1H	2S (impossible negative)
	♦AQxx	2NT (asking)	3H (4-4-4-1, 11–12 HCP)
	♣Axxx	etc.	

Now let's look at some non-fitting hands. Opener's hand remains the same.

E. ♠xxxx   1C   1D
    ♥ x   1H   1S (warning!)
    ♦ xxxx   2C (17–21 HCP, NF)   P (whew!)
    ♣ Qxxx

F. ♠Kxxx   1C   1D
    ♥ x   1H   1S (warning)
    ♦ Qxxx   2C   3C (5–8 HCP)
    ♣ Qxxx   X*(may pass
                   or try for game)

G. ♠ Kxxx   1C   1D
    ♥ x   1H   2NT (9+HCP,4-1-4-4)
    ♦ Qxxx   3C (ask)   3H (11–12 HCP)
    ♣ AQxx   X (GF) note –
                   when singleton is
                   in opener's suit, 1st step=9-10,not,7-8

H. ♠ Qxxx   1C   1D
    ♥xx   1H   1S (warning)
    ♦Jxxx   2C   2NT (5–bad 7 HCP, no fit)
    ♣ Axx   P or3NT

I. ♠KJxx   1C   1D
    ♥xx   1H   1S (warning)
    ♦xxxx   2C   3NT (good 7–8 HCP no fit)
    ♣ Axx

Repeating opener's hand: ♠ Ax ♥AKJxx ♦ Kxx ♣ KJxx

With at least a 5-card suit and 0-2 cards in opener's suit, the suit can be bid directly or after a warning bid.

J.	♠ QJxxx	1C	1D
	♥ xx	1H	1NT (5-8 HCP, 5 spades)
	♦ QJxx	etc.	
	♣ xx		

K.	♠ xxx	1C	1D
	♥ Qx	1H	2C (5–8 HCP, 5+clubs)
	♦ xxx	etc.	
	♣ A10xxx		

L.	♠ xx	1C	1D
	♥ x	1H	1S (warning)
	♦ xxxxxxx	2C	2D or P (0–4 HCP)
	♣ Qxx	P	

Sometimes responder may return to 2 of opener's major with only 2-card support but remote prospects for game.

M.	♠ Qxxx	1C	1D
	♥ xx	1H	1S (warning)
	♦ xxxx	2C	2H (game prospects not great—
	♣ Axx		may be best to sign off)

The 2H rebid supposedly shows 0–3 HCP and 3 trump, but 2H may be the best spot to play, especially at matchpoints. Responder is allowed to make a judgement call.

When the auction goes 1C-1D-1S, responder's rebids are essentially the same as those for hearts. Obviously, 1NT no longer shows 5+ spades. It is the "warning bid." As the cheapest bid, it becomes the second negative. It also handles the weak raise and non-fitting 4-4-4-1 and 4-4-3-2 bids. Direct 2C, 2D, and 2H bids show 5+card suits and less than 3 spades. Bids of 2S (4-6 HCP) and 3S (7-8 HCP) are normal raises. Jumps to 2NT, 3C, 3D, and 3H are "impossible negatives".

Here is a typical 1C-1D-1S hand and some responding hands:

Opener:♠ KQxxx ♥ Ax ♦ AKxx ♣ Qx

A.	♠ Jxx	1C	1D
	♥ xx	1S	1NT (warning bid)
	♦ Jxxx	2D	2S (0–3 HCP, 3+spades)
	♣ xxxx		

B.	♠ Jxx	1C	1D
	♥ xxx	1S	2S (3+ spades, 4–6 HCP)
	♦ Qxxx	P or game try	
	♣ Kxx		

C.	♠ Axxx	1C	1D
	♥ Qx	1S	3S (3+ spades,7–8 HCP,
	♦ Qxxx	4S no singleton)	
	♣ xxx		

D.	♠ xxxx	1C	1D
	♥ Kxx	1S	3D (impossible negative)
	♦ x	3H (asking)	3S (7–8 HCP, singleton D)
	♣ KJxx	4S	

E.	♠ AJxx	1C	1D
	♥ KQxx	1S	3C (impossible negative)
	♦ QJxx	3D (asking)	3NT (13–14 HCP,4-4-4-1)
	♣ x	4C (aces? controls? you pick) 4D would be RKCB	

F.	♠ x	1C	1D
	♥ KQxx	1S	2NT (9+HCP, singletonspade)
	♦ Qxxx	3C (asking)	3D (9–10 HCP)
	♣ Kxxx	3NT	P

Opener:♠ KQxxx ♥ Ax ♦ AKxx ♣ Qx

G. ♠ x   1C   1D
    ♥ Kxxx   1S   1NT (warning)
    ♦ xxxx   2D   P (whew!)
    ♣ xxxx

H. ♠ x   1C   1D
    ♥ Kxxx   1S   1NT (warning)
    ♦ Qxxx   2D   3D or 2NT (5–8 HCP—most likely 7–8)
    ♣ Kxxx   3NT

I. ♠ xx   1C   1D
    ♥ Kxxx   1S   1NT (warning)
    ♦ Qxx   2D   2S or P ?
    ♣ xxxx   (2S=known 5-2 fit; diamonds may be 4-3 or 5-3)

J. ♠ xx   1C   1D
    ♥ Kxxx   1S   1NT
    ♦ Qxx   2D   2NT (probably 7–8 HCP; with 5–6 HCP
    ♣ Kxxx   3NT   would probably bid 2S)

K. ♠ xx   1C   1D
    ♥ QJxxx   1S   2H (5+ hearts, 5–8 HCP)
    ♦ Qxx   2NT? P?
    ♣ Jxx

L. ♠ xx   1C   1D
    ♥ x   1S   2D (5-8 HCP)
    ♦ QJxxxx   3D   4C (game try)
    ♣ AJxx   5D

M. ♠ x   1C   1D
    ♥ xx   1S   1NT
    ♦ xxx   2D   3C (0–4 HCP, 6/7-card suit)
    ♣ Kxxxxxx

Now let's vary the 1C opener.

N.	♠ QJxxx	♠ xx	1C	1D
	♥ AKx	♥ Qxx	1S	2D
	♦ Ax	♦ Kxxxx	2NT	P
	♣ Axx	♣ Qxx		

O.	♠ Kx	♠ Qxxxx	1C	1D
	♥ AQJxx	♥ xx	1H	1NT (5+ spades,5-8 HCP)
	♦ Kxxx	♦ Qxx	2D	2H
	♣ Ax	♣ Qxx	2NT? P?	

P.	♠ AKJxx	♠ xx	1C	1D
	♥ AQxx	♥ Kxx	1S	2C
	♦ Axx	♦ Kxx	2H	2NT
	♣ x	♣ Q10xxx	3NT	

Q.	♠ Axx	♠ Kxxxx	1C	1D
	♥ AQxxx	♥ x	1H	1NT (5+spades, 5–8 HCP)
	♦ AKx	♦ Qxxx	2S	P
	♣ Kx	♣ xxx		

R.	♠ KQxxxx	♠ Jx	1C	1D
	♥ KQx	♥ xxx	1S	2D
	♦ Ax	♦ KQxxx	2S	3S
	♣ Ax	♣ xxx	4S	

S.	♠ KQxx	♠ xxx	1C	1D
	♥ AJxxx	♥ xx	1H	2C
	♦ Kx	♦ Axx	P?/2S?/2NT?	
	♣ Ax	♣ KJxxx		

After the 1C-1D-1M-2M (M=Major) sequence, opener can use the same long- and short-suit game tries that are used after 1S-2S or 1H-2H. (See "Constructive Raises," page 31). The cheapest bid starts the long-suit tries (LSGT), and the next three bids are short-suit tries (SSGT). When opener starts the long-suit try, responder can ignore the relay and bid a short suit of his own.

Here are some examples:

A.	♠ AKxxx	♠ Qxx	1C	1D
	♥ xxx	♥ xx	1S (forcing)	2S (4–6 HCP)
	♦ AQx	♦ Kxxx	2NT (relay-LSGT)	3C (forced)
	♣ Ax	♣ xxxx	3D (LSGT)	4S
B.	♠ AKxxx	♠ Qxx	1C	1D
	♥ xxx	♥ xx	1S	2S
	♦ AQx	♦ xxxx	2NT	3C
	♣ Ax	♣ Qxxx	3D (LSGT)	3S

On B, it turns out the doubleton heart is useful, but 4 spades needs a lot of luck. You'd have to be pretty desperate to bid it.

C.	♠ AKxxx	♠ Qxx	1C	1D
	♥ xxx	♥ Ax	1S	2S
	♦ AQx	♦ xxxx	2NT (relay-LSGT)	3C (forced)
	♣ Ax	♣ xxxx	3D (LSGT)	3H
			3S or 4S	
D.	♠ xxx	♠ xx	1C	1D
	♥ AKJxx	♥ Qxx	1H	2H
	♦ AQx	♦ Kxxxx	2S (relay-LSGT)	2NT (forced)
	♣ Ax	♣ xxxx	3D (LSGT)	4H
E.	♠ xxx	♠ Qxx	1C	1D
	♥ AKJxx	♥ Qxxx	1H	2H
	♦ AQx	♦ xxx	2S (LSGT)	2NT
	♣ Ax	♣ Qxx	3D	3H

With a singleton, the responder may ignore the relay and bid his short suit. When 2S is the relay, 3H shows a singleton spade.

F.	♠ xxx	♠ x	1C	1D
	♥ AKJxx	♥ Qxxx	1H	2H
	♦ AQx	♦ xxxx	2S (relay-LSGT)	3H (ignoring relay,
	♣ Ax	♣ Qxx	4H	singleton spade)

G.	♠ xxx	♠ xxxx	1C	1D
	♥ AKJxx	♥ Qxx	1H	2H
	♦ AQx	♦ x	2S (relay-LSGT)	3D (ignoring relay)
	♣ Ax	♣ QJxxx	3H	

H.	♠ Ax	♠ Kxxx	1C	1D
	♥ AKJxx	♥ Qxx	1H	2H
	♦ AQx	♦ xxxxx	2S (relay)	3C (ignoring relay)
	♣ xxx	♣ x	4H	

With a better raise (7–8 HCP), responder either raises to 3 of the major or makes a mini-splinter raise with 4 trumps and a singleton. This bid is made even without perfect 4-4-4-1 distribution. There is no danger of confusion with a "real" impossible negative (9+ HCP, 4-4-4-1) because opener can use the cheapest bid over the splinter to ask for clarification.

Some examples:

I.	♠ AJxxx	♠ Kxx	1C	1D
	♥ Kx	♥ Qxxx	1S	3S (7-8 HCP)
	♦ KQx	♦ Jxxx	4S (3NT possible)	
	♣ AJx	♣ Qx		

J.	♠ AJxxx	♠ Kxx	1C	1D
	♥ Kx	♥ Qxxxx	1S	3S (only 3 trump)
	♦ KQx	♦ Jxxx	4S	
	♣ AJx	♣ x		

K.	♠ AQxxx	♠ Kxxx	1C	1D
	♥ Kx	♥ Axxxx	1S	3C (4 trumps, singleton)
	♦ KQx	♦ Jxx	3D (asking)	3H (7-8 HCP)
	♣ AJx	♣ x	3NT (baby 1430)	4H (2 KC)
			6S	

Standard Strong Two Bids in the Majors

So what happens when the 1C opener has an old-fashioned strong 2-bid or a hand the modern standard bidder would open 2C? Very simple: at his second turn, he jumps in a new suit or in his first-bid suit. This forces responder to bid again. If responder has shown at least 4 HCP, the jump is forcing to game. If he has made a warning bid, it is forcing for one round.

Here are some examples:

L.	♠ AKJ10xx	♠ xx	1C	1D
	♥ AQJx	♥ Q10xx	1S (forcing)	1NT (warning)
	♦ AQ	♦ Jxxx	3H (forcing)	4H
	♣ J	♣ xxx		

M.	♠ AK	♠ Qxx	1C	1D
	♥ KQJ109xx	♥ xx	1H (forcing)	2C
	♦ A	♦ xxx	4C (RKCB-1430)	4D (1KC)
	♣ KJx	♣ Axxxx	6H	

N.	♠ AQ	♠ xxx	1C	1D
	♥ AKQxxx	♥ x	1H (forcing)	1S (warning)
	♦ KQ10xx	♦ J9xx	3D (forcing)	4D
	♣	♣ xxxxx	6C (void)	6D

Once the game force is established, standard slam tries (cue bids, etc.) are employed to try for slam. The only difference from a standard 2C auction is that if responder gives an initial negative response to the 1C opening, opener has a pretty clear immediate picture of the limits of the hand. Because of the low level of the opener's rebid, responder can then further define his hand by making a "warning bid", giving partner a well-defined raise, or bidding a new suit (showing 5–8 HCP).

Of course, if responder makes a positive response to 1C, opener knows the partnership is at least in marginal slam territory right away. Again, the low level of the auction after the initial two bids allows lots of room for leisurely slam exploration. There is enough bidding space for TAB, DTAB, SAB, splinter bids, fitting jumps, or any other favorite treatments that a pair may wish to employ.

CHAPTER 7

Big Suit-Oriented Hands (Minors)

When opener has a big (but not ostentatious) 1C opener (17–21 HCP) with a long minor, he has a couple of options. If the hand is truly unbalanced, such as having a singleton or void, he makes a simple rebid of 2C or 2D. With a semi-balanced hand-say, a 6-3-2-2 hand and 17–19 HCP-he may occasionally decide to rebid 1NT. This will allow responder to easily transfer into a major and may cause the defense problems when they try to figure out the hand. At any rate, opener does not have to jump to the 3 level to show strength.

A unique part of the system occurs when opener has the equivalent of a strong 2-bid (usually 21- 22+ HCP) and a long minor. As we shall see in an upcoming section, we have a special scheme to describe those hands.

1C-1D-2C/2D Rebids

After 1C-1D-2C, responder is allowed to pass. However, with 5 or more HCP, he should make an effort to keep the bidding alive. A 2D bid at this point is semi-artificial. It denies a 5-card major and invites opener to bid a 4-card major or 2NT. A bid of 2H or 2S is natural, showing a 5+-card suit and 5–8 HCP. Also natural is 2NT, showing a maximum 1D response (7–8 HCP) and tenaces in at least two suits outside clubs. A simple raise, 3C, shows 3+ clubs and 5–8 HCP. Jumps to 3D, 3H, 3S, and 3NT are the impossible negative, guaranteeing 9+ HCP and 4-4-4-1 distribution. A bid of 4C is a 7-8 HCP club raise with 4+ trumps and a side singleton.

After 1C-1D-2D, the auction is more cramped. Responder has no way to ask for a 4-card major at the 2-level. The good news, however, is that opener will rarely have one. With 17–20 HCP, 5+ diamonds, and a 4-card major, he should open 1D and use a

"1D with muscles" sequence (see pages (9-11). With 7-4 distribution, he may open 1C. If so, he'll probably have to bid his major at the 3 level if he can. At any rate, most of responder's rebids will be identical to those used after 1C-1D-2C. Bids of 2H and 2S will show 5–8 HCP and a 5+ card suit, as will 3C; 2NT still shows 7–8 HCP and tenaces; 3D and 4D are still the simple and jump raises; and 3H, 3S, 3NT, and 4C are still impossible negatives (9+ HCP, 4-4-4-1 distribution, and a singleton in the bid suit).

   If all this is not yet crystal clear, I will try to outline all of the major rebids discussed above in the form of a chart:

1C-	1D
2C	Pass = 0-4 HCP
	2D = semi-artificial, denies a 5-card major
	5–8 HCP, invites opener to bid a 4-card major or 2NT
	2H/2S = 5+ card suit, 5–8 HCP
	2NT =7–8 HCP, tenaces
	3C = 5–8 HCP, 3+ clubs 4C = 7–8 HCP, 4+ clubs
	3D/3H/3S/3NT (clubs) = singleton,4-4-4-1, 9+ HCP
1C-	1D
2D	Pass = 0–4 HCP
	2H/2S/3C = 5–8 HCP, 5+-card suit
	2NT = 7–8 HCP, tenaces
(opener unlikely to have a	3D = 5–8 HCP, 3+ diamonds, 4D = 7–8 HCP;
4-card major—would open	4+ diamonds)
1D-then reverse or jump-	3H/3S/3NT (diamonds)/4C = singleton,
shift—see "1D with muscles")	4-4-4-1 shape, 9+ HCP

Standard Strong Two-Bids in the Minors

As we have seen, the fact that 1C-1D-1H and 1S are forcing frees 1C-1D-2H for use as a standard 2NT opener. It also frees jump rebids of **2S and 2NT** for a very useful purpose. These jump rebids **can now be used as standard strong 2-bids in clubs and diamonds**. They provide the same advantage over standard bids as the 1C-1D-2H sequence. Starting two denominations lower than the standard bids leaves more room for responder to describe his hand.

To cite one obvious example, it is very hard to use 3C as a second negative response after a standard auction of 2C-2D-3C or 2C-2D-3D. In the latter case, it is downright impossible for responder to transfer to 3H. As we shall see, with this system we can do those things and more.

Before getting into specifics, I'd like to make a couple of general observations. Big hands with long minor suits are among the most awkward hands for standard bidders to handle. The auctions get too high too quickly, and they invariably seem to wind up with the weak hand declaring the hand and the strong hand exposed as dummy. Big hands with long diamonds are by far the worst. That is why several bidding theorists have come up with 2D opening bids that combine big diamond hands with other secondary meanings. The bids I have included in this system may not solve all the problems inherent in these hand types, but they are at least an improvement over standard bidding.

One defect we can't get around is the wrong-siding of a lot of diamond contracts. When responder has to respond 1D to a 1C opening, he obviously will be declarer if the contract ends up in diamonds. There are, however, mechanisms built into the bidding scheme to allow the strong hand to play a substantial majority of the major suit and NT contracts. This alone is a good reason to give this scheme a try.

Let's start with the strong standard 2-bid in clubs. This will be handled with an opening bid of 1C. **After a 1D response, a jump rebid of 2S shows 5+ clubs and approximately 22+ HCP.** Responder can now bid 3C as a super-negative (0–3 HCP). This removes the game force. Opener can conceivably pass. A 3D bid shows 4-8 HCP and is semi-artificial. It denies a 5-card major and invites opener to bid a 4-card major or 3NT.

A 3H rebid by opener now presents no problems. He is unlikely to hold two 4-card majors. Responder can raise to 4H or relay to 3NT by bidding 3S. Of course, he can also go back to 4C. A 3S bid by opener presents more of a problem. If there is no 4-4 spade fit, responder will have to choose between playing 3NT from the weak side or going for the minor suit game.

If responder has a 5-card major, he can transfer into it. How? To use my favorite overworked word, "Simple."A bid of 3H is an obvious transfer to spades. But 3D is already spoken for. How do we transfer into hearts? We treat 3S as a "flip-flop transfer," showing 5+ hearts. In either case, opener can accept the transfer with 3 or more cards in responder's suit or bid 3NT or 4 of his own suit without a fit. If the responder has 6 or more of the major, he can retransfer (4D = 6+ hearts, 4H = 6+ spades) at the 4-level.

Of course, responder may just want to give partner an immediate raise. There are two bids available for the purpose: 3NT and 4C. My preference would be to use 3NT for a strong (7–8 HCP) raise and 4C for a weaker (4–6 HCP) raise. Others may choose different definitions. After either raise, 4D by opener asks for keycards (1430, 0314, and Texas are all possible. You pick.)

Finally, what does responder do with an impossible negative? He could jump to the 4-level, but that is going to get the auction very high and inhibit careful investigation for a possible grand slam. It is far more efficient to use an unused bid at the 2-level: 2NT.

One of the basic tenets of the system is that weak hands never bid NT if they can avoid it. But using both 2NT and 3NT as good raises in this scheme makes sense. If responder has 4 clubs and a side singleton, the contract will probably wind up in clubs, not NT. If he has a singleton club, the hand will probably play pretty well from his side. And the NT bid by a presumably weak hand will almost certainly wake up opener and remind him that something unusual is happening.

Responder's 2NT bid will show any 4-4-4-1 hand with 9+ HCP. Opener bids 3C to ask for the short suit. A 3NT reply shows a singleton in clubs. After the short suit is determined, 4C asks for responder's range (4D = 9–10, 4H = 11–12, 4S = 13–14, etc.). A cue bid of the singleton asks for keycards (again, your choice of convention), or is simple Blackwood if clubs is the short suit.

The setup is very similar when the suit involved is diamonds. **After 1C-1D, a jump to 2NT shows approximately 22+ HCP and 5+ diamonds,** the equivalent of a strong 2-bid in diamonds. Responder's 3-level bids are identical to those after the 1C-1D-2S auction. A bid of 3C is the super-negative, 3D shows 4–8 HCP, and 3H and 3S are the flip-flop transfers. The weaker diamond raise (4–6 HCP) can be handled by bidding 3D and then rebidding 4D if appropriate. This also gives opener a chance to bid 3NT, which could very likely be the best contract, while 4D is still the maximum (7–8 HCP) raise.

The major difference is the handling of the impossible negative. Obviously, 2NT is not available to handle those hands. The simplest solution is to use the obvious available jumps to show the specific singletons immediately. A bid of 3NT shows a singleton diamond, and jumps to 4C, 4H, and 4S show shortness in those suits.

Opener then makes the cheapest continuation bid to ask responder's range. A bid of 4NT is key-card-asking (0314, 1430, or Texas, depending upon your preference. Once again, a chart may help clarify the entire scheme.

Response Similarities

- 3C = always acts as a second negative; 0–3 HCP, removes game force.
- Flip-flop transfers = bid of major by responder shows 5+ cards in opposite major. Strong hand always becomes declarer if fit found.
- 3D = always shows 4-8 HCP, may not be a suit- invites opener to bid a secondary 4-card major. Strong hand always becomes declarer if 4-4 major fit is found.
- Weak hand avoids bidding NT; strong hand declares almost all 3NT contracts.
- Immediate NT rebids by responder at second turn (otherwise avoided) show 4-4-4-1 shape,9+HCP, or good raise.

1C-1D-2S=(5+ Clubs, 22+ HCP) Responder bids:

- 3C = second negative—(0–3 HCP, no K, may be passed)
- 3D = 4-8 HCP, no 5-card major
- 3H = 5+ spades (4–8 HCP)
- 3S = 5+ hearts (4–8 HCP)-"flip-flop transfer"
- 3NT = good club raise (7–8 HCP)
- 4C = natural club raise (4–6), can also bid 3D-aiming for 3NT
- 2NT =shows all 9+ HCP 4-4-4-1 hands, then:
- 3C asks singleton; 3D, 3H,3S, 3NT (clubs) show it.

1C-1D-2NT=(5+ Diamonds, 22+ HCP) Responder bids:

- 3C-second negative (0–3HCP) (can be passed)
- 3D = 4-8 HCP, no 5-card major; may be start of 4–6 HCP raise.
- 3H = 5+ spades (4–8 HCP)
- 3S = 5+ hearts (4-8 HCP)-"flip-flop transfer"
- 3NT (diamonds) 4C, 4H, 4S = 9+ HCP,4-4-4-1
- 4D = natural diamond raise (7–8 HCP)

1C Opener / Jump in Suit to 3 level -minimum/but solid suit

Since a jump to 3C or 3D is not needed for the 22+ HCP-type hand, we can assign those bids a specific meaning. That would be a hand that is in the minimum 1C range but has 8 or 9 running tricks. Examples would be:

    ♠x ♥ Kx♦ AJx♣ AKQJxxx   ♠AK♥ x♦ AKQxxxxx♣ Kx

These bids would be more likely to be made in a minor but could also be useful and descriptive in a major (if not using those jumps as asking bids).

   1C–   *1D*
- 3C/3D/3H/3S—probably only 17–20 HCP, but very good suit, with 8-9+ tricks

CHAPTER 8

Positive Major Suit Responses to a
1C Opening/Special Rebids

So far we have only seen 1D responses from the partner of the 1C opener. Believe it or not, it is legal for responder to have a decent hand. Your partner may never have anything, but some players do occasionally hold 9 or more points. In this system, that constitutes a positive response. In the next several sections, we will go through the various positive responses to 1C. In some cases, the positive response is just one part of a two-way bid. We will have to go through both meanings of those bids as a single entity.

In general, the following statement holds true for every one of the bids we are about to discuss: a positive response to a 1C opening bid shows at least a very good 8–9 HCP and is essentially forcing to game. After an auction that starts with such a response, jumps are unnecessary unless they are used to show very specific holdings.

The continuation structure after a positive major suit response to 1C will incorporate some of the same principles we have built into other areas of the system. Many sequences have been designed to ensure that most contracts will be declared by the strong club hand and that such a hand may remain largely hidden. This is done by using transfers and suit switches to ensure that the 1C bidder is the first to mention NT or possible trump suits. Other sequences may be relatively natural.

When an immediate fit is found, both natural and conventional raises will be available to establish trump. However, when the best denomination is not clear, opener has several other options. He may bid a suit of his own, suggesting an alternative trump suit or a very unbalanced hand. He may also bid a conventional 1NT (or 1S over 1H) even if he just wants more information about responder's hand.

These rebids and responder's continuations are designed to result in the right-siding of most contracts that end in denominations other than responder's major. Other useful tools, which will be discussed in some detail, are strength-showing bids (SSB), strength-asking bids (SAB), the trump-asking bid (TAB), and the delayed trump-asking bid (DTAB). Asking bids will be confined to certain well-defined situations. They will generally be used to get certain specific information and then followed by standard slam exploration techniques.

1C—1H or 1S

The response of 1 heart or 1 spade shows at least a 5-card suit. It shows 9+ HCP, although an extremely good 8 HCP hand with a strong suit (say AKJ10xx) may qualify. This last comment should not be taken as approval for the current craze of upgrading at the slightest excuse. If responder has an 8-point hand, there is nothing wrong with starting with a negative 1D bid and then following up with a bid that shows 5-8 HCP. In fact, it is often much better to bid 1D first, because that allows opener to rebid 1NT in many cases. Responder can then use a transfer to place the contract in the stronger hand. If opener bids something other than 1NT, nothing is lost. Responder merely bids his suit at his second turn.

When the auction goes 1C-1H or 1C-1S, opener has three basic options:

1. He can raise responder's suit.
2. He can bid a suit of his own.
3. He can find out more about responder's hand before making a decision.

Option 1, the immediate raise, has a specific meaning. It shows 4 cards in responder's suit. It is often followed by conventional bids that indicate the chances for slam. With only 3-card support, opener can first show his strength and support responder's suit later.

Option 2, bidding your own suit, is used when opener has 5 or more cards in the opposite major or a long minor suit and an unbalanced hand. When the bid is the other major, this is not just a natural progression in the auction. It is also the first step in ensuring that the strong hand becomes declarer whenever responder's major is not destined to become trump. The second step is to structure the continuations so that the strong hand is usually the first to bid NT. In the case of a long minor, the opener may have shortness or a weakness in a major. Here the auction will be essentially standard, and a NT game may be bid from the weaker side if it has stoppers to cover opener's weakness.

Option 3, bidding 1NT with most balanced or semi-balanced hands, is often the best choice. Responder's next bid will usually tell opener if there are any slam prospects in the hand or if the target is simply the best game contract. It also allows opener to discover a 4-4 fit in the second major (if one exists) and ensures that he is the first to bid that suit.(A 1S bid in a 1C-1H-1S auction triggers continuations that perform the same functions.)

We will get to a detailed description of the bidding sequences following 1C-1H-1S and 1C-1H or 1S-1NT auctions in a moment, but first I need to describe and define some conventional bids and treatments that will be used in those sequences. I will also provide some acronyms as shorthand tools to refer to those bids.

Strength-Showing and Strength-Asking Bids (SSB/SAB)

After a positive major-suit response to 1C and a 1S or 1NT rebid, several of responder's next bids are artificial SSB. They may show minimum (9–12 HCP), marginal (13–14 HCP), or likely slam-going hands (15+ HCP). Several natural raises and same-suit rebids do the same thing. These bids tell opener whether or not slam is likely or if the combined hands are at least in the marginal slam range.

In auction examples, I may simply put SSB or a point range (such as 13+ HCP) next to the bid in question. In other cases, a bid may have a natural meaning but may simultaneously be a SAB. The most important example of a SAB is a direct single raise of responder's 1H or 1S response. The raise to 2H or 2S asks responder to give his strength by means of an artificial second bid. Again, the purpose is to immediately determine whether slam is a reasonable possibility.

There are at least two reasonable schemes we could use here. One simple method might be to use steps: first step=9–10 HCP, second step= 11–12 HCP, third = 13–14, etc. Another might be to use 2NT for any minimum (9–12 HCP) hand, with any suit bid showing a feature and 13+ HCP. This would be less precise as to HCP but would better indicate where useful cards might lie.

I have no strong preference. In example auctions, I will use the second scheme. Those who prefer the first one can simply figure out what the answer to the SAB would be in steps.

Whatever method is used, opener can now use the cheapest rebid of the prospective trump suit as a DTAB.(If responder's bid is too high for that, 3NT can serve as DTAB.) After responder's general strength and the quality of his trump suit are established, the opener can start exploring slam prospects with cue bids, Blackwood, and other standard methods. At this point, it might be a good idea to define trump-asking and delayed trump-asking bids.

Direct and Delayed Raises of Responder's Suits

TAB and DTAB—Trump-Asking Bids

Trump-asking bids are just what their name implies. They ask responder for a precise description of his length and honor holding in his suit. These bids are stolen (er, borrowed) directly from the Precision Club system

Earlier, I stated that a direct raise of opener's suit is often not the best choice for the 1C opener. This was not because I think it is a bad idea to support partner. It is because direct raises have also doubled as Precision asking bids in the previous editions of the system. A direct raise, therefore, could only be useful when the only information opener wanted was a description of responder's trump holding. This provided great information about possible trump losers, but it didn't answer a much more important question: do we belong in slam?

There are some hands where information about the length and strength of our trump suit is all we need to know in order to bid 6, but those are a small minority. Most of the time, we need to know more about responder's overall strength and distribution before we can make an intelligent decision. So, as usual, I decided to tinker with the original concept in order to make direct raises of responder's 1H and 1S bids more flexible.

My objective was to give a direct raise a specific meaning while retaining the ability to make a Precision asking bid with another nonessential call. The following scheme is the result of that quest and will heretofore be considered the default treatment for the system.

When the auction is 1C-1H or 1C-1S, a direct raise of 2 of the major will show a raise with at least 4 trump. With only a 3-card raise, opener will rebid 1S or 1NT in order to find out more about responder's hand. Since there is never any reason for opener to make a jump bid at this point in a game-forcing auction, we can now use the completely unnecessary jump rebid of 2NT as our Precision TAB in those infrequent cases where the only information opener needs to bid a slam is responder's trump holding.

After a 1C-1H or 1C-1S auction, an "impossible" jump to 2NT asks for responder's holding in his bid suit. As in the Precision Club, the answers to 2NT are shown by the following pattern: **0-1-2-1-2-3**. A DTAB may use the same answers as long as responder's length has not been clearly established. Here is the 0-1-2-1-2-3 set of responses:

- First step =0 of 3 top honors /5+ card suit (no exact length)
- Second step = 1 of 3 top honors /5 card suit
- Third step = 2 of 3 top honors /5 card suit
- Fourth step = 1 of 3 top honors /6 card suit
- Fifth step = 2 of 3 top honors /6 card suit
- Sixth step = 3 of 3 top honors / 5+ card suit (no exact length)

After a 1C-1H-2H or a 1C-1S-2S auction, responder will give a description of his strength by bidding 2S,2NT,3C,3D, or 3H (see previous discussion). Opener can now bid 3 of responder's major (DTAB) if interested in slam. Responder's answers are exactly the same: 0-1-2-1-2-3.

When opener rebids 1S or 1NT instead of making a direct raise, he may still make a DTAB inquiry in either major after responder has had a chance to give a better description of his hand. When responder raises opener's 1S rebid or bids and rebids his own suit, the cheapest NT bid is DTAB. When opener bids the other major and is raised, that will normally set trump; 3NT is then DTAB. If he goes back to responder's major, that will set trump and ask the same question that is asked by a direct trump raise: "How strong are you?"The answer scheme should also be the same. That answer will likely determine whether opener makes any move toward slam. He has three choices:

1. He can sign off in game.
2. He can bid three of the trump suit—or 3NT, if that is not possible (DTAB).
3. He can begin natural slam exploration by cuebidding any new suit.

On those rare occasions when opener's only interest is responder's trump holding or his holding in one particular suit, an immediate jump in one of responder's suits will also serve as DTAB for that suit. A follow-up bid in a second suit would then check on a specific control.

When responder's length in the suit in question is uncertain, the answers to DTAB remain the same as those above. One adjustment might be that if he has shown at least 6 cards in a suit, the steps might show 6/7 card length instead of 5/6.That would be a partnership decision.

When the exact suit length is known (as when responder has raised a second major with 4-card support), a simpler set of replies can be used. Here, DTAB is merely concerned with top honors. The answers are very simple: first step =0 of the top 3 honors; second step = 1of 3; third step = 2 of 3; and fourth step = all 3 top honors.

Second Suits

In the original version of Precision asking bids, a follow-up suit bid after a TAB is also an asking bid. Since opener may need information about more than one side suit and the answers take up quite a bit of bidding space, I have decided to confine second-suit asks to one very specific situation. That is the rare type of hand where opener can singlehandedly set the contract with one or two bits of information. That is, when opener's rebid after a 1H or 1S response to 1C is 2NT—the TAB.

Once opener has received TAB information about one suit, he can ask for controls in a second suit, The answers are as follows:

- first step = no control (3+ cards, no Q, K, or A)
- second step = third round control (Q or doubleton)
- third step = second round control (K or singleton)
- fourth step = first round control (A or void)
- fifth step= first and second round control (AK or singletonA)

A follow-up rebid of the same suit asks whether the control represents distribution (first step) or a high card (second step).Here is a TAB situation:

- 1C   1S
- 2NT**(TAB)   3H (5 spades, 2 of top 3 honors)
- 4D**(second AB)   4NT (first round control)
- 5D**(void or ace?)   5S (ace)
- 7S (opener was in complete control of the auction)

That type of auction is very rare. Another rare type of situation is when opener has a freak hand that only needs a specific ace or king to make a slam.

It will come as no surprise to anyone who has stayed with this tome this far that I also have a couple of possible methods to find specific honors. As a hint, I'll merely note that jump rebids to 3H,3S, 4C, and 4D by a 1C opener have no sensible use in an already game-forcing auction of 1C-1H or 1C-1S. Rather than push any readers already teetering on the edge of cerebral overload over the cliff, I'll merely refer anyone interested to Appendix G.

As noted, we will generally use a DTAB to check on trump quality and then use standard methods to look for possible slams. Here are a couple of DTAB situations:

1C	1H	1C	1H
1NT	2H (9–12 HCP)	1NT	2C (9–12 HCP)
2NT (DTAB)		2S	3S (4 cards)
		3NT (DTAB)	

In the first case, responder's heart length is uncertain. He might have 7 hearts, though 6 is certainly more likely. Therefore, I would use the regular TAB 0-1-2-1-2-3 steps with 6/7 lengths. In the second case, responder's exact length in spades is known. Therefore, DTAB is merely concerned with top honors. The answers are very simple:

- firststep = 0
- second step = 1
- third step = 2
- fourth step = 3

If one chooses to just assume that responder in the first case has exactly 6 hearts, either set of answers can be used (partnership choice).As a general observation, if a pair decides to use TABs, it is wise to have a thorough discussion about when they apply and which sets of answers are used in each situation.

Just to complicate things further, I have a suggestion about how to make the second auction more efficient. Instead of using a natural raise to 3S, one could use an artificial step response whenever opener asks about a fit in a second suit.

- first step = no fit second step = 4-card fit /or/
- 1st=no fit, 2nd =3-card fit, 3rd= 4 small, 4th= 4 to A, K,or QJ

This would let a 3H or 3S rebid serve as DTAB and let 3NT be natural or serve another purpose.

Now that we've explained all these special bids in painstaking detail, we can get back to the general topic: sequences following a major suit response to 1C. I apologize if parts of the next two sections seem a bit repetitive. We will first consider the bidding scheme used when the auction goes 1C-1of a major-1NT. This is mainly because some of the more exotic treatments that are introduced in this section will also be found in the section on suit rebids after 1C-1 of a major auctions. By explaining them in this context, I won't have to subject the reader to a second detailed explanation of the same bids later. A second reason is that the 1C-1H or 1S-1NT auction is likely to be the most common positive response sequence that a system user will encounter.

1C- 1H or 1S -1NT

Positive Major Suit Responses to 1C; 1NT Rebid

With any balanced hand (even if it contains 3 or 4 cards in responder's suit) and with many semi-balanced hands, opener should rebid 1NT. For one thing, it ensures that all NT contracts will be declared by the strong hand. For another, it takes up very little bidding room. Most importantly, though, just as with the 1S rebid, when opener rebids 1NT, the system provides a set of continuations by responder that the opener can use to immediately judge whether the partnership should be looking for slam or merely trying to settle on the best game contract.

Three of responder's 2-level rebids are artificial, describing his high-card strength within a fairly narrow range. They also narrow down the type of hand responder can have by a process of elimination. The remaining 2 and 3 level bids give both strength and distributional information (some explicit, some implied).

Let's start with the least complicated sequences, those coming after 1C-1H or 1S-1NT:

- **2C = 9–12 HCP**—This bid means that slam is unlikely, though not impossible. It also means responder does not have 6 of his major or 5/5 distribution. He may have a 4-card side suit or 5-3-3-2 distribution.
- **2 D= 13–14 HCP**—This bid means there are at least marginal possibilities for slam if opener is not at the bottom of his range. Distribution is less clear, but a strong 6-card holding in his major or 5/5 distribution is unlikely. Other bids are available to describe those hands.
- **2 of the opposite major =15+ HCP**—This bid means slam is very likely. Natural continuations are used to find suit fits. Since the hands are nearly equal in strength, right-siding the contract so that opener becomes declarer is not a major consideration.(Exception: When the auction goes 1C-1H 1S, a 2S bid is a natural raise, and 1NT shows any 15+HCP hand.)
- **2 of responder's major= 9–12 HCP, 6+-card suit**—lacking either the HCP or the suit quality for a stronger 3D or 3H bid

After those basic bids, we begin transfers into secondary 5-card suits:

2NT = transfer—9+ HCP, 5 Clubs / 5 of responder'"s major
>   3C = accepts transfer; also asks for short side suit.
>   Answers:
>>   3D= lower suit, 9–12 HCP / 3H= higher suit, 9–12 HCP
>>   3S= lower suit, 13+HCP / 3NT= higher suit, 13+HCP

3C =transfer—9+ HCP, 5 diamonds / 5 of responder's major
>   3D = accepts transfer; also asks for short side suit.
>   Answers:
>>   3H= lower suit, 9–12 HCP / 3S=higher suit, 9–12 HCP
>>   3NT= lower suit, 13+HCP / /4C=higher suit, 13+ HCP

One special feature of these secondary transfers is the ability of responder to make a transfer back into his own suit at the 3 level. This shows a semi-solid suit and 13+ HCP. A natural jump in his first-bid suit can now show a solid suit and 13+ HCP. So 3D is a special case. If responder's suit is spades, 3D is just a transfer into a 5-card heart suit. If responder's suit is hearts, then it shows a good 6+-card heart suit missing one top honor (i. e. AQJxxx) and 13+HCP. The same situation occurs when responder jumps to 3H after first bidding 1S. That shows a semi-solid 6+-card spade suit with 13+ HCP.

This summary may clarify matters:

3D= If responder's first-bid suit is spades, transfer to second suit (9+HCP, 5+ hearts/5+ spades)
>   3H = accepts transfer; also asks for short side suit.
>   Answers:
>>   3S= lower suit, 9-12 HCP / 3NT=higher suit,9-12 HCP
>>   4C= lower suit, 13+HCP / 4D=higher suit,13+HCP

If responder's first-bid suit is hearts—transfer back to his own suit (13+ HCP, semi-solid heart suit) 6+ hearts, missing 1 top honor; a suit likely to be playable for 1 loser opposite 2 small hearts in opener's hand

3H= If responder's first-bid suit is hearts—jump in his own suit (13+ HCP, solid 6+ card heart suit-AKQxxx)

If responder's first-bid suit is spades—transfer back to his own suit (13+HCP, semi-solid spade suit) 6+ spades, missing one top honor; a suit likely to be playable for 1 loser opposite 2 small spades in opener's hand

3S=If responder's first-bid suit is spades—jump in his own suit (13+ HCP- solid 6+ card spade suit—AKQxxx)

3S,4C,4D=If responder's first-bid suit is hearts, splinter bids-(0 or 1 card in suit), 6+ hearts, 13+ HCP

4C,4D,4H=If responder's first-bid suit is spades, splinter bids-(0 or 1 card in suit), 6+ spades, 13+ HCP

When responder bids 2C, it usually means that slam is not likely. Unless the 1C opener has extra strength or distribution that provides extra trick-taking potential, the auction will generally be a search for the best game. After a 2D or 2 of the opposite major rebid, opener will first try to set trump and then begin a control-showing sequence. Except for any DTAB or SAB bids that might occur, the auction will be quite standard.

Here is the complete rebid scheme:

Rebids after 1C-1H-1NT

1C	1H
1NT	?

2C*= artificial, 9-12HCP

2D*= artificial, 13+ HCP

2H = 6+ hearts, 9-12 HCP, as above

2S*= artificial, 15+ HCP

2NT = transfer; 5+ clubs, 9-12 HCP

3C = transfer; 5+ diamonds, 9-12 HCP

3D* =13+ HCP, 6+ hearts, semi-solidsuit

3H = 6+hearts, solid suit, 13+ HCP, as above

3S/4C/4D = splinter, 6+ GOOD hearts, 13+ HCP

After opener accepts the 2NT transfer to 3C or the 3C transfer to 3D, responder next shows his short suit in steps (first step= lower side suit, 9–12 HCP/ second step= higher side suit, 9–12 HCP)/ third step= lower side suit,13+ HCP/ fourth step= higher side suit,13+HCP). After 1C-1S-1NT, the bidding is essentially identical to that which follows1C-1H-1NT.

1C	1S
1NT	?

2C* = artificial, 9–12 HCP

2D* = artificial, 13–14HCP

2H* = artificial, 15+HCP

2S = 6+ spades,9–12 HCP

2NT = transfer,5+ clubs,5/5+, 9+ HCP

3C = transfer, 5+ diamonds, 5/5+, 9+ HCP

3D = transfer, 5+ hearts,9+ HCP

3H = 6+semi-solid spades, 13+ HCP

3S = 6+ solid spades, 13-16 HCP

4C,4D, 4H = splinters, 6+ GOOD spades, 13+ HCP

After opener accepts the 2NT transfer to 3C, the 3C transfer to 3D, or the 3D transfer to 3H, the same continuations apply.

Here are some example hands and auctions. They illustrate how responder's first bid and rebid can give a picture of his hand while opener's holding remains relatively hidden. They also illustrate the use of TAB, DTAB, and SAB. The use of asking bids is just one type of continuation scheme that might be used to explore for slam after responder's shape and strength is established. Many will prefer more natural methods.

A.	♠ AQxx	♠ Kxxxx	1C	1S (5+spades,9+HCP)
	♥ Kx	♥ Qxxx	1NT (SAB)	2C (5 spades, 9–12 HCP)
	♦ Axxx	♦ Kx	4S	(slam unlikely)
	♣ KQx	♣ Jx		

B.	♠ AQxx	♠ Kxxxxx	1C	1S (5+spades, 9+HCP)
	♥ A	♥ Jxx	2NT (TAB)	3S (6 spades, 1 top honor)
	♦ Axx	♦ x	4C (ask)	4NT (first round control)
	♣ KQx	♣ AJx	5D (ask)	5NT (second round control)
			6D (second ask)	6H (singleton, not king)
			7S	

C.	♠ AQxx	♠ Kxxx	1C	1H (5+hearts,9+HCP)
	♥ Kx	♥ Jxxxx	1NT (SAB)	2C (9-12 HCP, artificial)
	♦ AJxx	♦ x	2S (spades?)	3S (4 spades)
	♣ KQx	♣ AJx	4S	

D.

♠ AQxx	♠ xx	1C	1H
♥ Kx	♥ AQxxxx	1NT	2H (6+hearts, 9–12 HCP)
♦ AJxx	♦ x	2NT (DTAB)	3H (2 of top 3 honors)
♣ KQx	♣ AJxx	3S (1st-round control)	4C (1st-round control)
		4D (1st-round control)	4H (no other outside controls)
		5C (2nd-round control)	5D (2nd-round control)
		6H or 6NT	

E.

♠ AQxx	♠ xx	1C	1H
♥ Kx	♥ AQxxx	1NT	2NT (5H, 5C, 9+HCP)
♦ AJxx	♦ x	3C (ask)	3D (0-1 diamonds, 9–12 HCP)
♣ KQx	♣ AJxxx	4C (1430)	4S (2 KC)
		6C	

F.

♠ Kx	♠ AQxxx	1C	1S
♥ KJxx	♥ Axxx	1NT	2C (9-12 HCP, artificial)
♦ AQxx	♦ xx	2H (hearts?)	3H (4 hearts)
♣ AQx	♣ xx	3NT (DTAB)	4D (1 of 3 top honors)
		4H	

G.

♠ K10x	♠ AQJxxx	1C	1S
♥ Ax	♥ xxx	NT	3H (6+ semi-solid spades,
♦ AKxxx	♦ xx	4D	5C 13+ HCP)
♣ Kxx	♣ AQ	5D	5S
		6C	7C
		7S	

H.

♠ xxx	♠ AKQxxx	1C	1S
♥ AKx	♥ xx	1NT	3S (solid spades, 13+ HCP)
♦ Ax	♦ Qxx	4C	5C
♣ AQ10xx	♣ Kx	7S	

I.	♠ Axx	♠ KQxxxx	1C	1S (9+ HCP)
	♥ KQxx	♥ Ax	1NT	2S (6+spades, 9–12 HCP)
	♦ Ax	♦ xx	3S (DTAB)	4D (2 honors)
	♣ KQxx	♣ Jxxx	4H (DTAB)	5D (first round control)
			6S	

J.	♠ Qxx	♠ Kxxxx	1C	1S
	♥ AKx	♥ Qxxx	1NT	2C (9–12 HCP)
	♦ AKJxx	♦ x	2S (DTAB)	3C (5 spades, 1 top honor)
	♣ Kx	♣ AJx	3D	4C
			4H	4S
			5S (quality?)	P (weak suit)

Suit Rebids by the 1C Opener – 1C-1H- 1S

With 4 or more spades, opener rebids 1S after 1C-1H. For the sake of consistency and ease of memory, responder's continuations are very similar to those used when opener rebids 1NT. The main difference is that he has to be able to raise spades if he has support.

The artificial bids and transfer sequences are almost identical, with 2C and 2D still showing 9-12 and 13-14 HCP respectively. Since a bid of the other major can't be used to show 15+, 1NT is used for that purpose.(The 1NT here is so strong that right-siding the contract is not a major consideration.) All of the transfer sequences and jumps to the 3 level are identical.

The only new element is a method of raising opener's spade suit. We want to be able to differentiate between 3-and 4-card raises and also provide a way for responder to show his strength. Luckily, this can be done with the bids already in place plus one additional treatment.

That treatment is simple: all 4-card spade raises will be shown by a simple raise to 2S. Opener will then use 2NT to ask for responder's strength. Responder will show his HCP in steps. Opener can then ask for any shortness by bidding 3NT. Finally, he can sign off in 4S or ask for keycards in search of slam.

All 3-card raises will go through one of the strength-showing bids. Responder can use an artificial 2C bid and a delayed raise to show 3 spades and 9–12 HCP. He can bid 2D and then bid spades to show 3-card support and 13–14 HCP. He can bid 1NT and then 2S to show 15+HCP and 3 spades. Opener will use the cheapest bid over any strength-showing bid to let responder clarify his intentions. An immediate spade continuation will show the 3-card raise. Any other bid will basically be natural.

Responder also has two natural and several possible transfer rebids in his own suit. A simple rebid of 2H shows 6+ hearts and 9–12 HCP. A jump to 3H shows a solid 6+ card suit and 13+ HCP. A jump transfer of 3D shows 13-14 HCP and a semi-solid (AQJxxx, KQJxxx) 6-card suit. If one wanted to get even more precise, an artificial 1NT, 2C, or 2D bid followed by a 3H bid could show a less-than-solid 7-card suit with the appropriate point range. Finally, jumps to 2NT (transfer showing 5+ clubs) and 3C (transfer showing 5+ diamonds) can be used to describe a hand with 5-5+distribution and 9+ HCP.

This leaves artificial bids to cover any remaining possible hands. A bid of 2C shows any hand with 9–12 HCP that is not covered by any of the major suit rebids. With the 5-card heart suit already shown, the hand may have a side minor suit or 5-3-3-2 distribution. If no major fit is found, responder will bid as naturally as possible, maybe having to bid a 3-card minor to maneuver the contract into 3NT. If opener's bidding suggests weakness in one suit, responder may then bid NT from his side if that seems right.

A bid of 2D covers many of the same types of hands, except with a 13–14 HCP range. It may also be the start of a strong (but not solid) rebid with 6 hearts. The difference is that it is a signal that there is at least a mild possibility of slam in the combined hands. Continuations are similar to those after a 2C rebid. A bid of 1NT covers the same hands, with a strong implication that slam is possible.

Here is a chart of the continuations after a 1C-1H-1S auction:

1C	1H
1S (asking)	*Answers*

1NT** = 15+HCP (possibly a 3-card spade raise, 15+ HCP)

2C** = artificial, 9–12 HCP, may have a 3-card spade raise, 5-3-3-2 distribution, or 4+ clubs or diamonds

2D** = artificial, 13–14 HCP, may have a 3-card spade raise,5-3-3-2 distribution,4+ clubs or diamonds, or 6 hearts

2H = 6+ hearts, 9–12 HCP

2S= any 4-card spade raise, 9+ HCP (2NT asks HCP)

2NT = transfer 5+ hearts, 5+ clubs, 9+ HCP

3C =transfer 5+ hearts, 5+ diamonds, 9+ HCP

3D = 6+ semi-solid hearts, 13–14 HCP

3H = 6+ solid hearts, 13–14 HCP

3S = optional (spade raise with side void? your idea here)

3NT=***Alert =6+ hearts, **spade shortness**

4C, 4D =splinters = 6+ hearts, 13+ HCP, short in bid suit

** = **artificial asking bids**

When responder bids 1NT, 2C, or 2D, opener's bid of the cheapest suit is an asking bid. Opener should try to use this bid in most cases rather than try to describe his own hand. It allows responder to tell him whether he has 3 spades. The 1C opener can then rebid his spades, support partner's hearts, bid 2NT, or introduce a side minor suit after responder has given a further description of his hand.

Here is a thumbnail sketch of what responder should have for his follow-up bids after the auction goes 1C-1H 1S-1NT (15+ HCP):

2C (asking)

2D= 4 diamonds or 2-5-3-3 distribution, denies 3 spades or 6 hearts

2H = 6+ hearts, 0–2 spades, (no spade raise), 4–6 cards in the minors but no 5-card second suit, and minor suit holdings not suitable for a 2NT bid (no tenaces or weakness in one minor)

2S= 3-card spade raise, 15+ HCP

2NT= similar to 2D bid but with tenaces or fairly strong holdings in both minors

3C= second 4-card club suit (either 1-5-3-4 or 2-5-2-4 distribution likely nearly all values concentrated in hearts and clubs)

Here is what he might have after a 1C-1H 1S-2C (9–12 HCP) auction:

2D *(asking)*
2H=6+ hearts, denies 3 spades (occasionally might be a waiting bid with 2-5-3-3)
2S =3 spades (distribution and minor-suit holdings not suitable for NT)
2NT=likely 2-5-3-3 distribution, at least partial minor-suit stoppers
3C= second 4-card club suit (probably 1-5-3-4 or 2-5-2-4 distribution likely with nearly all values concentrated in hearts and diamonds)
3D= second 13+ HCP) 4-card diamond suit (probably 1-5-4-3 or 2-5-4-2 distribution, likely with nearly all values concentrated in hearts and diamonds)

Here is what he might have after 1C-1H-1S-2D (13–14 HCP):

2H *(asking)*
2S= 3 spades
2NT= 2-5-3-3 distribution
3C= second 4-card club suit, 2-5-2-4 or 1-5-3-4 distribution
3H= 6+hearts

When responder has a two-suited hand, he will forgo any of the strength-showing bids and instead use one of the transfers (2NT, 3C,3D,3H) to show 5+/5+ distribution. With a big one-suited hand, he will use one of the jump sequences discussed previously.

Note: A hand with 3-5-3-0 or 3-5-0-3 distribution might present a problem. Partners will have to decide whether the distribution or the 3-card raise should be given priority. Perhaps making the transfer and then jumping to 4S may be the answer. Alternatively, one could raise and then jump in the second suit.

Here are some example hands (notice DTAB can be used as a delayed inquiry tool in hearts):

A.	♠ AQxxx	♠ Jx	1C	1H
	♥ Kxx	♥ AJ10xx	1S	2D (13+HCP)
	♦ AKJx	♦ Qx	2H (ask)	3C (club suit)
	♣ x	♣ AKxx	3H (DTAB)	3NT (5 hearts, 1 of 3 top honors)
			4C (ask)	5C (first-and second-round control)
			6 NT	P

B.	♠ AJxxx	♠ x	1C	1H
	♥ Qx	♥ AKJ10xx	1S	3NT (0-1 S, 6+H, 3+HCP)
	♦ AQxx	♦ Kx	4NT	5D (3 KC—hearts assumed)
	♣ KJ	♣ Axxx	7H	

C.	♠ KJ10xxx	♠ Qx	1C	1H
	♥ x	♥ Kxxxx	1S	2C (9-12 HCP)
	♦ AQx	♦ Kxx	2D (ask)	2NT
	♣ AKJx	♣ Qxx	3S	4S

D.	♠ QJ10	♠ AKxxxx	1C	1S
	♥ Ax	♥ Jxx	1NT	2D (13+HCP)
	♦ KQJx	♦ Ax	2S (DTAB)	3S (6 spades, 2 top honors)
	♣ AQxx	♣ Kx	4C (ask)	4S (second-round control)
			5D (ask)	6C (first-round control)
			7S	

E.	♠ QJ10	♠ AKx	1C	1H
	♥ Kx	♥ AJxxxx	1NT	2S (15+HCP)
	♦ KQJx	♦ Ax	3H (DTAB)	4D (6 hearts, 1 top honor)
	♣ AQxx	♣ Kx	4S (ask)	5S (first- and second-round control)
			6NT	

F.	♠ QJ10	♠ Axx	1C	1H
	♥ Ax	♥ KQJxxx	1NT	2S (15+HCP)
	♦ KQJx	♦ Ax	3H (DTAB)	4H (6 hearts, 2 top honors)
	♣ AQxx	♣ Kx	4NT (1430)	5S (3 KC)
			5NT (kings)	6C (1)
			7NT (either black king should produce 13 tricks)	

Rebids of 2C and 2D After 1C-1H or 1S

When opener has a long minor suit and 17+HCP and gets a positive response of 1H or 1S to his 1C opening, he has a choice of rebids. With only a 5-card suit, a 1NT rebid is generally the best choice, assuming at least a semi-balanced hand. Even with 5-4-3-1 distribution and a singleton in responder's suit, a 1NT rebid may be the best way to get useful information on responder's hand and may also right-side any NT contracts.

A rebid of 2C or 2D, therefore, tends to show at least a 6-card suit. After a lot of exploration involving relays and other artificial continuation schemes to describe responder's distribution and point range, I finally came back to one that is fairly natural. It will use the cheapest second bid by responder (2D over 2C; 2H over 2D) as a waiting bid. Most other non-jump bids will be natural, and a few jump bids will show specific hands.

Responder usually will not try to indicate extra values immediately, since he is in a game-forcing auction, He will have later opportunities to indicate slam interest (by supporting opener's suit at the 4 level, cuebidding a side suit, making a splinter bid, etc.). He can rebid his suit with 6, bid a second 4-or 5-card suit, or support opener's minor with 3.The waiting bid will be used for many hands in the 9-12 HCP range. It will be used for any hand with no second biddable suit, no rebiddable 6-card major, and less than 3-card card support for opener's minor. A rebid of 2H over 2D may simply show a 5-3-3-2 hand with nothing else to bid. Another heart bid is needed to guarantee a 6-card suit.

There are basically only three immediate strong second bids available to responder. One is 2NT. This will guarantee honors in all suits outside opener's minor and show at least 13 HCP. Opener will be able to ask for the exact range (in steps) by bidding 3C (first step = 13–14, second= 15–16, third= 17–18, etc.). The second strong bid is a jump rebid in his major, which shows at least 13 HCP and a very good 6-or 7-card suit. The third is an immediate splinter, showing at least good 3-card support for opener's suit, shortness in the bid suit, and enough strength to invite slam. These bids may not be very sophisticated, but they should cause almost no memory strain.

Here are some example hands involving opener's 2C rebid:

A.	♥ Ax	♥ Qxx	1C	1H (9+ HCP, 5+ hearts)
	♠ x	♠ KQxxxx	2C	2H (6+ hearts, 9–12 HCP)
	♦ KQx	♦ Ax	2NT	3NT
	♣ AKJxxxx	♣ xx	P	
B.	♠ Kx	♠ Qxx	1C	1H (9+ HCP, 5+hearts)
	♥	♥ KJxxx	2C	2D (waiting)
	♦ AQxx	♦ Kxx	3C	3D (feature or suit)
	♣ AKJxxxx	♣ xx	3NT or 5C	P

C. ♠ x   ♠ QJxxx   1C   1S
  ♥ KQxx   ♥ AJxx   2C   2H
  ♦ A   ♦ Qx   3H (DTAB)   3NT (1 top honor)
  ♣ AKJ10xxx   ♣ xx   4NT (1430)   5C (1)
                               6H

D. ♠ Ax   ♠ QJx   1C   1H
  ♥ Kx   ♥ QJxxx   2C   2D (waiting)
  ♦ KQx   ♦ Jxx   2NT   3NT
  ♣ AQ10xxx   ♣ Kx

E. ♠   ♠ Qxxxx   1C   1S
  ♥ KQxx   ♥ AJxx   2C   2H
  ♦ Ax   ♦ Qx   3H (DTAB)   3N (1 top honor)
  ♣ AKJ10xxx   ♣ Qx   4C (control?)   4H (third-round control)
                               5C (honor or xx?) 5H (honor- Q)
                               7H

F. ♠ x   ♠ AQxxx   1C   1S
  ♥ Ax   ♥ QJx   2C   3C
  ♦ KQx   ♦ Ax   4D (Redwood)   5C (2 KC + Q of clubs)
  ♣ AKJxxxx   ♣ Q10x   5D (kings?)   5H (0)
                               7C (pushy?- at worst on 4–3 spade split;
                               heart finesse is bonus backup)

G. ♠ Kx   ♠ AQJxxx   1C   1S
  ♥ Qxx   ♥ x   2C   3H (splinter,13+HCP)
  ♦ AQ   ♦ Kxx   3S (DTAB)   4S (6+ spades, 2 of top 3)
  ♣ AQ10xxx   ♣ Kxx   5C (control?)   5S (second-round control,
                               6C or 6S   almost certainly the king)

Here are some example hands involving opener's 2D rebid:

A. ♠ Ax   ♠ KQxxxx   1C   1S
    ♥ x   ♥ Qxx   2D   2S
    ♦ AKJxxxx   ♦ xx   3S (DTAB)   4S (6+spades, 2 of top 3)
    ♣ KQx   ♣ Ax   4NT (1430)   5S (2 KC + Q)
                                6S

B. ♠   ♠ Qxx   1C   1H
    ♥ Kx   ♥ AJxxx   3D*(solid 7+ suit) 3H
    ♦ AKQxxxxx   ♦ xx   4C   5C
    ♣ Axx   ♣ Kxx   5H   6D
                                7D? (not unreasonable)

C. ♠ KQxx   ♠ AJxx   1C   1H
    ♥   ♥ QJxxx   2D   2S
    ♦ AKJ109xx   ♦ Qx   3S (DTAB)   4C (1 of top 3)
    ♣ Ax   ♣ xx   7S

D. ♠ Ax   ♠ QJxxx   1C   1S
    ♥ Kx   ♥ QJx   2D   3D
    ♦ AQ109xx   ♦ Kxx   4D (1430)   4H (1 KC)
    ♣ KQx   ♣ xx   4NT   P

E. ♠ KQxx   ♠ Axxxx   1C   1S
    ♥   ♥ AJxx   2S (TAB)   3C (5 spades, 1 top honor)
    ♦ AKJ109xx   ♦ xx   7S*(Could ask
    ♣ Ax   ♣ xx   about diamonds first.)

F. ♠ Ax   ♠ KQxxx   1C   1S
    ♥ x   ♥ Kxx   2D   2NT (13+)
    ♦ AQJxxxx   ♦ Kxx   3D   4D
    ♣ AQx   ♣ Kx   4H*(Redwood)   4S (1 KC)
                                5C**(kings?)   5D (0 or 3)
                                6NT (0 impossible)

** Depending on agreement, 5H might be the king-asking bid on hand F.

1C-1S-2H (Special Case)

When a 1C opener has 5 or 6 hearts and responder bids 1S, the bidding may get a bit cramped. A rebid of 2H by opener takes away any use of strength-showing minor-suit bids. There is barely enough room to confirm a possible 6-2 major fit or, failing that, stoppers in both minors for a possible 3NT contract.

The slightly imperfect solution is for opener to use the 1NT rebid with many semi-balanced hands containing 5 hearts. This conforms to the current fairly common practice of opening 1NT or 2NT with a 5-card major. In many cases, when responder continues with 2C or 2D, opener will have a chance to bid 2H and then rebid 3H to show his 5-card suit. On some occasions when the bidding makes it impossible to detect a 5-3 heart fit below the 3NT level, the NT game may be as good or better than one in hearts.

As a trade-off for this minor imperfection, we can define a 2H rebid by a 1C opener fairly narrowly. It should basically show one of three types of holding:

1. 6+ hearts
2. 5+ hearts and a 5+ card minor
3. 5+ hearts a nd a 4+ card minor with almost all of the strength confined to those two suits—i. e. xx AKQxxxx AKQx

When the auction goes 1H-1S-2H-?, responder's rebids become a bit vague; 2S must serve as a kind of waiting bid, and it may or may not show a 6-card spade suit. At this point, neither player can be sure of an 8-card major fit. We must rely on opener's continuations to clarify the situation.

If opener bids 2NT, he shows stoppers in both minors. He may have 5 or 6 hearts. This bid gives responder room to show delayed 2-card heart support, a 4+-card minor, or 6+ spades. If opener instead bids 3C or 3D, he shows either a real side suit or a 6-card heart suit with only 1 minor stopped. Responder can again show delayed heart support, rebid his spades with 6 or more, or bid 3NT with the unbid minor stopped. With slam-going strength and 4-card support, he can raise the minor suit to 4.

Other sequences are less complicated. Responder can show a real side suit by bidding a minor instead of 2S. He can show 3-card heart support with a direct raise to 3H. A jump to 3S would show a solid 6+ card suit.

A 3H rebid by opener would show a very good, if not solid, 6+ card suit. He could have shown a solid suit with extras by an immediate jump to 3H over 1S.

Bidding 3NT or 4 of either major shows an intent to play there, though that suggestion may be overruled by partner if he has undisclosed strength. With extra values, either partner may show slam interest by non-sign-off cue bids or splinter bids at the 4 level.

Here are some hands involving a possible 2H rebid by the 1C opener:

A.　♠ Ax　　　　♠ KQxxxx　　1C　　　　　　　　1S
　　♥ AKJxx　　♥ Qxx　　　　2H　　　　　　　　3H
　　♦ x　　　　♦ xx　　　　　3S (DTAB)　　　　4D (6+spades, 2 of top 3)
　　♣ KQxxx　　♣ Ax　　　　 4NT　　　　　　　　5S
　　　　　　　　　　　　　　　6S

B.　♠ —　　　　♠ AQxxxx　　1C　　　　　　　　1S
　　♥ AKQJxxx　♥ x　　　　　3H (solid 7+ suit)　3S (ace)
　　♦ AKJx　　 ♦ xx　　　　　4D (ace, no club ace)　4H
　　♣ xx　　　 ♣ KJ10x　　　5D　　　　　　　　5NT (club stop)
　　　　　　　　　　　　　　　P, 6H or 6NT (who knows?)

C.　♠ Kxx　　　♠ AQxxx　　　1C　　　　　　　　1S
　　♥ KQJxx　　♥ xx　　　　　1NT (SAB)　　　　2C (9-12 HCP)
　　♦ AKJ10　　♦ Qx　　　　　2S (DTAB)　　　　3C (5 spades, 1 of top 3)
　　♣ x　　　　♣ Axx　　　　 3D (ask)　　　　　3S (third round control)
　　　　　　　　　　　　　　　4D (ask)　　　　　4S (queen)
　　　　　　　　　　　　　　　5C (ask)　　　　　4NT (first-round control)
　　　　　　　　　　　　　　　6S

D.　♠ A　　　　♠ KQxxxx　　1C　　　　　　　　1S
　　♥ AKJxxx　 ♥ Qxx　　　　2H　　　　　　　　3H
　　♦ xx　　　 ♦ xx　　　　　3S (ace)　　　　　4C (ace)
　　♣ KQxx　　 ♣ Ax　　　　　4H (no diamond control) P

E. ♠ x   ♠ Axxxx   1C   1S
    ♥ AQJxx   ♥ x   2H   2S (waiting)
    ♦ AKQJx   ♦ 10xxx   3D   3NT
    ♣ xx   ♣ AJ10   4D   5C
                                  6D   P

F. ♠ x   ♠ AQJxx   1C   1S
    ♥ AKQxx   ♥ x   2H   3C
    ♦ A   ♦ xxx   4C (1430)   4NT (2 KC + Q of clubs)
    ♣ KJ10xx   ♣ AQxx   7C

CHAPTER 9

1NT and Two-Way Responses to 1 Club

An Overview

This chapter will cover several responses to the 1C opener which will have two or more possible meanings. The system already has several examples of this phenomenon (the 1D response to 1C, Sartor 2/1 responses to a major, Sartor jump shifts, etc.).This is not a bizarre attempt to create novelty. It is almost always done with two major objectives in mind. The first is to be able to describe multiple types of hands with limited bidding space. The second, and more compelling, is to make the 1C opener the declarer on as many hands as possible. This is done to keep the strong hand hidden as much as possible and to gain the advantage of the opening lead being made into, rather than through, the stronger hand. On any given hand, this may not matter, but I think the cumulative effect is significant.

The treatment will be seen in bids that are always positive game-forcing responses (1NT, 2C) and bids that may be either strong or preemptive (2D,2H). Responses from 2D through 3S will allow us to describe preemptive hands and differentiate between weak, invitational, and solid suits, while also arranging for the 1C opener to be the declarer in almost all cases.

Of all of these bids, the most essential are 1NT and 2C, which will be paired to describe balanced responses of different strengths while also covering certain unbalanced hands. This arrangement gives the 1C opener the first opportunity to bid NT when responder has any positive balanced response. Stayman then allows the strong hand to become declarer in either major if a 4-4 fit exists. The next two responses, 2D and 2H, combine specific positive diamond replies with preemptive bids in hearts and spades. Again, this allows the strong hand to remain hidden and receive the opening lead. The weak hand with the 7-card major comes down as dummy.

The system can certainly operate with standard preemptive responses rather than the various innovations I am suggesting, but I think the transfer effect they create makes it worth the effort to incorporate them. When you include all of the weakish hands covered by an initial 1D response to 1C and all of the hands that these two-way bids will cover, you wind up with the big club opener declaring a far greater percentage of contracts than in any other strong club or standard system that I know of.(For any grammar sticklers out there, change the end of that last sentence to "with which I am familiar.")

Let us now look at the bids in question.

1C-1NT

One of the major design flaws of the Precision Club is the use of 1C-1NT to show a balanced hand with 8-10 HCP. Of course, Precision was designed for simplicity, and this bid is simple and easy to remember. Unfortunately, 1NT is probably the most likely positive response in the whole system. The result is that a great number of NT contracts are declared by the weak hand, with the strong hand exposed as dummy. There is a solution for this problem, which will be explained in the next section. Suffice it to say, we have a better way to bid balanced 9–12 HCP hands.

The 1NT response can be improved by strengthening it. Its basic meaning—a natural balanced hand with game-forcing values-will remain the same. However, it will now show a balanced 13–15 HCP hand. The opening lead will no longer be going through a strong hand into a much weaker one. With that much strength, there should be no concern about responder declaring the hand. The possible opening lead advantage should be insignificant. Our main problem will be deciding if slam is a good idea.

Opener's initial rebids are quite straightforward. With a balanced or semi-balanced hand, opener bids 2C as Stayman. He may also have a 5-card club suit for this bid. Bids of 2D, 2H, and 2S are all natural, showing 5+ card suits. A 2NT bid shows a 6+ card club suit with no side suit.

At this point, any number of continuation schemes will work quite nicely. Some may prefer to make all of responder's bids natural, clarifying possible 8-and 9-card trump fits but making no attempt to define trump quality. Others may like a more artificial approach (see Appendix H).

I am going to present one fairly natural bidding structure, which I will treat as the preferred scheme for the system. I do not pretend that this is the only sensible way to handle the type of hands in question.

I also admit that some of the ideas proposed in subsequent sections are not indispensable. Some may choose simpler meanings for the 2D, 2H, and 2S responses instead of the two-way treatments outlined in these pages. This won'tdestroy the effectiveness of the basic system, although these bids do perform important functions. The strong (13-15 HCP) 1NT response outlined here combined with the two-way 2C response which will be explained later in this chapter are important to the overall system, however. They work together in tandem and cannot be sensibly separated from one another or from the system as a whole.

Here is my suggested natural structure for 1C-1NT auctions.

When Opener Is Balanced or Has Five Clubs

When the opener has a balanced hand and the auction goes 1C-NT, he bids 2C (modified Stayman). Responder's reply will either be a transfer showing a 4-card major or a bid denying a major but describing his hand's strength. To be specific, a 2D reply shows 4 hearts. Responder may also have a second suit. A bid of 2H shows 4 spades. It denies 4 hearts, but the hand may have a 4-card minor. A bid of 2S shows no major and a minimum (13–14 HCP). The hand will have 1 or 2 minors. A bid of 2NT shows no major and a maximum (15 HCP).Again, the hand will have 1 or 2 minors. Opener can then bid 2NT or bid a minor if he would consider bidding a minor suit slam. If he has 5 clubs, he may rebid 3C.

Opener's first goal is to establish a 4-4 fit in a major if one is possible. If he has a fit for responder's transfer suit, he bids it. If a trump fit does not exist in the transfer suit, opener bids a different suit, still looking for a combined 8-card trump holding. If responder's first rebid is 2D, showing 4 hearts, opener may still bid 2S, hoping he has both majors. Otherwise he can bid 2NT or a minor, still seeking a trump fit. Raises set trump. If no suit fit can be found, the contract will probably wind up in NT.

If opener has exactly 5 clubs, he still begins his trump exploration by bidding 2C. If he has a 4-card major, he may first bid 2C and then bid his other suit. If responder's first rebid of 2D or 2H immediately reveals a 4-4 fit, he may choose to establish the major as trump and show his clubs later as a slam try.

If a trump fit is found, standard slam exploration may ensue, with either partner able to suggest signing off by bidding 3NT or 4 of an agreed-upon major. Key-card asking bids will require partnership agreement. The chart and the example hands on the next three pages will illustrate why.

When Opener Has a Balanced Hand or Exactly 5 Clubs: A Chart

1C	1NT
2C (asking)	2D = 4 hearts (may have 4 spades)
	2H = 4 spades (denies 4 hearts)
	2S = no major, minimum (13-14 HCP)
	2NT = no major, maximum (14–15 HCP)

If responder bids 2S or 2NT, opener can try for a fit in either minor. If a fit is found, raises set trump and let either partner try for slam. A raise to the 4 level by the 1C opener can double as a key-card asking bid, while Redwood (Kickback) can be used if responder is the one who makes the raise.

When opener has any 5-card suit other than clubs, he bids 2 of that suit. He may also bid 2NT, which shows 6+ clubs. Each of these bids requires a slightly different set of continuations, but the general structure is pretty consistent. I'll go through each of them as a separate case.

Here are some possible auctions using these continuations:

A.	♠ Kxx	♠ Axxx	1C	1NT (13–15 HCP)
	♥ AQxx	♥ Kx	2C (Stayman)	2H (4 spades)
	♦ Ax	♦ Kxx	2NT (4 spades)	3C (4 clubs, non-minimum)
	♣ KQxx	♣ Axxx	3D (feature)	3H (feature)
			4C or 4NT (KC ask)	4D?5C?(KC answer)
			Likely ending in 6S	

B.	♠ Kxx	♠ Axxx	1C	1NT
	♥ AQxx	♥ Kx	2C	2H (4 spades, 2-3 hearts)
	♦ Ax	♦ Kxx	2NT	3C
	♣ KQxx	♣ Axxx	4C (KC ask)**	4S? (2) (KC answer)
			6C (**4D could be	
			Redwood/Kickback instead)	

C.	♠ AKJx	♠ Qxxx	1C1	NT
	♥ xx	♥ AKxx	2C	2D (4 H)
	♦ AKJx	♦ xx	2S	3S (4 spades)
	♣ Kxx	♣ Axx	4D (feature)	4H (feature)
			4NT	5S (KC answer)
			5NT	6C? 6D? (KC answer-1)
				or 5H (specific king)
			6H (minor Q?)	6S (nope-ends auction too)

D.	♠ Qx	♠ Axx	1C	1NT
	♥ KQ10x	♥ Ax	2C	2NT (non-minimum, no major)
	♦ KQxx	♦ AJxx	3D	4D
	♣ AKx	♣ J10xx	4H (KC ask)	4S? 4NT? (3 KC)
			6D (just as good as 4NT—bigger reward)	

E.	♠ KQxx	♠ Axx	1C	1NT
	♥ KQ10x	♥ Ax	2C	2S (minimum, no major)
	♦ Kxx	♦ Axxx	3NT	P
	♣ Ax	♣ J10xx		

As you can see, partners need to set up agreements about key-card asking bids. As one obvious example, in this system, a raise of a suit to the 4 level often sets trump and starts slam exploration. What does a bid of a new suit mean? Is it key-card asking? If so, what answers apply? Does Redwood (Kickback) apply? Is a new suit a cue-bid? If so, do you show any control (Italian style), or do you always cue-bid aces first, followed by kings later? What does 4NT mean in this situation?

As the ads for a prominent scandal sheet proclaim, "Enquiring minds want to know!" So do bridge partnerships that don't want to end up in homicide. Any set of agreements will work as long as both partners are on the same page. Of course, it helps if they are reading the same book.

As for myself I would suggest the following agreements:

1. If the 1C opener raises a minor to the 4 level, that sets trump and doubles as our key-card asking bid.
2. If the 1NT responder (the weaker hand) raises the minor and sets trump, Redwood (Kickback) applies—opener's bid of the next higher suit agrees on trump and asks for keycards.

3. The answering structure in either case shall be a partnership choice among 0314 keycard, 1430 keycard, and Texas responses. I prefer the latter, with the first step showing 0-1 keycards (unlikely- responder has 13-15 HCP) Opener can then use the cheapest rebid to find the trump queen if necessary. A more likely 2-step answer would show 2 keycards without the trump queen. The third step would show 2KC + the Q: the 4th, 3KC without, etc.

    However, in deference to all of those players who already use 1430, I will avoid a lot of confusion and use that set of responses on all of the example auctions in this chapter.

4. After the KC reply, the bid of a new suit or a rebid of the key-card asking suit can ask for kings. Does it ask for total or specific kings? A bid of 4NT is a suggestion to play there. (For simplicity, king inquiries will be for total number of kings outside of trump.)

5. After the king reply, any new suit bid asks for third round control and implies interest in a grand slam.

Others may choose completely different agreements. They may also decide on separate agreements for auctions in which opener shows a 5+ card suit.

Later we will see how a similar scheme applies when the auction goes 1C-2NT (16–18 HCP, balanced)

When Opener Has a 5+-Card Diamond Suit

1C-1NT-2D (5+-card diamond suit)

When opener has five or more diamonds, his first rebid after 1C-1NT is 2D. He will often have a 4-card major, so responder's rebids are very much like those used when opener bids 2C. He can bid 2H or 2S if he has a 4-card major or bid 2NT without one. If responder bids a major, opener may raise or bid 2S, 2NT, or 3C.

He may also rebid 3D if he has 6 or 7 diamonds. At this point, responder can bid a feature to suggest slam and show at least 3-card support.

Responder also has several types of raises available. A bid of any new suit at the 3 level should be treated as a fitting raise. This bid would specifically show 4 diamonds and 4 of the bid suit. That would immediately bring a possible diamond slam into the picture while also establishing a possible 4-4 side suit fit.

Once the initial rebids have clarified the suit fit (s) or lack thereof, bids of new suits would indicate slam interest. A bid of 3NT or 4 of an agreed-upon major would show an intention to stop in game.

There is another possibility. Since any 1C-1NT auction guarantees at least 30 HCP in combined assets, some may decide to treat the auction as forcing to 4NT. In that case, 3NT might simply be a natural continuation, giving or asking for further distributional information, rather than an attempt to sign off in game. That would have to be a matter for partnership agreement.

Here is a chart describing the bidding structure after a 1C-1NT-2D auction:

When Opener has 5 or More Diamonds: A Chart

1C	1NT
2D (5+ diamonds),	2H or 2S =natural, may have 2–3 diamonds (can make delayed 3-card raise to 3D or a delayed bid in a second suit or NT to deny 3 diamonds)
	2NT= no 4-card major,3+ diamonds
	3C= fitting raise, 4 clubs, 4 diamonds
	3D= 4 diamonds, no side suit (3-3-4-3)
	3H= fitting raise, 4 hearts, 4 diamonds
	3S= fitting raise, 4 spades, 4 diamonds
	3NT= no major,3 diamonds, maximum

Here are some possible auctions using these continuations:

A.	♠ Axx	♠ KQxx	1C	1NT (13–15 HCP)
	♥ Kx	♥Axx	2D (5+ diamonds)	2S (4 spades, 2-3 diamonds)
	♦ KQxxx	♦Ax	2NT	3C (4 clubs)
	♣ AQx	♣Jxxx	3NT (3S is possible- it might lead to a reasonable 4S contract)	P

B.	♠ Kx	♠ Axxx	1C	1NT
	♥AQx	♥ Kx	2D	2S (4 spades, 2-3 diamonds)
	♦ AQxxxx	♦ Kxx	3D (6+)	3H (3 diamonds, heart feature)
	♣ Kx	♣Axxx	4D (1430)*	4S (0-3)
			5C (K ask)	5H (1)
			7D	P

C.	♠ AKJx	♠ Qxxx	1C	1NT
	♥ x	♥ AKxx	2D	2H (may have 4 spades)
	♦ AKJxx	♦ xx	3D	3S
	♣ Kxx	♣ Axx	4NT (1430-spades)	5S (2 KC+Q)
			6S or 7S	

D.	♠ x	♠ AQ	1C	1NT
	♥ KQJ10	♥ Axxx	2D	3H (4H,4 D)
	♦ KQJxx	♦ Axxx	4D (KC ask)	4S? (3-however you show it)
	♣ AKx	♣ J10xx	5C (K ask)	5D? (0-however you show it)
			6H	P? 6NT?

4H could be used as Redwood / Kickback instead of asking with 4D.

E.	♠ A	♠ Jxxx	1C	1NT
	♥ Kx	♥ AQx	2D	2S
	♦ KJ10xx	♦ Ax	3C	4C
	♣ AQJxx	♣ Kxxx	4D (1430- clubs)	4S (0-3)
			5C (kings?)*	5D (0)
			7C	P

4H could be Redwood/Kickback for diamonds instead.

As mentioned, slam-bidding agreements are crucial and will require some serious partnership discussion no matter which treatments are chosen. A bid of 4S should be an ask for a side king. The next ask could indicate interest in a grand slam and ask for third round control in one of the two suits not shown by responder This would show responder's complete distribution and allow opener to bid 7.

When Opener Has a 5+-Card Major

When opener has a 5-card major, the response structure undergoes a few changes. There is much less room to describe various types of hands. The basic plan is to divide all of the balanced responses into one of three categories:

1. Hands that are unlikely to produce a slam
2. Marginal hands that may give a decent play for slam if they fit well with opener's hand
3. Hands that are very likely to produce a slam

It is necessary to use a couple of conventional treatments to divide the responding hands into some basic categories and then use 3-and 4-level continuations to try to separate them by strength and/or shape. In the interest of avoiding memory problems, we will make those treatments as consistent as possible for both majors.

The first such treatment is one we have seen before: the warning bid. Opener's rebid of a major has already taken up most of the 2 level. The 3 level cannot provide enough bidding space to describe all of the types of raises we would like to show. Therefore, we will use 2NT as a warning bid to separate various hand types. We have already seen a form of this bid in 1C-1D- 1 of a major auctions. In that context, it warned opener that he faced a non-fitting hand or a very weak raise. In this case, strength is not the crucial issue, though it has some relevance.

The 2NT bid will mainly function as a way to separate responding hands with poor or mediocre trump support from those with good support. Sequences using 2NT will show either 2 or 3 cards in opener's suit. When responder has only 2-card support, he will make his next bid in NT or a new suit. When he has 3-card support, he can make a delayed raise at his first opportunity after the 2NT bid. This raise will show 3 trump but will usually deny a high trump honor. By definition, this will be a bad 3-card raise, which the 2NT bid will help separate from good 3-card raises. We will discuss those good raises in a moment.

Responder may also choose to treat a raise as bad for other defects—minimum strength, too many "quacks"(queens and jacks), poor spot cards, or 4-3-3-3 distribution—but trump quality should be the first criterion. Therefore, when opener receives a delayed raise after a 2NT warning, he should assume he will be getting weak trump support.

Our warning bid will also tell opener he should explore possible alternative destinations for a final contract. It will tell him that the responder has exactly 2-card support for his major or a relatively bad hand with 3-card support. It will also allow him room to bid a second suit, looking for a possible 4-4 fit. It basically tells opener that slam prospects are not great unless he has extra (say 19–20 HCP) values or can find a good secondary fit. It suggests he may want to focus on finding the best game contract rather than pursuing a marginal slam. It also warns him of possible trump weakness if he should wind up declaring in his first major.

Having discussed hands that may make slam a doubtful proposition, let's turn to responding hands that are more promising. This brings us to our second conventional treatment: our method of showing a good 3-card raise. Any simple new suit bid will show exactly 3 of opener's suit (including at least 1 high honor) and 4 of the bid suit, usually with non-minimum (14–15 HCP) values.

One exception is a 2S bid over 2H. That shows 4 spades but does not guarantee 3 hearts. 3-card support for hearts may be shown later. A jump to 3S (in response to 2H) can be used for the specific raise described above—a non-minimum hand with 3 hearts and 4 spades. These two bids will ensure that we find any 4-4 major fits that might be missed if we were using some sort of immediate 3-card raise.

After any of these responses, opener can bid a new suit or rebid his first suit (waiting) to give responder a chance to finish describing his hand. A simple raise to 4 of opener's suit or a bid of 3NT by responder should then suggest a final contract. Any other bid can indicate slam interest.

Some otherwise good-looking hands with 3-card support for opener's major but no high trump honor have to be shown by bidding 2NT (the warning bid) and then making a jump raise. They may also be shown by strong later bidding in NT or a second suit.

The response most likely to encourage slam interest, of course, is a raise showing 4 cards in opener's major. A direct raise to 3H or 3S shows 4-card support. Opener can then use a simple rebid of 3NT to indicate a minimum, while any new suit should show extra values and slam interest. A new suit bid at the 4 level by responder can then show a feature and a maximum, while 4 of the agreed-upon trump suit would indicate a minimum. Opener can use 4 of an unbid suit, 4 of the opposite major, or 4NT to ask for keycards.

The charts on the next two pages show the continuations after auctions that begin with 1C-1NT-2H or 1C-1NT-2S.

Opener Has 5+ Hearts

1C	1NT
2H (5+ hearts)	2S= 4 spades, minimum, may have a delayed bad 3-card heart raise
	2N= warning bid–only 2 hearts, or a delayed bad 3-card heart raise
	3C= 4 clubs, 3 hearts (3H asks if minimum or maximum)
	3D= 4 diamonds, 3 hearts (3H asks if minimum or maximum)
	3H= 4-card heart raise (3S asks if minimum or maximum)
	3S= 4 spades, 3 hearts, good fitting raise
	3NT= 2 hearts, balanced maximum (likely 3-2-4-4)

Direct 4-level raises are rare. My suggestion would be to use them for "super" fit—raises showing 4 good trump and a very good side suit, or perhaps a hand with super trump. Any special meaning might prove useful.

> 4C= 4 hearts, very good clubs
> 4D= 4 hearts, very good diamonds
> 4H= 4 hearts, maximum, AKQ of suit (?)
> 4S = any bright idea

Here are some possible auctions using these continuations when opener has five or more hearts:

A.   ♠ Ax   ♠ KQxx   1C   1NT (13–15 HCP)

     ♥ Kxxxx   ♥Axx   2H   3S (4 spades,3 good hearts)

     ♦ KQxx   ♦Ax   3NT (waiting)   4D (feature)

     ♣ AQ   ♣Jxxx   4NT (1430)   5H (2 KC, no Q)

                                6S?(hoping it's
                                not on a club finesse)

B.   ♠ Kxx   ♠ Axxx   1C   1NT

     ♥ AQxxxx ♥ Kx   2H   2S (4 spades, 2-3 hearts)

     ♦ Ax   ♦ Kxx   3H   4C

     ♣KQx   ♣Axxx   4NT (1430-hearts)   5D (0-3)

                              6H?6NT? *(4D could
                              be Kickback for clubs.)*

C.   ♠ x   ♠ AKxx   1C   1NT

     ♥ AKJxx ♥ Q10x   2H   3S (4 spades, 3 good hearts)

     ♦ AKJx   ♦ xx   4D   4S

     ♣ Kxx   ♣ Axxx   4NT (1430-hearts)   5S (2 KC +Q)

                              6H P

D.   ♠ x   ♠ Axx   1C   1NT

     ♥ KQJ10xx ♥ Ax   2H   2NT

     ♦ KQx   ♦ Axxx   4NT (1430-hearts)) 5D (0-3)

     ♣ AKx   ♣J10xx   5NT   6C (0)

                              6H (?)   6NT (?)7H (?)

E.   ♠ Kx   ♠ Qxx   1C   1NT

     ♥ AQJxxx ♥ Kxxx   2H   3H (4 hearts)

     ♦ Kx   ♦ Axx   3NT (ask-min or max?) 4H (min, 4-3-3-3)

     ♣KJ10x   ♣ Axx   P (slam is iffy)

Opener Has 5+ Spades

1C	1NT
2S (5+ spades)	2NT=warning bid, only 2 spades, or a delayed 3-card spade raise in a minimum hand

3C= 4 clubs,3 spades (3D-cheapest bid-asks if minimum or maximum)

3D= 4 diamonds, 3 spades (3H-cheapest bid-asks if minimum or maximum if opener has a real heart suit, otherwise 3S asks if minimum or maximum)

3H= 4 hearts, 3 spades (3S asks if minimum or maximum)

3S=4 spades (3NT asks if minimum or maximum)

3NT= 2-3 spades, balanced maximum

4C=fitting raise, strong clubs, 4 spades, maximum

4D= fitting raise, strong diamonds, 4 spades, maximum

4H= fitting raise, strong hearts, 4 spades, maximum

4S =super trump? (AKQx),maximum / any other ideas?

Here are some possible auctions using these continuations when opener has 5 or more spades:

A.	♠ AJxxx	♠ KQx	1C	1NT (13–15 HCP)	
	♥ Axx	♥Kx	2S	3D (4 diamonds, 3 spades)	
	♦ KQxx	♦Axxx	4NT (1430 spades)	5D (0-3 KC-must be 3)	
	♣ AQ	♣Jx	5H (Q ask)	5NT (yes, but no side king)	
			6S, 6D or 6NT	P	
			(likely ending in 6S)		

B.	♠ Kxxxx	♠ Ax	1C	1NT	
	♥ AQx	♥ Kxx	2S	2NT (2-3 spades)	
	♦ Ax	♦ Kxxx	3C	4C	4NT
	♣ KQxx	♣Axxx	4D (Rosewood for C)	(2 KC, no Q)	

C.	♠ AKJxx	♠ Qxxx	1C	1NT	
	♥ x	♥ AKJx	2S	4H(4H, 4S)	
	♦ AKJx	♦ xx	4NT(1430-spades)	5S	6D(1)
	♣ Kxx	♣ Axx	5NT(kings?)	7S (pushy?)	
			6H(try for 7)		

D.	♠ KQJ10xx	♠ Ax	1C	1NT
	♥ x	♥ Ax	2H	2NT
	♦ KQx	♦ Axxx	4NT (1430)	5D (0 or 3)
	♣ AKx	♣ J10xx	5NT (kings?)	6D (0)
			6S (?) 6NT (?) 7S (?)	

E.	♠ AQJ10xx	♠ xx	1C	1NT
	♥ Kx	♥ AQJx	2S	2NT
	♦ KJ10x	♦ Axxx	3D	4D
	♣ A	♣ KJx	4H (Rosewood)	4NT (0)
			5C (kings?)	5H (1)
			6S (better than 6D)	P

When Opener Has 6+ Clubs

When opener has 6+ clubs, a slightly modified set of responses is required. This is because a long club suit is shown by a rebid of 2NT, starting further hand description at a high level and taking up valuable space.

Since space at the 3 level is limited, it is important to use it to get the information most likely to be of use to us. To me, that is whether there is at least 3-card support for clubs and whether the club bidder may have a 4-card major. Unless we have a 9-card fit, it is unlikely we will end up in a club contract. If all we have is a 6-2 fit, the contract will usually play just as well in NT. We also want to be able to find 4-4 fits in other suits at the 3 level, not a level higher.

With all these considerations in mind, we will make the 3C response a double-duty bid. It will show exactly 2 or 4 clubs. It will also serve as a Stayman-ish asking bid—asking opener to bid a 4-card side suit if he has one. If he bids 3H or 3S and responder has a 4-card fit, he may raise to game with minimum values or bid a new suit to show slam interest. If a 4-4 diamond fit is found, a raise to 4D is forcing to 4NT.

With no 4-card side suit, opener can bid 3NT (non-maximum but forcing to 4NT) or 4C (extra values/slam interest).This scheme will allow us to find any 4-4 fits that may exist and also let us evaluate slam prospects. Responder can bid 4C over 3NT with 4-card support or bid a new suit with excellent values and slam interest. When slam interest is indicated, a bid of an unbid major should be treated as key-card asking. Either partner may bid 4NT as a suggested final contract after the auction reaches the 4 level.

An immediate 3D, 3H or 3S response to 2NT will show exactly 3 clubs and 4 of the bid suit. It may possibly contain a second higher 4-card suit. If opener has 4 of the suit, he may raise it, especially if it is a major. If he doesn't have a fit, he may bid a higher-ranking major if he has one. He may also bid 3NT to indicate a minimum with no fit or 4 clubs to show extra values. A new suit at the 4 level cannot logically be natural, since the suit was bypassed at the 3 level. It should show a 4-card fit for responder's bid suit and slam interest, obviously with extra values. The same implications about slam apply.

Here is a chart describing the bidding structure after a 1C-1NT-2NT auction:

1C	1NT
2NT (6+ clubs)	**3C= 2 or 4 clubs**, usually at least one side suit (opener can then bid a 4-card side suit if he has one).Any secondary 4-4 fit will be found by bidding suits up the line. Either player may rebid 3NT with a minimum and/or no fit. Responder shows 4-card club support by bidding 4C.
	3D=3 clubs, 4 diamonds (may have 4H or 4S)
	3H=3 clubs, 4 hearts (may have 4S)
	3S=3 clubs + 4 spades (4-3-3-3)
	3NT=2 clubs, maximum
	4C= 4 clubs, maximum, no side suit (3-3-3-4)
	4D= 4 clubs, 4 diamonds, maximum
	4H= 4 clubs, 4 hearts, maximum
	4S= 4 clubs, 4 spades, maximum

Here are some possible auctions using these continuations:

A. ♠ A   ♠ KQxx   1C   1NT (13–15 HCP)
   ♥ Kx   ♥ Axx   2NT (6+ clubs)   4S (4 spades,4 clubs)
   ♦ KQxx   ♦ Ax   5D (1430)   5NT (2 KC + Q of clubs)
   ♣ AQxxxx   ♣ Jxxx   6C (missing 1KC,   6NT (or P)
                                likely ending in 6NT)

B. ♠ KQx   ♠ Axxx   1C   1NT
   ♥ AQ   ♥ Kx   2NT   3C (2 or 4 clubs)
   ♦ Ax   ♦ Kxx   3NT   4S (4 spades,4 clubs)
   ♣ K10xxxx   ♣ Axxx   4NT (1430)   5H (2 KC)
                                5NT (kings ?—we   6H (2 kings)
                                have all the KC)
                                7NT

C. ♠ AJx   ♠ Kxxx   1C   1NT
   ♥ x   ♥ AKQx   2NT   3H (4H, C)
   ♦ AJx   ♦ xx   4D (1430   4S (1 KC)
                                   for diam.)
   ♣ AKQxxx   ♣ Jxx   (4NT would
                                   be for hearts)
                                6C

D. ♠ A   ♠ Qxx   1C   1NT
   ♥ Qx   ♥ Axx   2NT (6+clubs)   3D (4 diamonds,3 clubs)
   ♦ KJ10x   ♦ AQxx   4D (1430)*   4NT (2 KC + Qof D)
   ♣ AQJxxx   ♣ Kxx   5H (kings?)   6C (0)
                                7D *(4H could be
                                Kickback instead.)

The use of otherwise unused jump rebids as asking bids was first mentioned in regard to 1C-1 of a major auctions in a previous chapter. Various possible answer schemes are discussed in detail in Appendix G. The scheme presented here is simply one I think is well-suited to a 1C-1NT auction.

Special Hands: Jump Rebids by 1C Opener

As you may have noticed, all of the examples given above involve simple rebids by the 1C opener after a 1NT response.. He simply makes the cheapest 2-level rebid that indicates his longest suit, whether he has 17 HCP or 25 HCP. He just wants to establish a trump fit if one exists and then make sure there are enough controls for slam.

In some cases, however, opener has the ability to set the final contract with absolute confidence if he can just find one or two specific cards. Generally, this will involve one of two types of hands:

1. A single-suited hand in which opener has no interest in any other trump suit and no more than one trump loser
2. A gigantic two-suiter missing 1 or 2 key cards in which opener has a willingness to give responder a choice between 2 possible trump suits after he sets the level for the final contract

The 1C opener has a simple method available to handle either of these hand-types. After the auction begins 1C-1NT, the entire 3 level is unused. The 1C bidder can show a special hand and begin asking for specific cards by making his first rebid a jump to the 3 level.*He may also first use a simple rebid to check on trump support and then jump to the 4 or 5 level to find a particular card.

Note that the definition of the jump rebid has nothing to do with HCP. It does not say that the opener has the equivalent of a standard 2C bid. It may just be a distributional freak with extraordinary playing strength. Responder's answers are relatively simple. They are as follows:

- cheapest step= no control of any kind (e. g. x-x-x)
- second step= Q (some may want to include a doubleton as third-round control)
- third step= K
- fourth step = A
- fifth step = AK

If opener now bids a second suit, the same answers apply. This may be a real suit or just a fragment. If he bids a third suit below the 6 level, it can still be asking. However, any bid at the 6 or 7 level is a strong suggestion that it be the final contract.

If that bid is in opener's first suit, it shows that he has a 1-suited hand and is setting the final contract. If he makes a bid in his second suit at the 6 or 7 level, he is setting the final level but is letting responder choose which of his suits should be trump.

Here are some auctions involving asking bids:

A. ♠	♠ Qxxx	1C	1NT
♥ AQJ	♥ Kx	3C (asking)	3NT (ace)
♦ KQ	♦ Axxx	4D	5C (ace)
♣ KQJxxxxx	♣ A10x	5H (asking)	6C (king)
		7C	P

B. ♠ AQJxxxx	♠ Kx	1C	1NT
♥ AQJxx	♥ Kxx	3S (asking)	4D (king)
♦ A	♦ QJxx	4H (asking)	5D (king)
♣ A	♣ K10xx	7NT	

C. ♠ AQJxx	♠ Kx	1C	1NT
♥ AQJxxx	♥ Kxxx	3S (asking)	4D (king)
♦ A	♦ QJx	4H (asking)	5D (king)
♣	♣ KQ10x	7H	P

D. ♠	♠ AKxx	1C	1NT
♥ AQJ	♥ Kxx	3D (asking)	3H (no honor)
♦ AQxxxxx	♦ xx	4H (asking)	5C (king)
♣ AK	♣ Q10xx	6D	P

E. ♠	♠ Kxxx	1C	1NT
♥ AKQJ	♥ xxx	3C (asking)	4C (ace, king)
♦ A	♦ QJxx	7C	P
♣ QJ10xxxxx	♣ AK		

F. ♠	♠ Qxxx	1C	1NT
♥ AQJxxx	♥ Kxx	3H (asking)	4C (king)
♦ KQJxxxx	♦ Ax	4D	5C (ace)
♣	♣ A10xx	7D (you choose)	7H
		P	

A hand such as these examples may come up only once in a millennium, but when you get one, you'll be ready!

1C-2C (Two-Way Bid)

As promised, I will now outline the better way to respond to a strong 1C opening with minimum positive balanced hands. In this system, they are defined as hands with 9–12 HCP, slightly stronger than the Precision equivalent. We will include these hands in our 2C response.

The 2C response to 1C is the first of four 2-level responses that have more than one meaning. These extra meanings allow the description of a wide variety of hands. This is a prime example.

The 2C response describes either a hand with 9+HCP and at least 5 clubs or a balanced hand with 9–12 HCP. Since the bid is forcing to game no matter which hand it shows, there is plenty of time to determine which it is. As to why this slightly more complicated method is worth the effort, it all comes down to the same two reasons cited throughout this little treatise:

1. The strong club opener will declare the hand and remain at least partially hidden The the weaker hand comes down as dummy.
2. The lead will come up to the strong hand, giving us a positional advantage.

Responder defines his hand with his second bid. A rebid of 3C is the most obvious way to show the 5+ clubs. There are some other bids that show clubs, plus side suits or singletons, but 3C is the primary vehicle. The balanced hand is often shown by a raise of 2NT to 3NT or by the use of 3D as Stayman. The entire scheme will become clearer when we outline opener's possible bids after 2C.

The simplest case is when opener has a balanced or semi-balanced hand. He bids 2NT. His point count is not important. There is no need to jump with a big hand. If responder has the balanced 9–12 HCP hand, he either bids 3D (Stayman) to find a 4-4 major fit or raises to 3NT. If he has clubs, he almost always bids 3C. Once in a while, he may reverse into 3H or 3S or splinter at the 4 level with 4D, 4H, or 4S to show a maximum hand.

When opener has a suit-oriented hand, he bids his long suit. If his suit is diamonds, one set of responses is used. If it is a major, a second slightly different set of bids is used. The responses follow some logical general rules that are intended to make them reasonably easy to remember. As always, they are meant to make the 1C opener the declarer in as many situations as possible.

The first general rule is that if responder bids 2NT, it has something to do with a major. Over 2D, it shows both majors. If the opener has a side 4-card major, he bids the suit and becomes declarer in any major suit game or slam. This is one of the few situations where having responder declare NT may actually be beneficial.

With an unbalanced hand, opener may be short in at least 1 major, and responder should have both of them covered. Over 2H or 2S, the 2NT bid shows a 4-card raise. Responder will never be declarer in that case.

The second rule is that if responder bids a major in response to opener's first rebid of 2 of a suit, he is denying 4 cards in the suit. Over 2D, it shows 4 cards in the opposite major. Over 2H or 2S, it merely shows a non-fitting balanced hand. A corollary of this rule is that a bid of 3D in response to 2H or 2S is artificial. It shows 4 cards in the opposite major.

The third rule is the most obvious. A bid of 3C shows 5+ clubs. It may be a non-fitting hand or contain a delayed raise of opener's suit.

The fourth rule is also not rocket science. A simple raise to 3 of opener's suit shows a 3-card raise. After both the 3 card and the 4 card raises, the cheapest bid is a form of Ogust, asking for strength and suit quality in steps. Those steps will be outlined in the system summary.

The fifth rule is that jumps to 4 of opener's suit and splinter bids in new suits both show 4-card support and a 5+-card club suit. Obviously, a splinter precludes any possibility that responder has a balanced 9–12 HCP hand. The jump to 4 of opener's major is merely the same hand with 5-4-2-2 distribution. The similarities between the two types of hands should make these bids easier to remember.

Finally, jumps to 4C indicate a very good suit and at least 13+ HCP. Again, this is hardly likely to confuse anyone. Here are the bidding schemes.

1C-2C-2NT

1C   2C (either 5+ clubs, 9+ HCP or balanced hand, 9-12 HCP)
2NT = 17+HCP, balanced or semi-balancedhand

Responder now defines his hand as follows:

3C = 5+clubs (may have a 4-card major)
3D = Stayman (balanced hand with at least one 4-card major)
3NT = balanced hand with no major

This leaves the rebids of 3H and 3S free for better than minimum hands with 5+ clubs and a side major. I would define them as having 13+ HCP, 5+ clubs, and 4 of the opposite major, which will make the 1C bidder the declarer in any 4-4 major fit.

So: 3H = 5+ clubs, 4 spades, 13+ HCP
3S = 5+ clubs,4 hearts, 13+ HCP

Others may choose to make them simply natural.

Bids at the 4-level all show good 6+ card club suits and 13+ HCP. A bid of 4C shows 6+ clubs and no short suit, while 4D, 4H, and 4S are all splinter bids. So, in summary:

- 4C = 6+clubs, 13+ HCP, no short suit
- 4D = 6+clubs, 13+ HCP, 0-1 diamonds
- 4H = 6+clubs, 13+ HCP, 0-1 hearts
- 4S = 6+clubs, 13+ HCP, 0-1 spades

When responder uses 3D as Stayman, he defines his hand as limited to 12 HCP. If opener is also balanced, he will usually not try for slam unless he holds at least 20 HCP. If responder signs off at 3NT, opener may bid a second suit at the 4 level, hoping for a 4-4 fit there. With no fit, responder can sign off again at 4NT. Any suit bid is a cue bid, confirming a fit in the second suit and some slam interest.

If a 4-4 major fit is found, responder can raise to 4 with any ordinary holding. With a maximum and slam interest, he may cue bid in a new suit rather than making a direct raise. Opener may sign off at 4 of the agreed-upon major or make a return cue bid to indicate slam interest. A bid of 4NT would be ace-asking (1430).

Here are some example hands for the 1C-2C-2NT sequence:

A.	♠ AJx	♠ Kxx	1C	2C
	♥ Kx	♥AQxx	2NT	3D (Stayman)
	♦ AQ109	♦ Jx	3NT	P
	♣ KJxx	♣ xxxx		

B.	♠ AQ10x	♠ Kxxx	1C	2C
	♥ Kx	♥ QJx	2NT	3C (9+ HCP, 5+ clubs)
	♦ KJxx	♦ x	3S	4S
	♣ AJx	♣ KQxxx	P or 4NT (1430)—may wind up at 5S	

C. ♠ Kx   ♠ Axx   1C   2C
    ♥ KJ10x   ♥ Axxx   2NT   3D
    ♦ AQxx   ♦ Jx   3H   3S (cue)
    ♣ AQx   ♣ Kxxx   4NT (1430)   5H
                                     6H (probably on 1 of 2 finesses)

D. ♠ AKQx   ♠ xxxx   1C   2C
    ♥ xx   ♥ Ax   2NT   3C
    ♦ AKxx   ♦ Qx   3S   4C (cue)
    ♣ Qxx   ♣ AKxxx   4D (cue)   4H (cue)
                                     5D (king)   6C (king)
                                     7C or 7S   7S or 7NT

E. ♠ QJx   ♠ Ax x   1C   2C
    ♥ Ax   ♥ x   2NT   3C
    ♦ KQ10xx   ♦ AJx   3D   4H (6+ C, 0-1 H,13+HCP)
    ♣ AQx   ♣ KJxxxx   4NT   5D (3 KC)
                                     7C or 7NT

F. ♠ K10   ♠ AQx   1C   2C
    ♥ AQJx   ♥ xxx   2NT   3NT
    ♦ Ax   ♦ Kxxx
    ♣ KQxxx   ♣ xxx

G. ♠ 109xx   ♠ AJxx   1C   2C
    ♥ KJ   ♥ Ax   2NT   3H (5+C,4S,13+HCP)
    ♦ AKQ   ♦ xx   3S   4H (cue)
    ♣ Axxx   ♣ KQxxx   4NT (1430)   5H (2KC, no Q)
                                     6C,6S, or 6NT

1C-2C-2D

1C   2C
2D= 5+ diamonds in an unbalanced hand.

Responder still answers as if it is a Stayman request for a 4-card major.
Responder's answers:

2H = denies 4 hearts, shows 4 spades
2S = denies 4 spades, shows 4 hearts
2NT = shows both majors, 9-12 HCP
3C = 5+clubs, no major
3D = balanced raise, 3+ diamonds
3H, 3S = splinters, hence 5+ clubs (and 4 diamonds)
3NT = balanced hand, 9-12 HCP
(good major stoppers / no 4-card major)
4C = 6+ clubs, good suit, 13+ HCP
4D = 4+diamonds, 5+ clubs, 13+ HCP

When responder shows a major, he may still have 5+ clubs. He may show his club suit
if he gets a chance to bid it below game.
    Here are some example hands:

A.	♠ x	♠ Qxxx	1C	2C
	♥ A109x	♥ x	2D	3H (splinter, 5+ clubs)
	♦ AKJxxx	♦ Qx	4NT (1430)	5H
	♣ KQx	♣ AJxxxx	6D	P
			*(4H could be Rosewood)	

B.	♠ AQx	♠ Kxxx	1C	2C
	♥ AQx	♥ xx	2D	2H (0-3 hearts, 4 spades)
	♦ KQJxxx	♦ xx	2NT (waiting)	3C
	♣ J	♣ AQxxx	3NT	

C.	♠ x	♠ KQxx	1C	2C
	♥ Ax	♥ Qxxx	2D	2NT (both majors)
	♦ AQJxx	♦ Kx	3C	3D
	♣ AQ10xx	♣ xxx	3H	3NT

D.	♠ KQx	♠ A	1C	2C
	♥ x	♥ xxx	2D	3C
	♦ KQxxxx	♦ Ajxx	3D	4D (1430)
	♣ AKJ	♣ Q10xxx	4NT	5H
			6D	

1C-2C-2H

1C   2C

2H = 5+ hearts - responder raises or rebids semi-naturally, showing or denying a second suit and/or shortness

   2S = no fit, denies 4 spades (opener rebids 2NT, 3H)

   2NT = 4+ card heart raise (9–12 HCP)-see follow-up suggestion at end of section*

   3C = 5+ clubs (may make delayed slam try of 4C,4D, or 4H after opener rebids 3D,3H,3S, or 3NT)

   3D = shows 4 spades (opposite major), balanced hand

   3H = 3 hearts, balanced*)-see follow-up suggestion at end of section

   3S = singleton spade, 5+ clubs,4 hearts (1-4-3-5 or 1-4-2-6) (9+ HCP-3NT asks range in steps)

   3NT = a balanced maximum (11–12 HCP), good major stoppers (use sparingly; can bid 2S to let opener declare NT)

   4C = 6+ solid clubs, 13+HCP

   4D = singleton diamond, 5+ clubs, 4 hearts [3415 or 2416] (13+HCP)

   4H = 4-card raise, shows 5 clubs, 4 hearts, 2-2 on side (13+HCP)

Here are some example hands:

A.	♠ A	♠ Qxx	1C	2C
	♥ QJ10xxx	♥ Axx	2H	3H (3-card raise)
	♦ AKx	♦ Qxxx	3S (cue)	4C (cue)
	♣ KQxx	♣ Axx	4NT	5H
			6H	
B.	♠ Kx	♠ Axx	1C	2C
	♥ AKQxx	♥ x	2H	3C
	♦ AQxxx	♦ Kxxx	3D	3S
	♣ x	♣ KJxxx	4D	5D
			6D	
C.	♠ KQx	♠ Jxx	1C	2C
	♥ AQxxxx	♥ Kxxx	2H	2NT (4-card raise)
	♦ AKJx	♦ Qx	3C	3H
	♣	♣ KJxxx	5C (exclusion BW)	5D (0)
			6H	
D.	♠ QJxx	♠ Kxxx	1C	2C
	♥ AKJxx	♥ Qx	2H	3D (4 spades)
	♦ x	♦ Qxx	3S	4S
	♣ AQxx	♣ Kxxx	P or 4NT (may wind up in 5S)	

1C-2C-2S

1C   2C

2S = 5+ spades- responder raises or rebids semi-naturally, with:

    2NT = 4-card raise (follow-ups—see suggestion at end of section))*

    3C = 5+clubs, may make delayed slam try of 4C, 4D, 4H

    3D = shows 4 hearts (opposite major)

    3H = denies 4 hearts, shows balanced non-fitting hand

    3S = 3 spades, balanced (3NT—follow-ups, see suggestion at end of section)*

    3NT = balanced 9-12 HCP, good tenaces

    4C = 6+solid clubs, 13+ HCP

    4D = singleton diamond, 5+ clubs, 4 spades [4315 or 4216] (13+HCP)

    4H = singleton heart, 5+ clubs, 4 spades [4135or 4126] (13+HCP)

Here are a few example hands:

A.	♠ AK109x	♠ QJx	1C	2C
	♥ x	♥ xx	2S	3C
	♦ AQxx	♦ xx	3D	3S
	♣ KJx	♣ AQxxxx	4C	4S
			4NT (1430)	5C (1 KC)
			5D (Q ?)	5S (yes)
			6C or 6S	P or 6S

B.	♠ QJ109x	♠ Kxxx	1C	2C
	♥ AKxx	♥ Jxx	2S	2NT (4-card raise)
	♦ KQx	♦ Ax	3C (Ogust)	3H (Hxxx) (see next page)
	♣ A	♣ QJxx	4NT (1430)	5H
			6S	

---

*Using 3H instead of 3S to show the spade singleton saves space and allows opener to pass at 3NT when responder shows a minimum in response to the 3S inquiry.

C.	♠ AQJxxxx	♠ K	1C	2C
	♥ Kx	♥ Axx	2S	3C
	♦	♦ Qxx	3S	3NT
	♣ AKxx	♣ QJxxxx	4C	4H
			5D	5S
			7C	

D.	♠ KQxxx	♠ Jx	1C	2C
	♥ AQJxx	♥ 109xx	2S	3C
	♦ AJ	♦ Qx	3H	4H
	♣ x	♣ AKJxxx	P or 4NT	
			(may wind up in 5H)	

For those unfamiliar with Ogust (mentioned in hand B), a highly modified version of that convention which might be used in these sequences is described on the next page.

Suggestion

One possible artificial treatment which might be useful whenever responder gives a direct 3- or 4-card raise to opener's major is a modified version of the Ogust convention. The cheapest bid (or the cheapest NT) after a raise could be used as an Ogust-like query about responder's holding in the prospective trump suit. The Ogust responses could be fairly simple. The first two bids could show minimum hands; the next three could show maximums. For a 3-card raise, good support might be defined as Qxx, Kxx, or Axx. Super would be 2 of the 3 top honors. Poor is Jxx or less. For a 4-card raise, Qxxx or better could qualify as good and two of the top three honors as super.

The general scheme might be:	for a 3-card raise	for a 4-card raise:
• first step =minimum, poor suit	xxx to Jxx	xxxx to Jxxx
• second step = minimum, good suit	Qxx to Axx	Qxxx to Axxx
• third step = maximum, poor suit	xxx to Jxx	xxxx to Jxxx
• fourth step = maximum, good suit	Qxx to Axx	Qxxx to Axxx
• fifth step = maximum, super suit	AJ10,AQx, KQx AQx	AJ10x, AQxx KQxx, AQxx

Note: Hxxx= one high honor (A, K or Q) and three small cards)
Hxx = one high honor and two small cards

This is certainly not the only way the three and four-card raises could be handled. The scheme I have outlined is just one possibility. Standard feature and control bids are one obvious alternative.

Two-Way Transfers To Long Suits

The next three 2-level responses to 1C all serve a particular purpose. They may have a primary positive meaning, but they all also function as ways to transfer contracts involving weak hands with long suits into the hand of the 1C opener. I believe the concealment and lead advantages they achieve are considerable.

1C-2D (Two-Way Bid)

The 2D response to a 1C opening bid has two distinct functions. It shows a 5+ card diamond suit and 9+ HCP (like Precision, Schenken, etc.) or it shows a 7+ card heart suit with less than 9 HCP and no more than 1 of the top 3 honors in the suit. The description I just gave of the diamond hand needs to be qualified. The 2D bid includes two specific positive diamond hands. Two other positive diamond hands are shown by the 2H response, which will be described in the next section.

Opener asks which hand responder holds with his first rebid, which is often 2H. Following our usual pattern, responder avoids bidding hearts first in almost all cases where the suit might become trump. When opener's first rebid is 2H, that takes care of the problem. When it is 2S or 2NT, the continuations are designed to make sure that the strong club bidder almost always declares the contract.

The continuation procedure is relatively simple. If opener has a minimum or non-fitting hand for hearts, he bids 2H. If he has a better hand—one that he wouldn't mind playing in 3H if necessary—he bids 2S or 2NT. Responder can now retransfer into 3H or even 4H if he has the heart hand. Any other bid shows the positive response in diamonds. After the definition of responder's hand, further bidding is fairly natural. Responder does try to avoid bidding NT first in situations where he might wind up declaring NT from his side. He may, however, bid NT conventionally when he holds the 7+-card heart suit, since the contract will generally wind up in hearts.

It will be easier to describe the entire bidding scheme if I give a precise description of exactly which diamond hands are covered by the 2D response. **Responder only bids 2D to show a positive diamond response when he has one of the following:**

1. **a single-suited hand with 6+(usually) diamonds**
2. **a hand with 5+ diamonds and a 4-card heart suit**

This limits the number of descriptive rebids he has to make.

Note: A hand with exactly 5 diamonds and 5-3-3-2 distribution falls between the cracks of our response system. If the suit is very solid (AKJ10x, KQJ10x, etc.), I would treat it as a diamond 1-suiter and bid 2D. With a mediocre suit, I would treat it as a balanced 9-12 HCP hand and bid 2C.

Here is an outline of the entire setup. After 1C-2D, opener knows partner has either:

- 9+HCP with 5+ diamonds and one of these specific holdings—5+ diamonds and 4 hearts or 6+ diamonds and no side 4-card suit *or*
- a preemptive hand with 7+ hearts and no more than one top honor (hands with diamonds and a black side suit willbe covered by the 2H response).

To begin his rebids, opener assumes the worst—that responder has a weak hand with 7 hearts. With a minimum hand or a hand that is a poor fit for hearts, he simply accepts the transfer or bids his own independent 6 or 7 card suit. Opener's rebids are as follows:

- **2H = willing to play 2H** opposite a very weak hand with 7+ hearts
- **2S = 5+-card spade suit,** willing to play at least 3H or 3S opposite a weak hand with 7+ hearts
- **2NT = extra strength or exceptional heart fit,** willing to play at least 3H opposite a weak hand with 7+ hearts
- **3C or 3D = natural, probably a good 6 or 7 card suit** with 0/1 hearts

Responder's rebids now become fairly easy, because there are only four possibilities: 9+ HCP with 5+ diamonds and 4 hearts; 9+ HCP with 6+ diamonds and no side suit; 0–4 HCP with 7+ hearts; or 5–8 HCP with 7+ hearts. After opener's 2H rebid, responder will clarify as follows:

- Pass = very weak hand with 7+ hearts
- 2S =relay to 2NT (This relay starts the description of all 5D, 4H hands)

(A 4-card spade suit is impossible; with a 4-card club or spade suit, responder's initial response would be 2H.) The following **direct 3-level bids (no 2S relay) show 6+ diamonds and 9–12 HCP:**

- 3C = 9–12 HCP, 6+ D, no 4-card side suit, 0-1 club
- 3D = 9–12 HCP, 6+ diamonds, no 4-card side suit or short suit
- 3H = 9–12 HCP, 6+D, no 4-card side suit, 0-1 hearts
- 3S = 9–12 HCP, 6+D, no 4-card side suit, 0-1 spades

All of those last four bids are game-forcing, and natural continuations ensue. Now let's flash back to **responder's continuations after his 2S relay. After 1C – 2D -2H - 2S- 2NT** (forced), responder continues with:

- **3C=9+HCP, 5D, 4H, 0-1C**
  3D now asks for a more precise description of responder's strength:
  3H = 9–12 HCP
  3S = 13–14 HCP
  3NT= 15+ HCP
- **3D=9+HCP, 5D, 4H, 2C, 2S**
  3H now asks exact strength:
  3S= 9–12 HCP
  3NT=13–14 HCP
  4C=15+ HCP
- **3H=9+HCP, 5D, 4H, 0-1S**
  3S now asks exact strength:
  3NT=9–12 HCP
  4C=13–14 HCP
  4D=15+HCP

When Opener Fails to Bid 2H

Opener will not always be considerate enough to bid 2H over 1C-2D. Don't forget that opener's 2H rebid can be passed. What if opener does not want to risk being passed in 2H? He must bid something other than 2H. With extra values and a 5+ card spade suit, he may bid 2S, with the understanding that he has to be able to handle a 3H contract or insist on a 3S or 4S contract. With extra general values or a good heart fit, he may bid 2NT, again saying he can make 3H opposite a weak hand. So we need a set of continuations for opener's 2S and 2NT rebids, which we will get to after a brief detour into the minor suits.

Opener may bid a super club or diamond suit after 1C-2D, though it might again be better to bid 2H and play there if partner's only values are in his long suit. At any rate, those bids are not forcing, but they are highly encouraging. Responder can pass with the worst possible hand. With a 5–8 HCP heart preempt, he can try to get to 3H via a 3D retransfer (if available) or a simple 3H over 3D. Any further bidding would be essentially natural.

Returning now to opener's 2S and 2NT rebids, responder needs to handle both his preemptive heart hands and the game-forcing hands with diamonds. As in other situations, our bids are designed to transfer all of the heart contracts into the hand of the 1C opener. After 2NT, that is accomplished by a retransfer bid of 3D. After 2S, however, it is more useful to have 3D show a 6+-card diamond suit without a spade fit.

Therefore, a conventional 2NT bid is used to show the heart preempt over opener's 2S. Given that opener may have very long spades and responder has a 7+-card heart suit, it should be very unusual for responder to end up declaring a NT contract. Here are the bidding schemes for those two situations:

After 1C-2D- 2S
Pass = 0–4 HCP, 1-2+ spades, not willing to make things worse by bidding
2NT= conventional 7+ hearts, 5–8 HCP (or very weak, void in spades, and willing to take a risk that he can get to a better 3H contract)
3C=9+ HCP, 5D, 4H,0-2S (3D asks spade length-3H=0-1   3S=2)
3D =9+ HCP, 6+ D, 0-2 spades
3H =9+ HCP, 5D,4H, 3-card spade raise
3S = 9–12 HCP, 6+ D, 3-card spade raise
4C =13+ HCP, 6+ D, 3S, 0-1 club
4D =13+ HCP, 6D, 3S, 2C, 2H
4H =13+ HCP, 6+ D, 3S, 0-1 heart

Notice that the 2NT bid tends to be fairly constructive—from 5–8 HCP with 7+ hearts. Occasionally, though, responder may just be making a desperate run from 2S with a pathetic hand and a spade void. In order to give him a last out, I suggest using a 2-way transfer acceptance scheme. With a hand that can make 4H opposite almost any 7-card heart suit, opener should jump to game.

If willing to be in game opposite a fair preempt (say 5-7 HCP) but happy to stop at 3H opposite real junk, he should bid 3H, letting responder pass or bid four. With a maximum, responder can even bid a singleton on the way to 4H.

Note:You will notice that 3C and 3D deny a 3-card spade holding, while 3H and 3S are simple 3-card spade raises. If responder should happen to have 3 spades and 7 hearts, he can first transfer with 2NT and then bid 3S.

After 1C-2D-2NT

3C = 9+HCP, 5+D/4H—opener can now bid 3D or 3H, letting responder bid out his
    shape—after 3D, 3H = 3-4-5-1   3S =1-4-5-3   3N =2-4-5-2; after
    3H, 3S=1-4-5-3   3N =2-4-5-2   4C = 3-4-5-1

3D = Retransfer (0–8 HCP, 7+ H), with 5–7 HCP and a decentsuit, responder will
    raise 3H to 4H or bid a side singleton

3H/3S = 9+HCP, 6+D, feature in suit

3NT = 9+ HCP, club feature

4C = 13+ HCP, 6+ D, 0-1 club, slam interest

4D = 13+ HCP, 6+ D, no short suit, slam interest

4H = 13+ HCP, 6+ D, 0-1 heart, slam interest

4S = 13+ HCP, 6+ D, 0-1 spade, slam interest

Here are some example hands:

A.	♠ AQx	♠ x	1C	2D
	♥ x	♥ K10xxxxx	2H (to play if weak)	P
	♦ KJxx	♦ Qx		
	♣ AQJxx	♣ xxx		
B.	♠ AQx	♠ xx	1C	2D
	♥ Jxxx	♥ AQxx	2NT	3C (4H, 5+D, 9+HCP)
	♦ KJ	♦ Axxxx	3H	3NT (2-4-5-2)
	♣ AQxx	♣ xx	4H	P
C.	♠ A	♠ Kxx	1C	2D
	♥ KJx	♥ Axxx	2NT	3C
	♦ KJxx	♦ AQxxx	3D	3H (3-4-5-1)
	♣ AQxxx	♣ x	3S	4D
			4NT (1430)	5S (2KC + Q of D)
			6D	

D.	♠ Jx	♠ x	1C	2D
	♥ AQJx	♥ Kxxx	2NT	3C
	♦ KQx	♦ Axxxx	3H	3S (1-4-5-3)
	♣ AQxx	♣ KJx	4NT (1430)	5H (2KC, no Q of H)
			6H	

E.	♠ Jx	♠ x	1C	2D
	♥ AQJx	♥ Kxx	2NT	3H (9+ HCP, 6D, H feature
	♦ KQx	♦ A109xxx	4C (cue)	4D (cue)
	♣ AQxx	♣ KJx	4H	4S (cue)
			5C	6C
			6D	

1C-2H (Two-Way Bid)

The 2H response to 1C covers two other possible hands with 5 diamonds as well as a preemptive hand with long spades, taking some of the pressure off the 2D response. It denies a 4-card heart suit. **If it is a positive reponse, it will specifically show 5+ diamonds and either 4 spades or 4 clubs.** Otherwise, it shows 7+ spades and less than 9 HCP. Again, opener generally makes a waiting bid (either 2S or 2NT) and lets responder clarify which type of hand he has with his second bid. As usual, the strong hand winds up playing any NT or spade contract, with the attendant lead and concealment advantages.

Opener should generally choose the 2NT rebid with most normal 1C opening bids. It simplifies subsequent bidding. It also immediately ensures that the strong hand will declare any NT contract. He should choose the 2S rebid as a kind of warning. It should say, "I have a minimum 1C bid and/or a poor fit for spades (often a void or singleton). Even 3S may not be makeable opposite a really weak spade preempt."

Whether opener's rebid is 2S or 2NT, responder's second bid immediately tells whether he holds 5 diamonds and 4 clubs, 5 diamonds and 4 spades, or 7+ spades. When opener has bid 2S, one extra bid (2NT) is available, but otherwise the responses are identical.

After experimenting with various complex methods of giving a complete picture of responder's exact distribution with his subsequent rebid, I finally settled on a much simpler semi-natural continuation scheme that gives the most important information without forcing users to remember a series of extended relays. It provides the information most likely to be of use in finding 4-4 and 5-3 major suit fits as well as possible minor suit games and slams.

When opener rebids 2NT, **a 3C continuation is natural, showing 5 diamonds and 4 clubs.** Opener may now bid 3D with a fit and no interest in either major suit. If the auction makes 3NT seem unattractive, it may lead to game or slam in diamonds. If opener holds a 5+ card major, he can look for a major suit fit by bidding 3H or 3S.(Since responder's 2H bid denies 4 hearts and the 3C rebid tends to deny 4 spades, this bid is searching for 3-card support.) Responder can either raise the major or bid 3NT. With 6 or more diamonds, he may also bid 4D. With stoppers in both majors, he may simply bid 3NT.

After the same 2NT rebid, **a 3D continuation shows 5 diamonds and 4 spades.** Opener can again bid 3H with five or more, bid 3S with 4, or bid 3NT with no obvious suit fit. He can also bid 4D if a diamond game or slam seems more viable than 3NT. (Since a 3S continuation over 2NT is not needed for other purposes, it could be used to show 5 diamonds, 4 clubs, and 4 spades.)

Finally, **a 3H bid in response to 2NT is a retransfer, showing 7+ spades and 0–8 HCP.** I would recommend that responder be allowed to jump to 4H as a"supertrans-fer"with a maximum hand (7–8 HCP) and a good (not likely to lose more than 2 trump tricks opposite 2 small cards) suit. That would make a 3H bid essentially invitational. Opener could bid 3S with most 1C hands or jump to 4S with extra strength.

When opener chooses to rebid 2S instead of 2NT after a 1C-2H auction, most of responder's continuations are the same. However, he does have two additional bids to choose from: pass and 2NT. Since the 2S bid is a warning that opener does not really like his hand in terms of a spade contract, responder should treat his opinion with some respect. With an average spade preempt (especially with a mediocre suit that might contain 3 or 4 losers on a bad day), pass is probably the right option. In order to give even an invitational raise, responder should have a pretty solid suit—one with good intermediate cards. It should be good enough to hold the trump losers to 2 opposite a singleton.

Should he choose to invite, he does have a useful tool: an artificial asking bid of 2NT. It asks opener whether there is a suit where a helping honor might increase significantly the value of his hand. If opener were to name a suit in which responder held the king, for instance, that might be enough to justify a jump to 4S. Without a useful helping card, a 3S sign-off would usually be best.

The 3C and 3D bids still show 5 diamonds and 4 clubs and 5 diamonds and 4 spades, respectively. Now, however, both 3H and 3S are available for any special meaning partnerships might attach to them. For instance, 3H could show the 4-0-5-4 hand (heart void), which would otherwise be very hard to describe at a reasonable level. A bid of 3S could show a decent spade preempt that is unlikely to suffer more than 2 trump losers opposite poor support. A bid of 3NT could show 13+ HCP and exactly 2-2-5-4 distribution. Opener could then use 4C or 4D to set trump and ask for keycards or cue bids from responder.

The following charts show all the basic 1C-2H continuations.

After 1C   2H

Opener   Responder

1C   2H = a preemptive hand with 7+ spades and 0–8 HCP or a positive hand with 9+HCP, 5+ diamonds and a 4-card black side suit- 5+D/4S or 5+D/4+C

2NT= generally at least semi-balanced, may have extra values or a strong spade fit (possibly even 5+ spades)—willing to play at least 3S

Responder can clarify with the following continuations:

- **3C** = 5+ diamonds, 4 clubs, 9–12 HCP, opener may bid 3D (diamond fit, no 5-card major), 3H or 3S (5+ card suit), or 3NT (no suit fit likely)
- **3D** = 5+ diamonds, 4 spades, 9–12 HCP; opener will bid 3S with 4+ spades, may bid 3H (5+hearts), 3NT, or 4D
- **3H** = retransfer—7+spades, 0–8 HCP
- **3S** = 5+ diamonds, 4 clubs, 4 spades, 9–12 HCP (optional)
- **3NT** = 5 diamonds, 4 clubs, 2-2 in majors, 13–14 HCP (4NT would show same hand with15+ HCP)
- **4C**= 5+ diamonds, 4 clubs, 13+HCP (optional; takes up space). The alternative is just to bid 3C, then bid on past 3NT with extras.
- **4D**= 5+ diamonds, 4 spades,13+ HCP (optional; takes up space). The alternative is just to bid 3D, then bid on past 3NT with extras.
- **4H**=super-retransfer—7+ spades, 7-8 HCP (optional, but recommended). The alternative is just to bid 3H on all 7+ card spade hands.

As you can see, the essential basic continuations are 3C,3D,3H, and 3NT. Bids of 3S and 4H also seem like quite sensible ideas, and I recommend them. Jumps to 4C and 4D may be useful to show strength, but they do take up a lot of bidding space. It may be better to find fits first and then have clear partnership agreements on how to indicate slam interest.

Opener   Responder
1C   2H = a preemptive hand with 7+ spades and 0–8 HCP *or* a positive
             hand with 9+HCP, 5+ diamonds, and a 4-card black side suit - 5+D /
             4S or 5+D /4+C

2S = a kind of warning—a minimum 1C bid and/or a poor fit for spades (often a void
or singleton). Even 3S may not be makeable opposite a really weak spade preempt.

After 1C   2H
2S
Responder's rebids:

- **Pass** = minimum, 7+ spades (0–4 HCP)
- **2NT**= maximum, 7+ spades (5–8 HCP, good suit). Also serves as an asking bid.
  Asks opener to bid a suit where a fitting honor would increase value of hand.
- **3C**= 9–12 HCP, **5+diamonds, 4 clubs**-often 5-4-2-2, 5-4-3-1, or 6-4-2-1 distribution

    After a 3C response, opener bids::
    3D -fit for diamonds
    3H or 3S- 5+-card suit
    3NT or a suit at the 4-level if 3NT seems unsafe

- **3D** = 9-12 HCP, **5+ diamonds, 4 spades**—often 5-4-2-2, 5-4-3-1 or 6-4-2-1
  distribution

    After a 3D response, opener bids:
    3H- 5+-card heart suit
    3S- 4+ spades
    3NT or a suit at the 4-level

- **3H** = 9–12 HCP, 5+diamonds, 4 spades, 4 clubs, 0 hearts. Not needed as re-transfer—this bid will allow the 1C opener to bid 3NT and right-side the hand.
- **3S** =6–8 HCP, 7+spades (decent suit—likely no more than two losers opposite poor support)
- **3NT**- should be avoided by responding hand
- **4C** =5+diamonds, 4 club, 13+ HCP (optional)
- **4D**=5+ diamonds, 4 spades, 13+ HCP (optional)
- **4H**- not really needed—responder would go through 2NT sequence with a good preemptive spade response

Slam Bidding After Positive 1C-2H Auctions

There are two possible ways that responder may indicate extra values that may produce slam. The first is to use jumps to 4C and 4D over opener's first rebid of 2S or 2NT as immediate slam tries. Those bids could show the same hands as 3C and 3D, but with greater (13+ HCP) strength. Continuations would be the same, just one level higher. The problem with these jumps is that they leave very little room for exploration.

Opener's first chance to introduce a major is to bid 4H or 4S. Raises have to be made at the 5 level. A bid of 4NT can be either to play or ace-asking, but one of those functions has to be abandoned.

The alternative is for responder and opener to describe their holdings at the 3 level, and then have two different types of 4-level bids available—passable raises to game and side-suit slam tries. I think this is the best choice. I will leave it to my fellow mad scientists to come up with special uses for jumps to 4C and 4D.

The slower method works like this (one possible structure).

After responder describes his hand with a **3C** bid:

Opener bids 3D; responder may continue with:
- 3H (relay to 3NT, 9–12 HCP)
- 3S (relay to 3NT,13+HCP)
- 4C (sets diamonds as trump—shows 13+HCP)
  (4D by opener now asks keycards—1430 or other methods)
- 4D (simple raise, 9–12 HCP—(some pairs may use 4H by opener here to ask for keycards; others may use 4H,4S as cue bids, looking for slam)

After responder describes his hand with a **3D** bid:

Opener bids 3H; responder may continue with:

- 3S (relay to 3NT, if opener has not already bid NT—denies 3 hearts—may be followed by a natural bid at the 4 level showing 13+ HCP but no more than 2 hearts)
- 3NT (to play, denies 3 hearts)
- 4C (4 clubs, fitting 3-card heart raise, 13+ HCP)
- 4D (6+ diamonds, fitting 3-card heart raise, 13+HCP)
- 4H (simple 3-card heart raise, 9–12 HCP)

Opener bids 3S; if responder's first rebid (3C) showed both minors, he may bid

- 3NT—less than three spades, 9–12 HCP, but may be followed by raise to 4NT (13+ HCP). Must have stopper in hearts if first bid showed clubs or diamonds.
- 4C (natural, no heart stopper)
- 4D (natural, 6+ diamonds)
- 4H (artificial 3-card spade raise,13+ HCP)
- 4S (simple 3-card spade raise, 9-12 HCP)

3S—If responder's first rebid was 3D (showing 4 spades), he may bid

- 3NT (shows heart stopper,9–12 HCP)
- 4C (artificial 4-card spade raise,13+ HCP, shortness in clubs)
- 4D (artificial 4-card spade raise,13+ HCP,4-2-5-2 distribution)
- 4H (artificial 4-card spade raise,13+ HCP, shortness in hearts)
- 4S (simple 4-card spade raise, 9-12 HCP)

Here are some example hands:

A.	♠ Jxxx	♠ AQxx	1C	2H
	♥ AKx	♥ xx	2NT	3D (5D, 4S)
	♦ Kx	♦ AQxxx	3S (4+ spades),	4D (4+S, 13+ HCP 4-2-5-2)
	♣ AQxx	♣ Jx	4H (cue)	4S
			4NT (1430)	5S (2 KC + Q of S)
			6S	P

B. ♠ Jxxx   ♠ Q109xxxx   1C   2H
    ♥ AKx   ♥ J   2NT   3H (7+ S, minimum)
    ♦ Kx   ♦ Jxx   3S or 4S (50/50)
    ♣ AQxx   ♣ xx

C. ♠ x   ♠ Q109xxxx   1C   2H
    ♥ AKJxx   ♥ x   2S (poor fit)   P
    ♦ KQx   ♦ Jxx
    ♣ Axxx   ♣ Q

D. ♠ AKJxx   ♠ x   1C   2H
    ♥ AQxx   ♥ Kxx   2NT   3C (5+D, 4C, 0-3 S)
    ♦ x   ♦ AJ10xx   3S   3NT
    ♣ QJxx   ♣ Kxxx   4C* P?   4S (2KC, no QofC)
                                4NT or 6C

    (*4C doubles as 1430 - some would pass 3NT rather than bid 4C)

E. ♠ QJx   ♠ xx   1C   2H
    ♥ AQxx   ♥ Kx   2NT   3NT
    ♦ AJx   ♦ KQxxx
    ♣ Kxx   ♣ Qxxx

Note: Remember-whenever the strong club hand raises 2 or 3 of a minor to 4 of that suit, it is not only a raise but also an ace-asking bid (1430, 0314, or straight Blackwood, depending on partnership agreement; see hand D).

When the weaker hand raises the strong club hand to 4 of a minor, the stronger hand should be the one to ask for aces. Therefore, Redwood (4D over 4C, 4H over 4D) is used. To clarify, compare the following two auctions:

1. 1C   2C   2. 1C   -1D
    2NT   3C   3C   4C
    4C

In auction1, the strong 1C opener raises to 4C, so that is both a club raise and ace-asking. In auction 2, the weaker hand has raised to 4C. That bid is simply a club raise. To ask for aces, the 1C opener has to bid 4D (Redwood).

1C-2S (Relay to 2NT) and Above

The 2S relay response to 1C starts transfer sequences into many long suits as well as hands with 9+ HCP and 5/5+distribution in the minors. In its original form, 2S forced 2NT; responder then bid 3C, 3D, 3H, or 3S naturally, showing 7-card suits with 2 of the top 3 honors. He could also raise 2NT to 3NT, showing any solid (AKQxxxx) suit.

With a little tinkering, however, a transfer scheme was developed to ensure that all contracts were played by the strong hand. It is slightly more complex, but definitely superior. In the new improved version, 2S starts transfer sequences into 3C, 3H, and 3NT. Transfers into 3D and 3S are made directly at the 3 level. If it helps, here is a memory aid: **Transfers into the lower minor (clubs) and the lower major (hearts) start with a relay at a lower level (2S). Transfers into the higher minor (diamonds) and the higher major (spades) are made directly at a higher level (simple 3-level transfers).**

So: 1C   2S (forces 2NT)
    2NT   3C = 7 clubs, 2 of 3 top honors (lower minor)
                3D = 7 hearts, 2 of 3 top honors (lower major)

    1C   3C = 7 diamonds, 2 of 3 top honors (higher level, higher minor)
                3H = 7 spades, 2 of 3 top honors (higher level, higher major)

This leaves 3 unused sequences for solid (AKQ) suits:

    1C   2S (forces 2NT)
    2NT   3NT = AKQxxx, any suit (uses lower bid-2S-only 6-card suit)

    1C   3D = AKQxxxx in a major (higher level—7-card solid suit)*
    1C   3S = AKQxxxx in a minor strongly suggests opener bid 3NT.

After 1C-3D: Opener simply bids his better major. Responder can then raise to 4 (7-2-2-2 distribution) or cue-bid shortness in a side suit. If opener is honorless in both majors and doesn't know which major responder has, he bids 4C; responder then re-transfers into his suit (4D = transfer to hearts / 4H = transfer to spades).

---

*With a bad 5 HCP, pass is a reasonable option.

After 1C-3S: If opener can tell which minor responder has, he bids 3NT. This bid is forcing to 4NT.(It is almost impossible to have a 1C opener that cannot take 10 or 11 tricks opposite a AKQxxxx suit.) Responder then bids a singleton at the 4 level or bids 4NT with a 7-2-2-2 hand. Over a singleton bid, 4NT is to play. Over any second bid by responder, the cheapest suit asks for aces.(5C over 4NT or 4S).

If opener is honorless in both minors (pretty unlikely), he can bid 4C (not sure of game in a minor) or 4D (willing to play in 5C or 5D). He may also bid a very good 5-card or 6-card major (willing to play there opposite a doubleton).

If you look carefully, you will see that the 1C opener plays all contracts—a big advantage. The weaker hand with the long suit always comes down as dummy.

Secondary Meaning: When responder is 5/5 in the minors with 9+ HCP

In addition to showing long suits, the 1C-2S sequence can be used to show positive responding hands with 5/5+ distribution in the minors. The bidding is very precise.

There are two unused 3-level rebids after the auction goes 1C-2S-2NT. They are 3H and 3S. It is simple to make these bids show singletons with 5/5+ in the minors. Thus 1C-2S-2NT-3H shows a singleton heart and a likely 2-1-5-5 shape. The sequence 1C-2S-2NT-3S shows a singleton spade and probable 1-2-5-5 distribution.

Follow-ups are also very straightforward. Opener can sign off with 3NT,4H, or 4S (natural to play) or try for a minor suit game or slam with 4C or 4D (usually setting trump but perhaps just getting information), which are RKCB for the bid suit. If more precision is desired, all of the 4 level is also available after 1C-2S-2NT. For example, one could define these bids as follows: 4C =1-1-5-6, 4D = 1-1-6-5, 4H = heart void,4S = spade void. Other meanings are also possible, depending on partnership agreements.

Here are some example hands:

A. ♠ Axxx   ♠ xx   1C   2S (relay to 2NT)
    ♥ Kx   ♥ AQxxxxx   2NT   3D (transfer to 3H-7+card suit)
    ♦ AQJ   ♦ xxx   3NT or 4H
    ♣ Kxxx   ♣ x

B. ♠ AKJxx   ♠ xx   1C   3S (solid 7-card minor)
    ♥ Kx   ♥ xxx   6NT (played from right side)
    ♦ xx   ♦ AKQxxxx
    ♣ AKQx   ♣ x

C. ♠ AKJxx	♠ xx	1C	3D (solid 7-card major)
♥ xx	♥ AKQxxxx	6H	
♦ AKQxx	♦ xx		
♣ x	♣ xx		
D. ♠ AKJxx	♠ x	1C	2S
♥ xx	♥ xxx	2NT	3C (7+ clubs, 2 of top 3 honors)
♦AKQxx	♦ xx	P	
♣ x	♣ KQxxxxx		
E. ♠ AJ10	♠ x	1C	2S
♥ AQxx	♥ xx	2NT	3S (0-1 S, 5+ C, 5+ D/9+HCP)
♦ Kxxx	♦ AQ10xx	4D (1430)	5C (2-K of C+ Q of D))
♣ Kx	♣ AQxxx	5H (kings?)	5S (0)
		6D	
F. ♠ AKxxx	♠ x	1C	2S
♥ QJ9x	♥ xx	2NT	3S (1-2-5-5 distribution)
♦ A	♦ KQJxx	3NT	
♣ Kxx	♣ AQxxx		

1C-2NT- BalancedHand—16-18 HCP

The 2NT response to 1C shows a balanced 16–18 HCP. Since that means the partner-ship has at least 33 HCP, it is essentially forcing to slam. Therefore, many sequences which sound like an attempt to set the final contract (such as a simple raise to game) are forcing. Some pairs may want to allow the auction to stop at a certain level below slam (perhaps 5NT). That is a matter for partnership agreement. In order to minimize memory strain, we will use a natural continuation scheme almost identical to the one used after a 1C-1NT auction.

Natural Continuations (One Possible Scheme)

Again, this method and the artificial method I will present later actually share one similar set of bids: the rebids and original continuations used when opener has a bal-anced hand.

When the opener has a balanced hand and the auction goes 1C- 2NT, he bids 3C (Stayman). Responder's reply will either be a transfer showing a 4-card major or a bid denying a major but describing his hand's strength. To be specific, a 2D reply shows 4 hearts. Responder may also have a second suit. A bid of 2H shows four spades. It denies 4 hearts, but the hand may have a 4-card minor. A bid of 2S shows no major and a minimum (16–17 HCP). The hand will have 1 or 2 minors. A bid of 2NT shows no major and a maximum (17+/18 HCP).Again, the hand will have 1 or 2 minors.

Opener can bid 2NT or bid a minor if he would consider bidding a minor suit slam and has discovered a 4-4 fit If opener has a fit for responder's transfer suit, he bids it. If no trump fit exists in the transfer suit, opener bids a different suit, still looking for a combined 8-card trump holding. Raises set trump. If no suit fit can be found, the contract will probably wind up in NT. If a trump fit is found, standard slam exploration will ensue.

Key-card asking bids will require partnership agreement. I would suggest using Kickback (the suit or denomination directly above an agreed-upon trump suit) at the 4 or 5 level to ask for keycards. Since both hands contain at least 16 HCP, I would use the Texas responses (with the first step raised to show 2 KC without a trump Q, the second showing 2 KC with the Q, the third showing 3 KC with no Q, etc.) rather than 1430.It is almost impossible for either hand to have less than the minimum response.

With a 5-card or longer suit, opener can bid 3D, 3H, 3S, or 3NT (showing 5+ clubs). over 2NT. Responder's replies after opener bids a major will follow a consistent pattern, but rebids after 3D and 3NT require slightly special treatment. In nearly all cases, direct raises show 3-card support. Simple NT rebids suggest 2-card support, but may contain a delayed 3-card raise. Most new suit bids in a lower suit are fit-showing. They show 4 cards in the bid suit and a 4-card raise for opener'smajor. New suit bids in a higher suit may be an attempt to find a 4-4 fit rather than settle for 5-3, or they may contain a 4-card raise and suggest a possible side source of tricks for slam. Here is an outline of the entire structure:

When Opener Is Balanced

1C	2NT
3C	3D= 4 hearts (may also have 4 spades or either minor)
	3H= 4 spades (may also have a 4-card minor)
	3S= no 4-card major, 16-17 HCP
	3NT= no 4-card major, 17+/18 HCP

Opener can now bid responder's suit or bid a second suit, looking for a 4-4 fit. He can bid 3NT as a waiting bid when no trump fit is found at the three level.

When Opener Has a 5 + Card Minor

1C	2NT
3D (5+ diamonds)	3H, or 3S =natural, may have 2-4 diamonds (can make delayed 3-card raise to 4D)
	3NT= no 4-card major, 2 or 3 diamonds, minimum
	4C= fitting raise; 4 clubs, 4 diamonds
	4D= 4 diamonds, 3-3-4-3 distribution
	4H= fitting raise, 4 hearts, 4 diamonds
	4S= fitting raise, 4 spades, 4 diamonds
	4NT= no major, 2 or 3 diamonds, maximum

1C	2NT
3NT (5+ clubs)	4C=exactly 2 clubs, thus two side suits (opener can bid a 4-card side suit if he has one / any secondary 4-4 fit will be found by bidding suits up the line / 4NT by either player = no fit)
	4D= fitting raise 3 or 4 clubs, 4 diamonds
	4H= fitting raise, 3 or 4 clubs, 4 hearts
	4S= fitting raise 3 or 4 clubs + 4 spades
	4NT= any 3-3-3-4 hand, 4 clubs

As you can see, most of the fit-showing bids are retained, with one small alteration. Lack of bidding space makes it necessary to consolidate 3-card and 4-card fitting raises. They still allow us to find possible 4-4 fits in the majors while guaranteeing at least 5-3 fits in clubs. A later bid of 5C would suggest 4-card club support and slam interest.

When opener has a 5-card major our structure is very similar to the minor suit structure.

When Opener Has a 5+-Card Major

1C	2NT
2H (5+ hearts)	?

2S= 4 spades, may have delayed 3-card or minimum 4-card heart raise

2NT= 2 or 3 hearts, waiting (minimum if a delayed heart raise)

3C= 4 clubs, 4 hearts, fitting raise

3D= 4 diamonds, 4 hearts, fitting raise

3H= 3 hearts, good 3-card raise

3S=4 spades, 4 hearts- fitting raise, maximum

4C= 4 clubs, 4 hearts, fitting raise, maximum

4D= 4 diamonds, 4 hearts, fitting raise, maximum

4H= 4 hearts, 3-4-3-3, maximum

The spade structure is almost identical to that used for hearts.

1C	2NT
2S (5+ spades)	?

2NT= 2 or 3 spades, waiting (minimum if a delayed heart raise)

3C= 4 clubs, 4 spades, minimum fitting raise

3D= 4 diamonds, 4 spades, minimum fitting raise

3H= 4 hearts, 4 spades, minimum fitting raise

3S= 3 spades, good 3-card raise

3NT= 2 or 3 spades, balanced maximum

4C= 4 clubs, 4 spades, maximum fitting raise

4D= 4 diamonds, 4 spades, maximum fitting raise

4H= 4 hearts, 4 spades, maximum fitting raise

4S= 4 spades, 4-3-3-3 maximum

Here are some possible auctions using natural continuations:

A.	♠ Axxx	♠ KQxx	1C	2NT (16-18 HCP)
	♥ Kx	♥Axx	3C	3H
	♦ KQxx	♦Ax	3S (4 spades)	4C
	♣ AQx	♣Kxxx	4NT (1430-spades)	5C (0 or 3)
			5D (Q ask)	6C (yes + K of C)
			7S	

B. ♠ Kxx	♠ AQxx	1C	2NT (16-18)
♥AQxx	♥ Kx	3C (Stayman)	3H (4 spades)
♦ Ax	♦ KJx	3NT	4C (natural)
♣ KQxx	♣AJxx	4D (1430-clubs)	4H (0-3)
		4NT (kings?)	5H (2)
		7C or 7NT (only	
		12 sure tricks)	
C. ♠ AKJxx	♠ Qxxx	1C	2NT
♥ x	♥ AKQx	2S	3H (4H,4S, minimum)
♦ AKJx	♦ xx	4D (ace)	4H (ace)
♣ Kxx	♣ AJx	5C (king)	5H (king)
		6D (king)	7S (can count 13
			tricks with D ruff)
D. ♠ x	♠AKQ	1C	2NT
♥ KQJ10xx	♥Ax	3H	3NT
♦ KQx	♦Axxx	4NT (1430)	5C (0-3 KC, no Q of H)
♣ AKx	♣J10xx	5NT	6S (K of S) or 6D (1)
		7NT (13 sure tricks)	

1C-3NT (Balanced 19+ HCP)

This bid will occur about as often as Halley's Comet will appear above Los Angeles. It's only real function is to provide the 2NT response with an upper limit. I won't waste time outlining a response scheme. Should it ever come up, just use the scheme for the 2NT bid, with every bid 1 level higher.

Afterthought

Note:I mentioned that some might be interested in a more artificial continuation scheme involving asking bids after a 1C-1NT or 1C-2NT auction. I decided to discuss such a scheme as a separate topic. Anyone interested in such an idea will find a complete outline of a possible artificial structure for auctions beginning 1C-1NT in Appendix H. Also included is the corresponding scheme for 1C-2NT.

CHAPTER 10

Interference Over a 1-Club Opener

With any strong club system, it is essential to have a good structure to handle interference over a 1C opening bid. The conventional wisdom, of course, is that continual hyperactive use of overcalls is the best way to limit the effectiveness of strong club bidding.

The counter-interference structure I have devised is designed to use enemy interference to our advantage whenever possible. It is most effective over doubles and 1-level overcalls, where it allows us to find major suit fits before the opponents can engage in disruptive preemption. It allows us to describe 4-and 5-card major suit holdings as well as strength levels immediately, as well as transferring potential major-suit and NT contracts into the 1C bidder's hand in many cases.

It is not quite as effective when opponents overcall at the 2 level and above, but it still allows us to find reasonable contracts with at least some accuracy. Our most effective weapon against really obnoxious and overenthusiastic preemption, of course, will always be the penalty double. Whenever the opponents interfere to the extent that we cannot confidently expect to find a makeable contract of our own, the double should be our default action. Nothing discourages kamikaze overcalls like a few 800s or 1100s on the scoresheet.

After a double or 1-level overcall, there is plenty of room for constructive bidding. Some use very simple advances in this situation (i. e. pass = 0–4 HCP, double or re-double= 5–8 HCP, any bid = 9+ HCP). I prefer a more definitive set of bids. I especially want to be able to find 4-4 major fits, which can get lost if the doubler or overcaller's partner raises to the 2 or 3 level. A scheme like the one I am about to outline certainly requires a lot more partnership practice than the simple advances I just mentioned, but the importance of this area justifies the extra work. Interference over a 1C opening may come up several times in a session. The frequency of this situation justifies a little extra attention and memory work.

The next several pages contain an outline of my proposed "official" structure.(As usual, prospective system users are free to completely ignore my ideas and come up with their own competitive structures.)

Actions After a Double of 1C

When the opening bid of one club is doubled, opener's partner may have to make an immediate choice of tactics. Of course, if he holds a wretched (0–5 HCP) hand without any extraordinary distribution, there is little to think about. He simply passes. With a stronger or more distributional hand, however, he has several possible courses of action.

The first bid available to him is redouble. This shows at least 9 HCP and is essentially game-forcing. However, he may choose not to show his strength at once. When the opponents are vulnerable and we are not, the best choice may be to lurk in the shadows in hopes of getting a big penalty. A delayed double after an initial pass shows at least 9 HCP and a relatively balanced hand. Since a double of a strong 1C bid often shows the majors, it suggests strength in those suits. It does not deny one or even two 4-card majors (though a 1NT bid is available for that hand). It is a strong suggestion that our best score may lie in defending a doubled contract. If partner doubles but later bids rather than continuing to seek a penalty, the auction is game-forcing.

Another choice may be whether to immediately show a major suit. With exactly 4 hearts or 4 spades, it will almost always be best to transfer into the major. This will avoid any chance of losing the suit entirely if the opponents quickly raise the bidding to a high level. With a 5-card or longer suit, however, other actions are available.

Responder's 1-level transfer to a major will generally show between 5 and 12 HCP. With a 5-card major and a hand in this range, the transfer is certainly one good option. With a stronger (13+ HCP) hand, he may want to first redouble and then bid his suit. This sequence should suggest slam possibilities.

Should responder transfer, opener will usually accept the transfer with 3 cards in the suit, while often bidding 1NT with 1 or 2. If the opponents compete over the transfer, he can show a 3-card fit with a support double or bid the suit with 4. If opener gets the chance to bid 1NT, responder can use Puppet Stayman and standard transfers to uncover 8-card fits in either major.

A unique situation arises when opener decides to bid 1NT after the redouble. If the redoubler had planned to show his 5-card suit at his second turn, he has to change his plan. Instead of bidding his suit directly, he must switch to Puppet Stayman with 4-suit transfers, similar to the situation in which responder has used a 1-level transfer. If the opponents bid to the 2 level, it is still possible to use 4-suit transfers (starting with a 2NT transfer to clubs), though some may prefer to bid suits naturally. After 3-level competition suits should probably be bid naturally. There isn't much room to use anything fancy, though 4-level transfers are certainly possible.

With a 6-card (or bad 7-card) major, jump transfers are available at the two level. Seven card suits can be transferred into at the 3 level. These bids are the same as the ones used when there is no interference (See p.204, p.216), so they present no additional memory problems. Transfers to 7-card club and heart suits begin with the 2S relay to 2NT. Transfers to diamonds and spades are made directly at the 3 level. Solid majors and minors can also be shown with bids of 3D and 3S.

Here is a complete outline of the bidding scheme following a double of a 1C opening bid:

- After 1C[double],pass = 0–4 HCP or 9+ HCP with no 5-card major (possibly trapping for penalty; a later double shows 9+ HCP, with the auction having to end in game or a doubled enemy contract)

- Redouble = 9+ HCP (game-forcing), either a balanced hand in a situation that does not favor a trap pass (i. e. when vulnerable vs. non-vulnerable opponents) or an unbalanced hand with game-forcing values. If opener should rebid in a suit, natural bidding will follow. A new suit bid will generally show at least 5-card length, though a 4-card minor is possible. If opener's first rebid is in NT, responder can use Puppet Stayman and 4-suit transfers to advance the auction.

- With a balanced hand, opener can pass over any bid RHO may make or bid 1NT and wait to hear partner's continuation. With an unbalanced hand, he can bid his suit.

- 1D = 5+ HCP, 4 or 5 hearts—opener may bid 1H with at least 3 hearts. With a 5-card suit, responder can raise to 2H (5–6 HCP) or 3H (7–8 HCP) or bid an artificial 1S, followed by a forcing heart raise. (Responder can't have 4 spades. He would have bid 1NT or 2NT with both majors.) With only 4 hearts and minimum values, he can bid a non-forcing 1NT, 2C, or 2D. With 9+ HCP and only 4 hearts, he can bid the artificial 1S and then make a game-forcing bid of a new suit.

- If opener does not have at least 3 hearts, he may bid 1NT or a suit. Often, the best choice is 1NT. Even with a slightly unbalanced hand, it may be the best contract if responder is weak, It will also allow him to use Puppet Stayman and 4-suit transfer advances if he has extra values. This means the spade fit won't be lost if opener bids 1NT with a 5-card spade suit.

- 1H = 5+ HCP, 4 or 5 spades—Opener bids 1S with at least 3 spades. With a 5-card suit, responder can raise to 2S (5–6 HCP) or 3S (7–8 HCP). With only 4 spades and minimum values, he can bid a non-forcing 2C or 2D. With 9+ HCP, he can bid an artificial 2H (he can't have 4 hearts—he didn't bid 1NT or 2NT) and then raise spades, bid NT, or bid a minor. Just as with the transfer to hearts, if opener lacks 3 spades, he bids 1NT (first choice) or a suit of his own. The same continuations apply.

- 1S= 5-8 HCP, no major—either balanced or containing a 5+ card minor, which responder may bid if opener bids 1NT. This bid almost serves as a re-lay to 1NT, though opener may choose to bid a suit if he is unbalanced. With 20+HCP, opener may choose to jump in a suit or NT. This should be essentially game-forcing. Responder may pass opener's 1NT or bid a non-forcing 2C or 2D. He may invite game with 2H (5+ clubs),2S (5+ diamonds), or 2NT (balanced hand).

- 1NT = 4-4+ in the majors-9+HCP. This runs counter to my usual aversion to having the weak hand bid NT. However, since a double of the 1C opener gen-erally shows the majors, it is unlikely to have to be used very often. Its most important function is to allow the bids of 1D (hearts) and 1H (spades) to show one specific major. At least opener will be able to invite or raise to game in NT with some assurance of major suit stoppers. With a major suit fit, he can bid a non-forcing 2H or 2S or a forcing 3H or 3S. Major suit contracts will thus be played from the strong side.

- 2C = 4–4 in the majors, 5–8 HCP, and 5+.This is simply a weaker version of the 1NT response. Again, it won't come up too often, but it will allow any major suit contracts to be played by the 1C opener. He can bid a non-forcing 2H or 2S or a forcing 3H or 3S if he finds a fit.

Most of the bids above 2C are transfers into long suits. Bids of 2D and 2H show decent 6-card or poor 7-card holdings in the majors. Starting with the 2S relay to 2NT, the bids are essentially the same as would be made if the opponents hadn't doubled: 7-card suits with 2 of the top 3 or all 3 top honors (See p.204, p.216) or hands with 9+ HCP and 5/5 in the minors (see page 159).

2D = transfer, 6+ hearts (if 7, 0-1 top honors)
2H =transfer, 6+ spades (if 7, 0-1 top honors)
2S through 3S – see pages (155-6)

Actions Over a 1D Overcall

There are at least two reasonable ways to handle a 1D overcall by the opponents. (Actually, there are probably dozens, but I'm trying not to make this tome longer than *War and Peace*.)

The first way would be to essentially ignore the interference and give almost every bid the same meaning it would have had without the overcall. There would only be two slight changes. Pass would now serve as a negative response, showing 0–5 HCP. Double could now serve as a semi-positive bid, showing any 6–8 HCP hand. All other bids would retain their original meaning.

A second choice would be to use a modified version of our scheme following 1C-double. This would again emphasize protecting our possible 4-4 major suit fits from enemy jumps to the 3 level. A quick summary of one fairly simple scheme would look like this:

After 1C-[1D]-
Pass = 0-4 HCP or 9+ HCP, trap passing (shown by later double or cue bid)
Double= 5+ HCP, 4 or 5 hearts (continuations would be the same as after 1C-double-1D)
1H = 5+ HCP, 4 or 5 spades (same continuations)
1S = 5-8 HCP, no major (may have a 5+card club suit). This bid will often let opener bid 1NT to play.
1NT = 8-11 HCP, good diamond stopper
2C = 5+ HCP (unlimited), 4-4+ in majors
2D = 9+ HCP (asks partner to bid 2H with at least 3 cards in that suit—will raise with 5+ hearts or bid a new suit or NT if the bid is not based on a heart suit). Opener can bid 2NT or a suit of his own with 0-2 hearts.
2H = 9+ HCP, 5 or more spades (asks partner to bid 2S). Responder will bid 3S with 6 or bid something else with only 5.

2S = relay to 2NT- good 7+ card club or heart suit (shown by 3D rebid-a transfer to3H)

2NT= 12+ HCP, good diamond stopper

3C = good 7+ card diamond suit

3D= solid (AKQxxxx) major

3H = good 7+ card spade suit

3S = solid 7+ card (AKQxxxx) minor

Again, this is just one of many possible structures.

Actions Over a 1H or 1S Overcall

When the opponents overcall our 1C opening with 1H or 1S, our scheme deviates from many other strong club systems. The most important deviation is the use of a standard negative double, showing exactly 4 cards in the other major. When a double of 1H or 1S is used merely as an indicator of a certain point range, as in many strong club systems, it is far too easy to lose 4-4 major fits. This is especially true if the overcaller's partner immediately raises to the 3 level. An immediate negative double solves that problem.

Another useful idea is to use the cuebid of the overcaller's suit to show 9+ HCP and a 5+-card holding in the other major. In addition to creating a game force, it ensures that game or slam contracts in that suit will be played by the concealed strong hand. A natural bid of the other major is limited to 5–8 HCP.

Responder has other descriptive bids available for balanced or minor-oriented hands. Artificial 2C and 2D advances are essentially negative and positive doubles, emphasizing the minors. Certain jumps (transfers in some cases) show game-forcing 1-suited hands. Most minor-suit sequences give the strong club bidder the chance to right-side any NT contracts.

Here is the complete structure:

After 1C-[1H]-P =0-4 HCP* or trap pass

Double = 5+ HCP (unlimited) exactly 4 spades

1S = 5–8 HCP, 5+ spades

1NT = 8–11 HCP, double stopper in hearts

2C = artificial, 5–8 HCP, denies 4 spades (kind of a negative double for the minors— may have a 5+ card club or diamond suit

2D = artificial, 9+ HCP, denies 4 spades (kind of a game-forcing negative double for the minors—may have a 5+ card club or diamond suit

2H = 9+ HCP, 5+ spades (a cuebid of the opponent's major shows a game-forcing hand with 5+ cards in the other major)

2S = transfer, 9+ HCP, 6+ clubs—good suit (2H already handles GF hands with spades)

2NT = 12 + HCP, balanced, double stopper in hearts

3C = transfer, 9+ HCP, 6+ diamonds—good suit

3D = transfer cue bid—slam values—asks about controls in opponents' suit

answers = 3H =no control

        3S =one-half control

        3NT =king

        4C=singleton

        4D =ace or void

        4H =AK

After 1C-[1S]-P = 0–4 HCP* or trap pass

Double = 5+ HCP (unlimited), exactly 4 hearts

1NT = 8–11 HCP, double spade stopper

2C = artificial, 5–8 HCP, denies 4 hearts

2D = artificial, 9+ HCP, GF, denies 4 hearts

2H = 5–8 HCP, 5+ hearts

2S = 9+ HCP, 5+ hearts, GF

2NT = 12+ HCP, double stopper in spades

3C=transfer, 9+ HCP, good 6+ diamond suit

3D=flip-flop-transfer -9+ HCP, good 6+ card club suit

3H = transfer cue bid—slam values—asks for controls in opponents' suit

answers = 3S =no control

        3NT =king

        4C = singleton

        4D =ace or void

        4H =AK

(If the various transfers—especially the transfer cue bids—strike you as over the top, jumps to 3C and 3D can simply be treated as natural 6+ card suits with 9+HCP. Keep the cue bids of 2H and 2S, but forget the others.)

---

* With a bad 5 HCP, pass is a reasonable option.

Actions After 2-Level and 3-Level Overcalls

After 2-level overcalls, there is much less room for an elaborate structure. I would use a simple natural scheme along these lines:

Pass = 0-6 HCP or no clear action, possible trap pass
Double = 7+ HCP, standard negative double; major suit oriented
Simple suit bids = 7+ HCP, forcing 1 round
Cue bid at the 3 level = general game force, usually aiming toward 3NT or slam
3C = artificial GF, denying major suit
3D = artificial GF, showing opposite major or both majors (at least 4-3)

A Couple of General Principles (repeated for emphasis)

- If the opponents use hyperactive interference tactics and you have no reason to believe that you are a favorite to make game (or you are unsure which game to bid), you should probably be willing to settle for reasonable pluses by doubling at the 3 level and above.
- When no action is clear and our side clearly has a majority of the points, try to convert negative, artificial, and reopening doubles to penalty doubles.

Alternative schemes can be found in Appendix E.

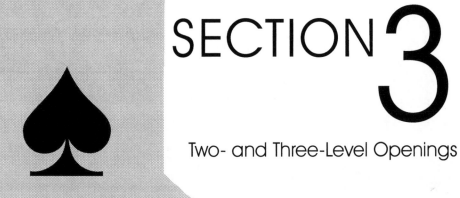

SECTION 3

Two- and Three-Level Openings

CHAPTER 11
The Fun Zone / Two-Way Two-Level Openings

Because opener's first suit rebid after a 1C opening bid always shows a 5-card suit, it is necessary to have a bid showing a big 4-4-4-1 hand. In the original version of the system, that bid was a simple 2D. It had only one meaning- a good (16+ HCP) hand with 4-4-4-1 shape. The 2H and 2S bids were standard weak 2 bids. Then the mad scientist in me complicated matters.

I wanted to have a way to differentiate between good preemptive hands and the junk that modern players preempt with. I did come up with a good method for doing this, but there was a minor problem:I had to use the 2S opening bid for my brainchild. That left only two bids—2D and 2H—to describe three different hands:a weak 2 bid in hearts, a weak 2 bid in spades, and a big 4-4-4-1 hand. The only way to solve this problem was to make these bids do double duty. Thus were born the Schizoid 2D and 2H opening bids.

- **The Schizoid 2D bid** shows either a weak 2 bid in hearts or a 4-4-4-1 hand with 16+ HCP and a singleton in a black suit. Thus *it always guaranteesat least 4 hearts.*
- **The Schizoid 2H bid** shows either a weak 2 bid in spades or a 4-4-4-1 hand with 16+ HCP and a singleton in a red suit. Thus *it always guarantees at least 4 spades.*

Those guaranteed suits are important. The ACBL is deathly afraid of Multi, where a 2D opening shows a weak 2 bid in either major. They think that American players are not smart enough to handle defending against such a complicated convention, though millions of Europeans seem to handle it quite easily. Their main contention is that having a weak 2 in an unknown suit is unfair.

My schizoid bids unequivocally meet their objections. The major suit in question is always known. Opener will either have a weak hand with 6 of a specific major or a very good hand with 4 of that suit. Defenders will almost never want to play in the anchor suit.

I also provide a simple and logical defense for these bids. There should be no possible way to argue that using them is taking advantage of inexperienced players. However, because some ACBL directors may forbid their use, I will also outline the original set of bids alluded to earlier at the end of this chapter (See p.248). Another suggestion is provided in Appendix F.

Using the Schizoid 2D and 2H allows the use of the Sartor 2S bid for good preempts. The Sartor 2S describes all preempts containing either 2 of the top 3 honors or AKQ in any suit. That means all 3-level preempts can have no more than 1 top honor. It also creates a kind of "transfer Gambling 3NT" as a side benefit.

These three bids constitute the "fun zone" of the California Club system. They are useful, logical, and fun to use. A detailed summary of each bid follows.

The Two-Way 2D Bid

As stated in the fun zone summary, the Schizoid 2D bid shows either a **weak 2 bid in hearts or a good 4-4-4-1 hand with a singleton in a black suit**. It thus always guarantees at least 4 hearts. I estimate that it will be a weak 2 bid about 95 percent of the time. It is therefore usually a transfer to 2 hearts, exposing the already known weak hand as dummy and leaving partner's hand concealed.

The response system is designed to ensure that the opener's hand winds up as dummy if it is indeed a weak 2 bid. The cheapest response, 2H, shows a willingness to play that contract if partner is weak. The next response, 2S, indicates a good enough hand to be willing to play at least at the 3 level if opener has the weak 2 bid. Of course, if opener shows up with the good 4-4-4-1, then the 2S response is forcing to game. Opener's rebids define exactly which hand he has.

Here they are in chart form:

After 2D-2H, opener bids as follows

Pass= weak 2 bid in hearts

2S = 4-4-4-1, club singleton, 16–17 HCP (cheaper of each pair of bids = lower black
    singleton / next bid = higher black singleton)

2NT = 1-4-4-4, spade singleton, 16–17 HCP

3C = 4-4-4-1, club singleton, 18–19 HCP

3D = 1-4-4-4, spade singleton, 18–19 HCP

3H = 4-4-4-1, club singleton, 20–21 HCP

3S = 1-4-4-4, spade singleton, 20–21 HCP

3NT = 4-4-4-1, club singleton, 22–23 HCP

4C = 1-4-4-4, spade singleton, 22–23 HCP

4D = 4-4-4-1, club singleton, 24+ HCP (unlikely but why not?)

4H = 1-4-4-4, spade singleton, 24+ HCP (when pigs fly)

(Actually, I've seen this hand once.)

You don't have to memorize all these bids—just count on your fingers.

Responder now places the final contract. In the rare instance when slam is possible, a cue bid of the singleton would ask for aces.

After 2D-2S, game or slam is more likely, and a different set of rebids is used—one that lets responder ask for controls if slam is possible. The cheapest rebid shows the 4-4-4-1 hand with the lower singleton (this allows a convenient cue bid of the singleton, which can now ask for point range).

The next two bids show bad and good weak 2 bids (this maintains the transfer—the weak 2 bidder never bids his actual suit). Bids above that show the 4-4-4-1 hand with the higher singleton and give the point range immediately (again, merely the most efficient use of space). Here's a memory aid: the 4-4-4-1 hands with the higher singleton always start at 3 of the possible weak two suit.

After 2D-2S

2NT = 4-4-4-1 club singleton, any range (to ask, responder bids the cheapest suit,
which conveniently is also a cue bid in the stiff- 3C. Opener replies in steps:
first step = 16–17 HCP, second step = 18–19 HCP, third step=20–21 HCP, etc.)

3C = poor (5–7 HCP) weak 2 bid in hearts; responder may sign off at 3H or bid game

3D = good (8–10 HCP) weak 2 bid in hearts; since both partners have shown values,
3H is now invitational, 4H to play, and other bids are slam tries.

3H = 1-4-4-4 -singleton spade, 16–17 HCP (cheapest bid, 3S, now asks for controls,
starting at 0-4)

3S = 1-4-4-4 -singleton spade, 18–19 HCP (cheapest suit bid, 4C, now asks for controls, starting at 0–6 / 3NT is to play)

3NT = 1-4-4-4 singleton spade, 20–21 HCP (4C still asks for controls)

4C = 4-4-4-1 singleton spade, 22–23 HCP, etc.

One important issue essential to avoiding misunderstandings is how to handle interference. Unless firm agreements are in place, disasters are possible. These bids offer more
protection against such dire results than Multi because we have a guaranteed anchor
suit, but confusion is still possible without discussion.

Let's start with an opponent's double of the opening bid. Obviously, with a weak
nondescript hand, responder will just pass. With a weak hand and a fit for the anchor
suit, he may bid 2, 3, or even 4 of that suit. How high he competes will depend on distribution and vulnerability. With a good hand, especially one with a strong holding in the
suits most likely to be bid by the opponents, responder should redouble. With a weak 2
bid, opener will have to use his judgment on whether to retreat to his suit immediately;
pass and possibly play a redoubled contract in a second suit; or go for a penalty. At least
he will have more than guesswork to go on. Should the opener have the good 4-4-4-1
hand, the carnage may be spectacular. Both partners should double at every turn to bid.

When an opponent makes a direct overcall, responder's first responsibility will be
to double if he has a strong holding in that suit and reasonably good values. Opener can
pull the double with a minimum weak 2 and poor defensive values. A pass will leave it
up to opener to compete if he has the good hand. With a good fit for the anchor suit,
responder can bid it at an appropriate level.

Where confusion may set in is when the overcall is passed around to opener. If our
agreement is that responder will double rather than trap pass with a hand that might
yield a big penalty, there is no need to have opener reopen with a double to show shortness and the good 4-4-4-1. Any action other than pass will show the good hand and
also usually reveal opener's short suit. He can double or bid NT with a strong holding

in the overcaller's suit. This will almost certainly pinpoint his singleton as being in the other suit of the same color. If he bids that suit, it will almost always show shortness in overcaller's suit. This scheme may not be perfect, but it should allow responder to always have a good picture of opener's hand. It will also ensure that an underhanded opponent (like me) cannot get away with psyching us out of a fit.

Here are somehands involving the 2D opening bid:

A. ♠ Jx   ♠ AQxx   2D   2H (willing to play
    ♥ KQ10xxx ♥ x   P   2H if weak)
    ♦ xxx   ♦ Kxx
    ♣ xx   ♣ QJxxx

B. ♠ x   ♠ AQx   2D   2S (willing to play
    ♥ AKJ10xx ♥ xx   3D (good weak 2)   4S   at least 3H)
    ♦ xx   ♦ KJxx
    ♣ J10xx   ♣ A98x

C. ♠ x   ♠ Qxx   2D   2S
    ♥ KQxx   ♥ Axxx   3H (1-4-4-4,16-17 HCP)   4S (1430 for H)
    ♦ AQJx   ♦ Kx   5C (3)   5D (Q of H?)
    ♣ AJxx   ♣KQxx   6C (yes,+ K of C)   6H

D. ♠ AQxx   ♠ Kxxx   2D   2S
    ♥ AQxx   ♥ x   2NT (4-4-4-1,singleton C)   3C (range?)
    ♦ KQxx   ♦ AJxx   3D (16–17 HCP)   3S (1430)
    ♣ x   ♣ Axxx   4H (2 KC + Q of S)   6S

E. ♠ x   ♠ xxxx   2D   2S
    ♥ AKQx   ♥ J109xx   3H (1-4-4-4, 16–17 HCP)   3S (1430 for H)
    ♦ KJxx   ♦ Ax   4C (3)   4D (Q of H?)
    ♣ A109x   ♣ KQx   5D (yes, + K of D)   6H

The Two-Way 2H Bid

Like the 2D bid, the 2H opening bid shows one of two hands. It is either a **weak 2 bid in spades or a 4-4-4-1 hand with 16+ HCP and a singleton in a red suit**. Just as 2D guarantees 4 hearts, 2H guarantees 4 spades. It also essentially serves as a transfer to spades, just as 2D does with hearts.

After 2H-2S or 2H-2NT, the pattern is exactly the same, only one denomination higher in each case. Here's the chart form.

2H-2S (willing to play 2S opposite weak 2bid)
Pass = weak 2 bid in spades
2NT = 4-4-1-4, singleton diamond (lower red suit), 16–17 HCP
3C = 4-1-4-4, singleton heart (higher red suit), 16–17 HCP
3D = 4-4-1-4, singleton diamond, 18–19 HCP
3H = 4-1-4-4, singleton heart, 18–19 HCP
3S = 4-4-1-4, singleton diamond, 20–21 HCP
3N = 4-1-4-4, singleton heart, 20–21 HCP
4C = 4-4-1-4, singleton diamond, 22–23 HCP
4D = 4-1-4-4, singleton heart, 22–23 HCP
4H = etc.
4S = etc.

Again, you don't have to memorize all these bids. Just count on your fingers.

2H-2NT (good fit or values / willing to play at least 3S)
3C = 4-4-1-4 hand, singleton diamond, any range (3D asks HCP, first step =16–17,
     second= 18–19, third = 20–21, etc.)
3D = poor (5–7 HCP), weak 2 bid in spades
3H = good (8–10 HCP), weak 2 bid in spades
3S = 4-1-4-4 hand, singleton heart, 16–17 HCP
3NT = 4-1-4-4 hand, singleton heart, 18–19 HCP
4C = 4-1-4-4 hand, singleton heart, 20-21 HCP, etc.

Here are some example hands:

A.	♠ AQ10xxx	♠ xx	2H	2S (to play if weak)
	♥ x	♥ Qxx	P	
	♦ QJx	♦ A10xxx		
	♣ xxx	♣ Kx		

B.	♠ KJxxxx	♠ AQxx	2H	2NT
	♥ Kxx	♥ AQxx	3D (poor weak 2S)	4S
	♦ x	♦ Axx		
	♣ xxx	♣ xx		

C.	♠ AKxx	♠ QJ10x	2H	2NT
	♥ x	♥ Jxxx	3S (16–17, 4-1-4-4)	4H (1430 for spades)
	♦ KQJx	♦ Ax	5C (2 KC)	5D (kings?)
	♣ K10xx	♣ AJx	5NT (2)	6S

Note: 4C, 4D would have been 1430 for those suits. 4H takes over key-card-asking duty for spades. A bid of 4S would be a sign-off.

D.	♠ QJ10x	♠ 98xx	2H	2S
	♥ AQJx	♥ Kxx	3D (18–19 HCP, 4-4-1-4)	3S
	♦ x	♦ xxx	4S? P?	
	♣ AKQx	♣ xx		

E.	♠ QJ10xxx	♠ Axxx	2H[double]	3S or 4S
	♥ xx	♥ xx	(opposition may compete to 5-level)	
	♦ KQxx	♦ x	5S?	
	♣ x	♣ xxxxx		

F.	♠ KQJx	♠ Axx	2H	2NT (
	♥ AKQx	♥ x	3C	3D (ask)
	♦ x	♦ xxx	4C (22+HCP)	4D (
	♣ AKxx	♣109xxxx	4NT (2)	6C (Banzai!)

Note: There is no way to use 1430 here; 4H, 4S, and 5C would all be sign-offs. When that is the case, simple Blackwood should be the default agreement. Since opener has only 2 aces, responder can reasonably infer he must have all 3 kings plus some queens to have 22+HCP. Hence, 6C. (As for responder's bidding 2NT, he wants to give a false impression of strength. He knows they have a huge club fit if opener is 4-1-4-4 or 4-4-1-4 He also knows his side has almost no defense against the red suits if partner has a weak 2 spade bid. Either way, he'd like to keep the opponents out of the auction if possible.)

Defense Against the Schizoid 2D, 2H

In introducing the 2D and 2H bids, I noted that they might be considered highly un-usual methods by some directors, who might decide to ban or restrict them. Actually, there is a simple common sense defense to these methods. It can be printed on an index card and explained in a couple of minutes.

In explaining the defense, the first point to be made is that each bid has a definite anchor suit. The 2D bid will always show hearts. The 2H bid will always show spades. Opener will always have 4 of the anchor suit in a very good hand or 6 of the anchor suit in a weak hand. In either case, it is very unlikely that that the opponents are going to want to play in that suit. This actually gives them an extra bid with which to compete effectively.

They can use a cue bid of the anchor suit for a classic takeout double (showing shortness in the anchor suit and good support for the other suits). Double can now be used to show any nondescript hand with minimum (12–15 HCP) opening values. All other bids are natural. Overcalls in any suit other than the anchor are exactly what they would be over a normal weak 2H or 2S bid. A direct 2NT overcall will show the usual 15–18 HCP. A double followed by a NT bid can show a hand too big for a 2NT bid.

If opponents are given the following outline, there should be no way anyone can possibly claim that that these methods place an undue burden on them.

Over 2D:

Double = 12–15 HCP, balanced or semi-balanced

2H = takeout double, short in hearts

2S, 3C, 3D = natural overcall

2NT = 15–18 HCP

Double, then 2NT or 3NT = 18–19+HCP

Double, then bid in suit that could have been shown by simple overcall = 18-19+ HCP

Jump overcalls = optional (Leaping Michaels ?)

Over 2H:

Double = 12–15 HCP, balanced or semi-balanced

2S = takeout double, short in spades

3C, 3D, 3H = natural overcall

2NT = 15–18 HCP

Double, then 3NT = 18–19+ HCP

Double, then bid in suit that could have been shown by simple overcall = 18–19+ HCP

Jump overcalls = optional (Leaping Michaels ?)

The Two-Spade Opening Bid
(Used to describe all good preempts)

The 2S bid is now not needed as a standard weak 2 bid. It becomes available for a special purpose—describing various good or solid preemptive opening bids. This, in turn, allows us to give much more definition to 3-level preempts. All opening 3 bids are limited to 1 top honor at most. Separating good and bad to-mediocre preempts allows responder to pass or bid games with a fair degree of certainty rather than merely guessing.

The 2S bid shows one of the following hands:

- Any 7-card suit with 2 of the 3 top honors (AKxxxxx, AQxxxxx, or KQxxxxx)
- A 7-card minor suit with all 3 top honors (AKQxxxx).This is essentially a gambling 3NT, but played from the right side.

After a 2S opening, responder can do the following:

- Place the contract if he's sure of the suit or knows that the suit will run no matter what it is.
- Bid 2NT,*the asking bid (which incidentally right-sides any eventual NT contracts).
    o   With only 2 of the 3 top honors, opener bids 3 of his suit.
    o   With AKQxxxx, opener bids 3NT, with the contract being played from the correct side (if responder has two open suits, he can bid 4C, asking partner to correct if that isn't the correct suit).
    With game-forcing values, responder can bid 4H to ask for a singleton or 4S to ask opener to transfer into 5 of his minor (4 NT = transfer to 5C, 5C = transfer to 5D).
- Jump directly to 4H or 4S (to play, with a strong hand and a very good 6+(7 would be better) card suit.

Important Notes

In third seat (or fourth), there may be no point in differentiating between a good and bad preempt. I would recommend using 2S only for the solid suits in third and fourth seats, with standard preempts. The main emphasis in those seats should be buying the contract and/or disrupting the opponents' ability to bid comfortably. The only exception might be a case where the passed hand has 10–11 scattered points and might be able to bid 3NT if he knows dummy will provide a solid 7-card suit. The 2S bid would allow him to do that and would also right-side the contract.

I would also recommend a partnership agreement that a passed hand is not allowed to raise a third-seat non-vulnerable preempt. This will allow for "creativity" on the part of the third-seat bidder. Creativity (read temporary insanity) may include making an offbeat 3-bid with a bad opening hand or suggesting an opening lead with an audacious AQxxx and out in a minor.

After a 2S opening, neither regular Blackwood nor RKC Blackwood is necessary. Opener cannot have an opening hand, so only five holdings are possible. He may hold a minor suit with AKQxxxx and no side ace or king. (With solid minor and a side card, he would open 1D or 2C. With a solid 7-card major, opener would open 1H, 1S, 4H or 4S rather than opening 2S.)

After opener's 3NT rebid, which shows this hand, responder can simply place the contract or bid 4C (pass or correct to 4D) with 2 open suits. Since the solid suit can only be a minor, responder can use 4H, 4S, or 4NT (opposite minor) rebid over 3NT to ask opener to show no control (1 step), second round control (2 steps), or first round control (3 steps) in that suit. If he simply wants to play 4H or 4S, he has to bid it directly over 2S.

If opener bids 2S and rebids 3C, 3D, 3H, or 3S in response to 2NT, he can only have:

- KQxxxxx with no side ace
- KQxxxxx with a side ace
- AQxxxxx with no side ace
- AKxxxxx with no side ace (any stronger hand would be a 1-bid)

Since no-0 reply to an ace-asking bid is possible, the following sequences can replace Blackwood or RKB after a 2S opener and a suit rebid. After a rebid of 3C,3D,3H, or 3S, the cheapest suit should ask suit description. A bid of 3NT would have to be natural, so 4C would be the asking bid over 3S (or 3S could remain natural, with 4C used over either minor).

The answers would be :

- First step = KQxxxxx with no side ace (weakest possible holding)
- Second step = AQxxxxx with no side ace
- Third step = AKxxxxx with no side ace
- Fourth step = KQxxxxxwith a side ace (one could also use all bids from the-fourth step on to show this hand with a specific ace if desired.)

Partnerships may alter the responses to fit their taste. A second request for information is also possible. The second cheapest bid could ask for a singleton if responder is not interested in aces. Another possible scheme would be to always use 4C as the suit-quality asking bid, with all new suit bids natural or singleton-asking. If a major is used as an asking bid, it could be agreed that a rebid of that major at the 4 level is natural and to play. Also, a jump to 4 of a major over 3C or 3D and a jump to 4S over 3H should be to play. In fact, any bid of 4H or 4S that cannot be an asking bid should be to play. These ideas are just suggestions, with partnerships encouraged to use any they happen to like. Here are some examples of the Sartor 2S bid:

A. ♠ xx   ♠Kxx   2S   2NT
   ♥ KQ109xxx   ♥Ax   3H   3NT
   ♦Qxx   ♦Kxxx   P
   ♣ x   ♣Axxx

B. ♠ x   ♠ QJxx   2S   2NT
   ♥ Jx   ♥ Kx   3NT (AKQxxxx)   P
   ♦ xxx   ♦ AQxxxx
   ♣ AKQxxxx   ♣ x

C. ♠ AKxxxxx   ♠ Qxx   2S   2NT
   ♥ Q   ♥ xxxxx   3S   4D (asks singleton)
   ♦ xxx   ♦ A   4H   6S
   ♣ xx   ♣ AKxx

D. ♠ xxx   ♠ AQ   2S   2NT
   ♥   ♥xxxx   3NT (AKQxxxx)   4H (asking)
   ♦ AKQxxxx   ♦xx   5C (first round control- 7D
   ♣ xxx   ♣ AKQxx   must be a void)

E. ♠ AQxxxxx   ♠ x   2S   4H (I know my suit
   ♥ x   ♥ AKQxxxxx   is better than yours.)
   ♦ Jxxx   ♦ Q
   ♣ x   ♣ Axx

F. ♠ xx   ♠ QJxx   2S   2NT
   ♥ KQJxxxx   ♥ x
   ♦   ♦ J10xxx
   ♣ Qxxx   ♣ KJx   3S   P

Alternate Two-Level Bids

As noted earlier, the original set of 2-level bids was not likely to raise the ire of many ACBL directors. Should it be necessary to abandon the fun-zone scheme in order to satisfy official objections, here is,an alternative: 2 hearts and 2 spades become standard weak 2 bids, with whatever accompanying conventions a partnership may prefer. The 2D bid handles all 4-4-4-1 hands with 16 or more HCP.

The responses to 2D are relatively simple. The cheapest bid in a major is non-forcing. It may even be a 3-card suit, if responder has a weak hand and 4-3-3-3 distribution. Opener passes if it is one of his suits or makes the cheapest rebid if opener has bid his singleton. Responder will usually have a second place to play and will either pass or bid his other suit. Opener needs a very good hand (19+ HCP) to raise responder's 2H or 2S bid to the 3 level and needs an absolute monster to raise him to game. He needs to remember he may have forced responder to bid with a complete Yarborough.

The only other weak response to 2D is 3C. This necessarily shows both minors, since responder would bid 2H or 2S if he held clubs or diamonds and a major.

With decent values and/or a single long suit, responder bids 2NT. Opener then bids his singleton. He bids 3C, 3D, 3H, or 3S with 16–19 HCP. Responder can either invite game (if there is room at the 3 level) or just jump to game. A raise of the singleton is natural, showing at least a good 6-card suit.

With 20+ HCP, things get a little more interesting. A simple jump to 4C, 4D, 4H, or 4S is the easiest way to show the hand, but it is very space-consuming. For those who enjoy making things complicated, a rebid of 3NT can be used for any 20+ hand, allowing each partner to bid suits up the line in order to find a fit at the 4 level. This would allow for more leisurely slam investigation. I'm sure any readers who have gotten this far without having their brains explode are perfectly capable of working out their own extensions and variations of this bidding scheme.

Using this simplified scheme also eliminates the 2S bid's ability to differentiate between bad, good, and solid preemptive bids. Pairs will simply use whatever preempting style they are comfortable with. The next section describes the type of 3-level preempts that are compatible with the fun zone bidding scheme.

Three-Level Preempts

Because the 2S opening bid covers all good preemptive bids (at least all of those in first or second seat), 3-level bids are by definition limited to no more than one top honor. That does not mean they are ridiculously weak. In first or second seat, I promise a suit that I would not be ashamed to have led if my partner is on opening lead. If the lead of an unsupported king would be embarrassing, I'd rather pass. Sitting non-vulnerable in third seat, I'd rather bid a frivolous 3X with AQ10xx than with a monstrosity like J9xxxxx. With a terrible 7-card major, a 2D or 2H bid might be a better choice if you can't bring yourself to pass.

A typical first or second seat preempt will look something like:

AJ9xxxx   KJ10xxxx   K109xxxx   QJ10xxxx

Third seat preempts (especially non-vulnerable) may be more creative, as earlier noted. A 6-card lead-directing bids is certainly reasonable, and I have been known to throw in an occasional 5-card preempt when I thought it was the right thing to do. It helps if you have an ironclad agreement that your partner is not allowed to sacrifice based on your third-seat preempt.

Whatever style of preempts you settle on, knowing that you will need a fairly substantial fit if you plan to run the preemptor's suit in 3NT or bid a close game may improve your percentage of correct guesses in close bidding decisions.

Four-Level Preempts

As a matter of personal preference, I would play the Namyats 4C and 4D to show very good 4H and 4S openers, with an opening 4H or 4S showing less slam potential. If it is decided to use Namyats, I would recommend the following set of responses and continuations:

- Accepting the transfer is a sign-off.
- Bidding the intervening suit is a relay to 4 of opener's major and may have two possible purposes:
  - Responder may want opener to play the contract (he may not have any tenaces to protect or he may feel his partner is a better declarer than he is).
  - Responder may want to make a slam try after opener bids his major. Some may use simple cue bids or ace-asking bids for that purpose. I would suggest using the cheapest bid as an asking bid, with opener showing keycards immediately via the "Little Bit West of Texas" responses discussed earlier. Thus 4S would ask over 4H and 4NT would ask over 4S. Since opener has suggested a very good hand with his Namyats opening, the steps could be:
  - first step = 1 KC + the Q of trump;
  - second step = 2 KC, no Q;
  - third step = 2KC + the Q ;
  - fourth step =3KC, no Q; etc.

Enterprising pairs might wish to combine the relay idea with direct bids above the trump suit, getting the benefits of each scheme.

SECTION 4

Defense, Carding, Appendices

CHAPTER 12

Defense

There obviously is no official California Club defense system. I'll merely use this section to mention a few pet ideas and conventions. It will be mercifully brief.

Transfer Advances of Overcalls

A serendipitous benefit to using the Sartor 2/1 response scheme to major suit opening bids is that it gives us a ready-made system for advancing overcalls of 1H or 1S. We can use transfer advances for a variety of hands that are difficult to handle in standard methods.

The scheme does force us to make one fairly major trade-off. Advancer can no longer make a natural response of 1NT, which in some cases may be our best contract. In exchange, however, we gain the ability to bid many otherwise unbiddable hands. We also can make lead-directing raises of opener's suit, and show both invitational and forcing values by means of natural and transfer raises. The bids are simple and logical, and they put very little strain on the memory.

Transfers are especially useful when advancer has a long suit and a weak hand. He is able to improve the contract without having the auction rise to a dangerous level. Here is an example from actual play:

```
LHO-1C          Partner-1S          RHO-Pass
You:   ♠A   ♥J1098xx   ♦xxx   ♣xxx
```

You don't have to be a soothsayer to predict that a 2H contract will be much better than 1S.(Your hearts will usually be useless in spades, but should take several tricks in hearts.) Unfortunately, a standard 2H response will mislead partner and get you too high. (It will also cause your partner to have serious questions about your judgment and/or your intelligence.) Transfer advances solve the problem. You make a transfer advance of 2D and pass partner's 2H bid. The transfer should almost always be accepted, unless he has a very good suit of his own.

With a different hand—♠ Jxx♥AKx♦ xxxxx♣ xx—you could use the transfer into hearts and then pull it to 2S. This could be a raise with heart values and would get partner off to a good lead if you wound up on defense. A pull to 3S could be the same hand with greater values. A cue bid of opener's suit could still show a limit raise +. As a side issue, a partnership will have to decide what constitutes a transfer to hearts when opener's suit would be the normal transfer bid. If opener had bid 1D, would 2D by you be a transfer or a cue bid? My preference is to keep it simple and always have advances be transfers to the next suit. A transfer cue bid into opener'ssuit can serve as the substitute for a standard cue bid to show a limit raise +.

With at least near-opening values, good support, and a side suit that will provide a source of tricks, fit-showing jumps may be a useful adjunct to our scheme. An alternative would be to use jumps in new suits as mini-splinters.

Jump Overcalls

It seems to be taken for granted in modern bridge thinking that weak jump overcalls are appropriate in any situation and at any vulnerability. I beg to differ. I can think of several adjectives to describe what I think of the use of weak jump overcalls when vulnerable versus non-vulnerable opponents. The most diplomatic of these is *foolhardy*. A less polite term would be *stupid*.

If a pair were to double the opponent's vulnerable weak jump overcall whenever their side holds better than half the points in the deck and seems to hold 4 or 5 of the enemies' trumps, I think they would show a large profit over time.

When the vulnerability is unfavorable, the scoring mathematics alone make the weak jump overcall a foolish gamble. If our side has enough points to make 8 or 9 tricks on offense, we usually have enough to inflict a 1-trick set on the opponents. Plus 200 gives us a better score than all the others making a part score in our direction. Even if we occasionally misjudge the situation, we'll probably still wind up getting 3 tops for every bottom we receive. Of course, at IMPs we may have to let them off the hook a little more often.

The scoring advantage for doubling continues all the way up the line. When we have enough for game, we are very likely to be able to set them 2 for 500. If they talk us out of a non-vulnerable slam, plus 1,100 is often available.

This unsolicited tirade is all a way of providing a rationale for my own slightly out-of-the-mainstream approach to this area of defensive bidding. I use weak jump overcalls, but not when vulnerable against a non-vulnerable foe. In that situation I use intermediate jump overcalls. I define these as hands with 12–16 HCP and a good 6-card suit. These bids are very descriptive and are often helpful in getting to game when partner might otherwise hold back with mediocre trump support. They also identify a source of running tricks at NT.

But the constructive aspects of intermediate jumps are not their most valuable feature. Their biggest virtue is quite simple: they force me not to do anything stupid when holding a weak hand and a 6-card suit, vulnerable, when a non-vulnerable opponent opens in front of me. Even if I had the inclination to put my head on the chopping block with a silly weak jump bid, my partnership agreements prevent me from doing anything idiotic. They have probably saved me thousands of points over the years.

When both sides are vulnerable, my point requirements are lower (usually 8–12 HCP), but I still require a good suit. Of course, with QJ109xxxx and 3-4 HCP, I make the same jump everyone else will probably make. When non-vulnerable, my weak jumps are pretty much like everyone else's.

The philosophy I try to follow is simple: avoid doing anything stupid. I just have an aversion to unnecessary self-induced disasters.

Leads and Carding

Again, there is no official California Club system of leads and carding. The reader is encouraged to use whatever methods he finds most effective. Among my personal lead preferences are the following:

- Rusinow honor leads (lower of two touching honors) except in suits freely bid by partner
- leads of the 10 or 9 from internal sequences (KJ10, K109, Q109)
- third and fifth best leads vs. suits
- fourth best leads vs. no trump

Carding

Touching suit discards the discard of:
- 2,3,4 = shows strength in a lower touching suit
- 5,6,7 = shows strength in the suit discarded,
- 8,9,10 = shows strength in a higher touching suit

- Or

- **Upside down attitude signals** (low card encourages)

Defense against 1NT

- double = club or diamond one-suiter or both majors (2H rebid)
- 2C = clubs and a higher suit
- 2D = diamonds and a major
- 2H = natural
- 2S = natural

Defense Against 2H, 2S

- double= takeout
- overcalls = natural
- cue bid (3H or 3S) = asks for 3NT with stopper—often long-running minor
- 4C = Leaping Michaels (5+clubs, 5+card major)
- 4D = Leaping Michaels (5+diamonds, 5+ card major)

APPENDIX A

Alternate 1D-2C Bidding Schemes

As I mentioned during the discussion of the "1D with muscles" continuations, the 1D - 2C sequence does present some special challenges. Ideally, you would like to show the big 17-20 HCP hand with a simple reverse to 2H or 2S. This would leave lots of room for slam exploration. Unfortunately, it also prevents a 1D opener with an ordinary 11-16 HCP hand from conveniently showing a 4-card major. That opener is forced to make a "waiting" 2D bid and then show his major at the 3 level if he has one. If responder bids 2H or 2S over a 2D, that doesn't really solve his problem. If you recall, that may just be a feature rather than a real 4-card suit. It requires some special agreements to determine if a 4-4 fit exists if opener raises the suit to 3H or 3S. Of course, you could make responder's immediate jump to 3H or 3S over 2D show a real 4-card suit, but that also takes up space. I will present two conceivable alternatives to our default scheme here, but I can't honestly suggest that they are improvements. They may, however, suggest lines for further experimentation for those dissatisfied with my system choice.

Here is just one possible scheme:

Scheme A – (where a second bid of 2H or 2S shows 17-20 HCP)

Opener	Responder
1D	2C
2D (waiting)	
	2H or 2S = (GF) natural, 4+ card suit .*or* a feature (Axx, Kxx,
Then:	etc.)- 2nd bid of suit shows 4
Cheapest	
X-2nd waitng bid	**2NT** = 11–12 HCP, invitational
over 2H or 2S	**3NT** = 13–16 HCP, no slam interest
to see if	**3C** = 11–12 HCP,6+ clubs, invitational
responder	3D, 3H, 3S = 13+ HCP, real 4-card suit,
has 4	
1D	2C

2H or 2S= 17–20 HCP, 5+ diamonds, 4-card major ("1D with muscles")
3D=6+ diamonds, 15–16 HCP, semi-solid suit

1D	**3C** = semi-preemptive, 6–9 HCP, 7+ or 6 very solid clubs

Scheme B- where a 2nd bid of 2H or 2S by opener could be either "normal" or a strong reverse

Opener	Responder
1D	2C
2D (waiting- 11-16 HCP)	**2H/2S**-,feature or suit / 2NT- 11-12 HCP
2H or 2S = natural,	**3H, 3S** = 11-12+ HCP, real 4-card suit,
11-16 HCP or 17-20 HCP	**4H,4S** =13+ HCP no singleton
	jump shift to 3S, 4H-singleton, 4 trump, 13+HCP

Scheme B-(continued) when opener has big 17-20 HCP hand

Opener	*Responder*
1D	2C

2H or 2S = natural,	**3H, 3S** = 11-12+ HCP, real 4-card suit,
11-16 HCP, or 17-20 HCP	
jump shift to 3S or 4H- singleton, 17+HCP	

1D	2C
2H or 2S = natural,	**2NT**= 11-12+ HCP
11-16 HCP, or 17-20 HCP	
jump shift to 3S or 4H-singleton, 17+HCP	
4C=3 or 4 clubs, 17+ HCP, singleton or void in other major	
4D=5-4-2-2 distribution, 17+ HCP	

Similar 4-level bids would be needed if responder were to raise clubs or diamonds. On the whole, it seems like these alternate schemes are more complicated than simply using a jump rebid of 3H or 3S after a 1D – 2C auction to show the "1D with muscles hand". Add to that the fact that "normal"1D openers are far more common than big reverses and that the combination of the big 1D facing a 2C response will only occur occasionally, and I think it makes a lot of sense to stick to our original choice as the default treatment for the system.

APPENDIX B

An Alternative to Two-way Raises to 4 of a Major

In our system's current version, a raise of 1 spade to 4 spades or 1 heart to 4 hearts has two possible meanings. It may show a fairly weak distributional raise with 5 or more trumps, as in Standard American. It may also show a fairly balanced 13–16 HCP hand that, in responder's judgment, has little prospect for slam opposite a limited opening bid. This is fine in the vast majority of cases. Strong players'estimations of slam potential are usually pretty accurate. Opener will rarely be tempted to disturb the game contract.

There is, however, one case that puts opener in an awkward situation. He may hold a very distributional hand (usually a 2-suiter) that only requires a couple of aces from responder to make slam. At the same time, the hand may go down at the 5 level if the opener gets adventurous and finds that responder holds an aceless distributional raise. Here is an example:

Opener:		♠ KQ10xxx	♥ x	♦ AKxxx	♣ x
Responder:	A.	♠ AJxx	♥ Axx	♦ Qx	♣ Qxxx
	B.	♠ 10xxxx	♥ Kxx	♦ x	♣ Kxxx

Responder may raise 1S to 4S with either hand using our system treatment.

Opposite hand A, 6S is a big favorite. Opposite hand B, opener will very likely go down at 5S, losing an almost certain game in the process. Is there a way to avoid this problem?

Here is my suggested solution: we can separate the two meanings by making use of the rarely used direct response of 3NT for the major-suit raise with the minimum opening hand. If the responder really wants to suggest 3NT as a final contract, he can bid a forcing 1NT and then bid 3NT after opener's rebid instead. After the 3NT balanced raise, opener will probably bid the major suit game 95 percent of the time. However, on the rare occasion when all he needs are a couple of aces to make a slam, he can bid 4C as Gerber (aces only, simple keycard, Texas, or 1430, depending on partnership preference).

At this point, I need to make an additional suggestion that will complicate matters slightly. This scheme works very well for spades, but not quite as well for hearts. This is simply because there is less room for responder to answer to 4C without going past game in hearts. My slight additional tweak is to switch the meanings of a 3S and a 3NT response to a 1H opening. Make 3S the balanced raise to 4H and make 3NT a splinter in spades. This lets opener use 3NT to ask for aces or keycards, giving us one extra answer before we go past 4H.

To clarify, this would be the scheme:

1♠—3NT=13-16 raise to 4♠   1♥—3♠=13-16 raise to 4♥
    [4♣ Gerber/4♠ to play]   [3♠ Gerber/4♥ to play]
    direct 4♣,4♦,4♥—splinters   3NT (♠),4♣,4♦—splinters
    direct 4♠—weak, 5+ ♠   direct 4♥—weak 5+ ♥

The reason for the adjustment in the heart scheme is that it allows opener to ask for keycards even if an answer showing 2 keycards would not be sufficient to bid slam. Let's say a pair chooses a very simple Gerber response scheme:

- firststep—0 keycards
- second step—1 keycard
- third step—2 keycards
- fourth step—3 keycards

If the 3NT raise and the 4C Gerber ask were used, a 2 key-card answer would be 4S, forcing opener to the 5 level. If opener needed 3 keycards to bid the slam, he could sign off at 5H, but that might be a little precarious. Using the tweaked scheme, a 2 key-card answer would be 4H, and opener could pass at a safer level.

If the answer scheme were 0314 or 1430, the same problem would be present. An answer showing 2 keycards (with or without the queen of trump) would always force the auction to the 5 level. Of course, one could say that opener has no business asking if he can't bid the slam opposite 2 keycards, and that may be true. But the switch of the 3S and 3NT responses is a practical way to avoid getting too high when responder has an inconvenient number of keycards.

APPENDIX C

The Kaplan Inversion

One adjustment that could add to the efficiency of our Sartor 2/1 response setup is the addition of the Kaplan Inversion to a 1H opening bid. This could be done without great disturbance to the rest of the structure. (Of course, since the ACBL restricts its use for many events, it might only be useful for certain major team competitions or at clubs with laisse faire attitudes toward conventions.)

This treatment simply involves switching the meanings of the 1S and 1NT responses to a 1H opening bid. In the original version, responder's first bid of 1S shows 0-4 spades. With 5 or more spades, he usually responds 1NT (there are a couple of other bids he may make with strong hands). Both responses are forcing for one round. Opener's 1NT rebid shows a 4-card spade suit. This essentially creates a modified version of the Flannery convention (4 spades/5 hearts). That is great for finding a 4/4 spade fit, but it severely limits the ability to stop in 1NT.

When opener has 5-3-3-2 distribution, he has a rebid problem. He is forced to bid a 3-card minor, just as in the commonly used forcing 1NT response to a major. This negates one of the inversion's major advantages: the ability to stop in 1NT with a minimum semi-balanced opener. Having the 1NT response guarantee at least 5 spades does, however, make it easier to find 5-3 spade fits. This is especially beneficial when responder holds a bare minimum standard 1S response in a 1H-1S auction.

Looking at the pluses and minuses of the original idea, though, I think the ability to rebid 1NT on more hands is more important than the chance to immediately find a 4/4 spade fit. I would therefore propose a slightly modified version of the convention.

In my version, the **1S response** to 1H is a kind of multipurpose waiting bid. It usually, but not always, **shows either 0-3 or 6+spades**. The "usually" covers a few hands that might present rebid problems if responder were to bid 1NT (see below). The **1NT response shows exactly 4 or 5 spades**.

After a 1H-1S sequence, my version gives opener the ability to rebid 1NT with many holdings with which a player using an ordinary forcing NT would have to bid a 3-card minor. A minor suit rebid therefore almost always guarantees at least 4-card suit, and often shows 5. Whenever opener has a 2-suited hand, he can simply bid as if he were using the basic continuation scheme, without the inversion. A bid of 2C or 2D would tend to deny more than normal opening strength. A bid and rebid of a second suit would show 5-5+ distribution. An immediate jump to 3C or 3D would show a maximum (15-16 HCP) 2-suiter. All of the systemic raises would still apply.

Of course, no method is perfect. In this scheme, responder will occasionally have a weak hand with 4 spades. He may choose to bid 1S (planning to pass 1NT) simply to avoid rebid problems that might occur if he bids 1NT. If opener also has 4 spades and rebids 1NT, a 4/4 spade fit may occasionally be missed. However, playing in 1NT in that case may not be the end of the world.

A secondary benefit of the 1S response is the ability to use it to show both invitational and game-forcing 3-card heart raises at a low level. The logic behind this is fairly simple. In this system, weak heart raises of any length are shown by transferring to 2H via a 2D bid. A constructive 2H bid covers hands in the 8–10 HCP range. Invitational and game-forcing 4-card heart raises are shown by a 2S bid or a 3-way jump shift. This leaves only 3-card raises with 11+ HCP needing a way to describe them.

As usual, I have a "brilliant" solution. I call it the "impossible 1S response." When responder replies 1S to a 1H opening, he is seemingly denying having a heart raise. If his first rebid is then an unlikely 2H or 3H, that should grab opener's attention. I choose to give this sequence a very specific meaning. The cheapest heart bid should show an invitational 3-card raise. The result of this is that a 1H-1S-1NT-2H sequence can show a balanced 3-card limit raise at the 2 level. A jump in hearts should show a game-forcing 3-card raise. So 1H-1S-1NT-3H shows that type of hand.(See chart on page 190.)

Of course, opener will not always rebid 1NT. If he bids 2C or 2D, showing 5-4 or 5-5 distribution, then 2H would simply be a weak sign-off in opener's first suit. Opener may also rebid 2H. After any of these bids, 3H would become the 11–12 HCP hand, and a jump to 4H would show the forcing hand. That loses the low-level advantage we get if the rebid is 1NT, but it just puts us in the same position as if the auction had gone 1H-4H—possibly a balanced opening hand. (see page 33 or Appendix B)

1H-1NT

Responder should use the 1NT response with most hands with either a 4-card or 5-card spade suit, but the bid requires good judgment. Just as with the 1S response, responder must consider how he will handle opener's rebid. If there is a good chance opener's next bid will put him in an untenable position, he may want to exercise an option available to those playing a strong club system but not available to standard bidders: he may want to pass 1H! With a weak responding hand opposite a limited opening bid, there is very little risk of missing a game. I'll discuss the cases when this may be the best option later. The situation will not occur often, but an occasional strategic pass may enable you to avoid a disastrous auction.

The basic idea is that a 1NT responder should either have enough points to make an invitational second bid or have 2-card heart support, so he can stop at 2H over opener's 2C or 2D rebid when he is weak. Of course, if responder has a clear heart raise and no reason to introduce spades, the whole discussion is moot. Responder simply makes one of the immediate raises discussed above.

Continuations After 1H-1S-1NT

After the auction begins 1H-1S-1NT, responder should pass most semi-balanced weakish hands, hoping that 1NT will score better than any other likely partscore contract. He will usually pass 2H if opener rebids a 6-card heart suit. He may bid a non-forcing 2S, showing 6+ spades and a weakish (6–9 HCP) hand.

Though we certainly want to make sure we land in a good spot when responder is weak, the most important goal of our continuation scheme should be making sure responder is able to accurately describe invitational and game-forcing hands. When the first response is 1S, this may often involve just raising opener's 1NT rebid to 2NT or 3NT. However, there are other options. (See continuation chart below.)

Assume opener rebids 1NT. Most of the continuations are pretty straightforward. They are highlighted in boldface black in the chart below. A few, however, are highlighted in italics. These represent personal brainstorms such as the 3-card heart raises that I discussed earlier, or the game-forcing 2D, which is only one possible use for that bid. Here are some of the basic auctions in chart form:

1H	1S
1NT	**2C** (natural, weak, 6+ clubs—to play)
	2D (**artificial**, **game-forcing**, possible slam or minor suit game interest—allows for slow exploration by both partners)
	2H (*natural, 3-card raise, 11–12 HCP*)
	2S (natural, weak, 6+ spades, 6–9 HCP)
	2NT (natural, invitational, 10–12 HCP)
	3C (natural, invitational, 6+clubs, 10–12 HCP)
	3D (natural, invitational, 6+ diamonds, 11–12 HCP)
	3H (*natural, forcing, 3 card heart - raise, 13+HCP*)
	3S (natural, invitational, 6+ spades, 10–12 HCP)

1H	1S
2C or **2D**	**Pass**—3+ card support, often 0-1 hearts, weak
	2H (likely only 2 hearts) weak, to play
	2S (natural, weak, 6+ spades)
	2NT (natural, invitational, 10–12 HCP, stoppers in other suits)
	Raise to 3C or 3D (natural, invitational)
	3C as new suit (6–7+ clubs, to play)
	3H (*invitational 3-card heart raise, 11–12 HCP*) *2H now weak*
	3S (invitational, good 6+-card spade suit) (with game-forcing hand and 6+ spades you jump shift to 2NT at your first turn)

If opener's rebid is 2H, responder's 2S, 2NT, 3C, 3H, and 3S bids would be the same as those used after 2C or 2D.

Let's now look at the other side of the inversion. When the first response to 1H is 1NT, our continuations are geared toward clarifying responder's exact strength and spade length whenever opener has at least 3 spades and some interest in that suit as a possible trump suit. Without that interest, opener's second and third bids are pretty standard—simply describing his own distribution.

Several of opener's rebid options are easy. With 4 spades, he bids 2S or 3S, knowing he has an 8-or 9-card trump fit. With 0-2 spades and a minimum opener, he can rebid a natural 2D or 2H. He can also bid **2C**, but that bid **may or may not show a real club suit**. That bid is needed for a **special purpose**, which we'll discuss in a moment. With a maximum (15–16 HCP) and good distribution and suit quality, he may jump to 3C, 3D, or 3H. Some may want to treat a 2NT bid as showing 5 hearts and 4 spades with a maximum. Others will prefer that bid to just show an opening NT with 5 hearts.

The 2C Asking Bid

Hands with 3 spades require special treatment. We need a way to determine responder's strength and exact length in spades. We also need a sensible rebid for an opener with 5 hearts and 4 or 5 clubs. As usual, I have come up with another of my fiendishly clever solutions for this problem. The answer is to use 2C as an artificial asking bid and to use responder's 2D reply as an artificial relay to 2H.

This relay sequence accomplishes two things. It allows responder to sign off in 2H when all he has is a weak hand with a faint hope of finding a 4-4 spade fit before settling for a 2H contract. More importantly, it also allows him to pull out of 2H to show an invitational hand with 5 spades (2S) or 4 spades (2NT). With a game-forcing hand, responder just bypasses 2D and bids 2S (with 5 spades) or 2NT (with 4) directly in response to the 2C inquiry.

When opener has a secondary club suit and no real interest in spades, responder's replies will allow the bidding to stop at 2H, 2S, or 2NT, or proceed to game. Opener will have a good idea of the proper final contract. Responder really doesn't need to know what kind of hand opener has unless he plans to explore for a club game or slam. The following chart will (I hope) help make all this a little clearer.

1H-1NT Rebids and Continuations

1H	1NT (4 or 5 spades)
2C (*either 4 clubs or asking bid*)	**2D** *relay to 2H*
2H	P—weak, to play
	2S—invitational, 5 spades
	2NT—invitational, 4 spades
1H	1NT (4 or 5 spades)
2C (*either 4 clubs or asking bid*)	*No 2D Relay*
	2H game-forcing, only 4 spades (could use 2NT instead for consistency)
	2S game-forcing, 5 spades

By bypassing the 2D relay, responder indicates a game-forcing hand. Either partner may then probe for the best game or explore slam possibilities by bidding new suits at the 3 level. If one of the minor suits seems to be a weakness, they may wind up avoiding a poor 3NT and playing in a 5-2 major fit or in 5C or 5D.

How the Kaplan Inversion Works with Other Game-Forcing Heart Raises

As discussed earlier, one part of our response scheme to one heart involves using the jump shift to 2NT for game-forcing hands (even some with slam potential) with good 6+ card spade suits. That bid already covers slammish spade hands with 17+ HCP - traditional strong jump shifts (see pages 49-50). We can add similar spade hands in the 12–16 HCP range to the existing structure with almost no memory burden. This means that the Kaplan 1NT response will rarely be used for a strong hand with a 6-card spade suit.(A good hand with a weak suit might be treated as if it were only the equivalent of a five-card suit on occasion.)The following chart will make it clearer (already existing bids are in black, and our new additions are in italics):

Opener		Responder
1H		**2NT** = strong (17–18+) jump shift in spades
	OR	mini-splinter (9–11 HCP, 4+ hearts)
	OR	maxi-splinter (15+HCP, 4+ hearts)
We will add:	OR	*intermediate game-forcing jump shift in spades* *(6+ spades, 12–16 HCP)*

Opener	Responder
1H	**2NT** =4-way jump shift
3C =*asking*	**3D = 6+ spades, 12-16 HCP**
	3H = mini-splinter (4+ hearts, 0-1 spades)
	3S, 3NT, 4C, 4D= all show strong jump shift in spades (off suits can show side features)
	4H=maxi-splinter (4+ hearts, 0-1 spades, 15+HCP)

As you can see, the chart shows several rebids that indicate that responder has the strong jump shift. The suggested specific meanings were originally discussed on pages 34-36. Following that scheme, most 3-level new suit bids showed the strong (17+) jump shift and side controls. The addition of the 12–16 HCP hand to the structure alters those bids slightly. It forces the side controls to be shown at the 4 level in some cases. This should not cause any major problems. The rebids showing the mini-splinter and maxi-splinter remain the same.

Creative players can probably come up with other variations on the basic multi-meaning jump-shift structure that I have proposed. One interesting area for exploration might be to do some computer simulations to determine whether I have

chosen the best ranges for the various splinter bids. Perhaps lowering the strength requirements for each bid by one HCP (8–10, 11–13, and 14+)might increase the frequency
and/or effectiveness of their use. Any math mavens who happen to read this are invited
to check out that hypothesis and let me know.

APPENDIX D

Alternate Major Structure
(For Use When Some of the More Exotic System Bids Cannot Be Used)

Major suit openings (1H/1S) show 11–16 HCP (you should avoid opening 11-point 5-3-3-2 hands; 11-12 HCP hands are optional openings). Responder may pass with up to 7–8 HCP and no prospect of game or improving the contract.

Types of Raises

Raises Using the Forcing NT

1NT (or 1S response to 1H, if playing that convention) is forcing. Responder may have the following:

- a weak (4–7 HCP) raise of opener's major
- a balanced hand with 10–11+/12 HCP (responder rebids 2NT next)
- a balanced hand with 12+/13–15 HCP (responder rebids 3NT next)
- a long suit with less than 10 HCP

Opener's bids after 1S–1NT:

- 2C = default bid (no 4-card heart suit, good 4/5+ diamond suit, or 6-card major; may be short)
- 2D =good 4-card or 5-card suit
- 2H = 4+ card suit
- 2S = 6+ card suit
- 3C/3D/3H = 15–16 HCP, 5/5+ in bid suits
- 3S = 15–16 HCP, very good 6+ card suit

Opener's bids after 1H-1NT:

- identical in all lower suits (2C,2D,3C,3D)
- 2H/3H identical to 2S/3S above
- 2NT = natural, 15–16 HCP (with minimum, would bid 2C or 2D)

Raises of Opener's Suit via a New Suit

A 2-level response in new suit is not game-forcing. The auction may stop at 2NT or 3-level if both partners are minimum (i. e. 1S-2C-2H-2NT-P /1H-2D-2NT-P /1H-2C-2D-2H-3H-P). Two of a new suit followed by a non-jump raise of opener's suit is invitational.

Weak (4–7 HCP) Raises

Responder bids 1NT (forcing), then 2 of opener's suit. Opener should almost never consider a game try after this sequence. The same sequence may also be used with a slightly better hand but with only 2 trump; that might be seeking a better spot—i. e., a hand with 2 spades and a 4-card heart suit, hoping for a fit in the second suit. Game is still unlikely, and the raise to 2 of opener's suit is almost always passed

Constructive Direct Single Raise (8–10 HCP)

After 1S-2S or 1H-2H, opener may try for game with either a long (help needed) suit or a short suit game try.

Long Suit Game Try by Opener (LSGT)

The cheapest bid is a relay—1H-2H-2S** or 1S-2S-2NT.** This tells responder to make the next cheapest bid (1H-2H-2S**-2NT**-forced).Opener then makes his long-suit try. If he bids trump now, he is making a try in the suit taken by the relay. Here is the outline:

1H-2H-	2S**-2NT **** (2S=relay/2NT forced)
Now:	3C= LSGT in clubs
	3D= LSGT in diamonds
	3H (trumps)= LSGT in spades (relay suit)

Similarly:	
1S-2S-	2NT**-3C**** (2NT=relay/3C forced)
Now:	3D= LSGT in diamonds
	3H= LSGT in hearts
	3S (trumps)= LSGT in clubs (relay suit)

Important note: Responder can ignore the relay to make his own short suit try. Any second bid other than accepting the relay shows shortness in the bid suit. A bid in the trump suit shows shortness in the relay suit, i. e. 1H-2H-2S**- 3C= shortness in clubs 3D= shortness in diamonds 3H (trump)=shortness in spades (relay suit).

Short-Suit Game Try by Opener (SSGT)

A bid other than the relay suit is an SSGT (showing a singleton or void). For example, after 1S-2S, direct 3C, 3D, and 3H bids are SSGT, because 2NT, the relay bid, was by-passed. After 1H-2H, there is a special case. Since 2S is the LSGT relay bid, 2NT is the SSGT in spades.

Here is the outline:

| 1S- | | 2S** |

Now:
3C (bypassing 2NT, which would start a LSGT)=short in clubs
3D= short in diamonds
3H= short in hearts

Similarly:

1H-   2H

Now:
2NT-short in spades (2S would be the relay)
3C= short in clubs
3D= short in diamonds

Responder evaluates game prospects in terms of the usefulness of the shortness shown and bids 3 or 4 of the agreed-upon trump suit.

A simple rebid of the opener's suit (1S-2S-3S /1H-2H-3H) probably shows an interest in the quality of responder's trumps. With extra length or honor strength, responder should bid game.

Jumps to the 4-Level After a Constructive Raise

Opener may jump to a new suit at the 4-level after a constructive raise with great playing strength, even though the partnership is limited to 26 HCP on the bidding. This would usually show a maximum with extra trump length or at least 5/5 distribution,15–16 HCP, and great playing strength. Slam is rarely in the picture after 1S-2S or 1H-2H, but it is not impossible.

Hands Worth a Limit Raise or Better

The system can be played with standard limit raises, but an improvement is the following: with a balanced 3-card raise, bid 1NT, then jump to 3 of the trump suit (or raise opener's rebid of his suit to 3). Sartor Raises (similar to Jacoby but not necessarily game-forcing) can be used for both limit raises and hands that have game and slam potential. A Sartor raise is a jump in the denomination directly above the trump suit (1H-2S***or 1S-2NT).

The 1H-2S sequence allows a more efficient system of descriptive rebids than 1H-2NT, as in Jacoby. The meanings of 1H-2S and 1H-2NTare simply reversed, with the 2NT showing a jump shift in spades, however the partnership treats that bid. A Sartor raise shows limit raise or better values and asks opener to describe his hand.

Opener is asked to describe his hand within the context of the 11–16 HCP range. Hand strength and shape are shown in steps:

- first step = minimum, no short suit)
- second, third, and fourth step=shortness, with a trump rebid showing shortness in the suit taken by the first step
- fifth step = maximum, no singleton   jumps to the 4 level = maximum hands with 5/5+ distribution

It is also possible to substitute Kokish responses here (first step asking responder to name the lowest suit in which he would accept a help-suit game try), but I think it is easier to ask opener to clarify his hand within its already narrow range. At any rate, here is the outline:

After 1S-2NT

3C= minimum (11–14), no singleton

3D= singleton/void (minimum if 5/5)

3H= singleton/void (minimum if 5/5)

3S= singleton/void in clubs (3C showed minimum, no shortness) but minimum (may be passed)

3NT= maximum (15–16 HCP), no singleton

4C= 5+ spades/5+ clubs, maximum (15–16 HCP)

4D= 5+ spades/5+diamonds, maximum (15–16 HCP)

4H= 5+ spades/5+hearts, maximum (15–16 HCP)

4S *** maximum with club stiff (this is needed so that responder may pass 3S with a limit raise that is not helped by a club singleton—or- with a max and a stiff club, bid 3C, supposedly showing a minimum, but then ignore any sign-off and cuebid at the 4 level or jump to 4S.*******.

With a maximum and 6+ spades, opener can bid 3NT or bid his shortness first and then jump or bid a new suit (possibly just showing an ace).

After 1H-2S
2NT= minimum (11–14 HCP), no singleton
3C= singleton/void (minimum if 5/5)
3D= singleton/void (minimum if 5/5)
3H= singleton/void in spades (since 2S was the Sartor raise) minimum (may be passed)
3S= singleton/void maximum
3N= maximum (15–16 HCP), no singleton
4C= 5+hearts/5+clubs, maximum (15–16HCP)
4D= 5+hearts/5+diamonds, maximum (15–16 HCP)
4H= open; perhaps maximum, 6+ hearts, no shortness
After opener's descriptive rebid, responder may sign off at the 3-level, bid game, or make a game/slam try in a new suit.

Weak Distributional Raise (1H-3H)/(1S-3S)

This bid may be made with 4+trumps, 3–7 HCP, and a singleton. It may also cover weak hands with 5 trump and 5-3-3-2 distribution, which may not be appealing to bid at the 4 level.

Raise to the 4-Level- alert !

Triple jump raises (1S-4S and 1H-4H) are two-way bids—either a standard weak distributional raise with 5+ trump or a balanced13–16 HCP hand that offers little prospect of slam opposite a limited opening bid. (Or use suggested treatment in Appendix B.)

Jump Shifts-Strong Traditional

17+ HCP—one of three types of hands:

1. A hand having a good fit for opener's suit
2. A hand having an independent suit
3. A strong and balanced hand (though 3NT could be used naturally for this hand)

Some may wish to use weak or fit-showing jump shifts instead.

Splinter Raises

Splinter raises are used often, either at responder's first or second chance to bid. Delayed splinters show a good second suit, shortness in the jump-bid suit, and usually 4+ cards in opener's trump suit.

Forcing NT
(May cover some strong hand types)

1. A weak raise of opener's major
2. A hand with 7–10 HCP, 2-card trump support for opener, looking for better fit
3. A balanced hand with 11–12 HCP (can rebid 2NT, non-forcing)
4. A better balanced hand, 13–15 or 17+, depending on meaning of a direct jump to 3NT (can rebid 3NT or 4NT)
5. A balanced 3-card limit raise (can jump or raise to 3M at next bid)
6. A limited hand with a long suit and poor fit for opener (can bid the suit at the next turn)
7. An invitational hand with a long suit and a poor fit for opener (can jump or raise to the 3 level at the next turn)
8. Special agreements for unused bids (for example, a double jump to the 3 or 4 level at responder's second turn might be used as a splinter bid with a void or a Swiss-type strong balanced raise with 3 or 4 trump and strength in the side suit.

Opener's Responses to a Forcing NT

2C is the default bid. It denies 6 of opener's major, 4 hearts (if spades are opener's bid suit),or a good 4- or 5-card diamond suit.

2D= 4 good or 5 diamonds

2H= 4+ hearts (if spades are opener's first bid suit)

A rebid of opener's first bid suit shows 6+ cards in the suit.

Jumps in a second suit show 5/5+distribution and a maximum hand (15-16 HCP).

As the reader can tell, this is a sort of California Club Lite. If this is still too complex, there's always Goren. Seriously, almost any common major suit structure will work without affecting the strong club part of the system or any of the other more esoteric opening bids.

APPENDIX E

Alternative Ideas for Coping with Two-Level Interference Over a 1C Opening

The approach to 2-level interference I outlined earlier on pages 49-52 is probably enough to handle most situations. However, in this appendix I am going to outline a couple of other reasonable approaches in a little more detail.

The first idea is to make all bids essentially natural along with a standard negative double. The second is to use the more artificial type of scheme that we already employ over 1-level overcalls, with 2N serving as a kind of Lebensohl relay to 3C. These are only two of many possible structures.

Generally Natural

1C   (2C)   double = 4-3+ in majors (6–7+ HCP, (may be strong)
               2D=5+ diamonds,6-7+ HCP (1 round force, may be strong)
               2H or 2S= 5+card suit,6–7+ HCP (1 round force, may be strong)
               2NT= 8+ HCP, at least one stopper
               3C= GF, no 5-card suit
               3D, 3H, 3S= GF, good 6+ card suit
               Pass= weak or trap pass (opener can use judgment about reopening
               double)

1C   (2D)   double = 4–3+ in majors, 6–7+HCP (may be strong)
2H or 2S= 5+ card suit, 6–7+ HCP (1 round force, may be strong)
2NT= 8+ HCP, at least 1 stopper
3C= 5+ clubs, 6-7+ HCP (1 round force, may be strong)
3D= GF, no 5-card suit
3H or 3S= GF, good 6+ card suit
Pass= weak or trap

1C   (2H)   double = 4 spades, 6-7+ HCP (may be strong)
2S= 5+ spades, 6-7+ HCP (1 round force, may be strong)
2NT=8+ HCP, at least one stopper
3C or 3D=7–8+HCP, 5+ card suit (1 round force, may be strong)
3H=GF, denies 4 spades, usually balanced, minor oriented
3S=GF, good 6+ card suit
Pass= weak or trap

1C   (2S)   double= 4 hearts, 6–7+ HCP (1 round force, may be strong)
2NT=8+ HCP, at least one stopper
3C, 3D =4/ 5-card suit, 6–7+ HCP (1 round force, may be strong)
3H= 5+ card suit, 6–7+ HCP (1 round force, may be strong)
[3C,3D,3H invite 3S (½ stopper) or 3NT (full stopper) by opener]
3S=8+ HCP, ½ stopper 3NT= 8+HCP, full stopper

Semi-Natural (with Transfers and Lebensohl)

1C   (2C)   double = 4 - 3+ in majors, 6–7+ HCP (may be strong)
2D= GF, 8–9+ HCP, balanced or with 5+-card minor
2H=5+ hearts, 6–7+ HCP (1 round force, may be strong)
2S=5+ spades, 6–7+ HCP (1 round force, may be strong)
2NT=Lebensohl, relay to 3D (6+diamonds) weak *or* 8+HCP, at least
1 stopper, GF (suit bid at next turn=1 stop/3NT =2 or more stops)
3C=transfer, 6+diamonds, good suit, GF
3D=transfer, 6+ hearts, good suit, GF
3H=transfer, 6+ spades, good suit, GF

1C   (2D)   double =4 - 3+ in majors, 6-7+ HCP (may be strong)

2H=5+ hearts, 6–7+HCP (1 round force, may be strong)

2S=5+ spades, 6–7+ HCP (1 round force, may be strong)

2NT=Lebensohl, relay to 3C (6+clubs) weak, *or* 8+HCP, at least 1 stopper, GF (a cuebid at next turn=1 stop. A bid of 3NT = 2 or more stops.)

3C=7–8+HCP, 5+ card suit (1 round force, may be strong)

3D=transfer, 6+ hearts, good suit, GF

3H=transfer, 6+ spades, good suit, GF

1C   (2H)   double= 4 spades, 6–7+ HCP (may be strong)

2S=5+ spades, 6–7+ HCP (1 round force, may be strong)

2NT=Lebensohl, relay to 3C (6+clubs or 6+diamonds) weak, *or* 8+HCP, at least 1 stopper, GF (suit bid at next turn=1 stop / 3NT =2 or more stops)

3C,3D=7–8+HCP, 5+-card suit (1 round force, may be strong)

3H=general GF, no 5-card suit, suggests opener bid 3NT

1C   (2S)   double =4 hearts, 6–7+ HCP (may be strong)

2NT=Lebensohl, relay to 3C (6+clubs, diamonds, or hearts) weak, *Or* 8+HCP, at least 1 stopper, GF (cue bid at next turn=1stop / 3NT =2 or more stops)

3C,3D,3H=7–8+HCP, 5+ card suit (1 round force, may be strong)

3S = general GF, no 5-card suit, suggests opener bid 3NT

Many pairs may have their own ideas on the subject. Any coherent scheme will probably work as long as both partners are on the same page.

APPENDIX F

Another Possible Opening 2D (4-4-4-1, 16+)
(When 2H, 2S, and 2NT Are Standard, Not Two-Way bids)

This is actually the structure I use in most of my casual California Club partnerships. It is simple enough to be used after the five minutes of discussion, and it is approved by the ACBL.

Opener
2D = any 4-4-4-1,16-18, or 19+HCP

Responder
2H,2S = non-forcing (at least 3 cards in the suit)
3C = non-forcing, with 6+clubs)
2NT = forcing (asks for singleton and HCP)

Opener's Answers to 2NT

- 3C = singleton diamond (16–18) (suit bid is one step below the singleton)
- 3D = singleton heart (16–18) (suit bid is one step below the singleton)
- 3H = singleton spade (16–18) (suit bid is one step below the singleton)
- 3S = singleton club (16–18) (suit bid is one step below the singleton)
- 3NT = singleton club (19+) (NT bid is one step below the singleton)
- 4C = singleton diamond (19+) (suit bid is one step below the singleton)
- 4D = singleton heart (19+) (suit bid is one step below the singleton)
- 4H = singleton spade (19+) (suit bid is one step below the singleton)

This structure is very easy to remember. The singleton is always the suit above the denomination that is bid. It also provides the most efficient way to ask controls—a very cheap cue bid of the singleton. This saves a whole level of bidding compared to bidding the singleton directly and then cue-bidding that suit again to ask for controls. Non–cue bids are now all natural, to play.

The answers to a cue bid depend on the level of the response. If opener showed 16–18 HCP, then the first step shows 0–3 controls (ace=2, king=1). The second step shows 4, the third shows 5, etc. If opener showed 19+HCP, the first step shows 0–5 controls, the second shows 6, the third shows 7, etc. This bid is obviously not as versatile as the version that includes the major-suit weak 2-bid option, but it will not arouse the ire of the directors at any ACBL tournaments.

APPENDIX G

Freak Asking Bids

Conventions are usually invented to handle a problem that some expert has run into at the table and was unable to solve with the ordinary bidding tools in his arsenal. They may be the product of "mad scientists" or "solid citizens." The famous expert Howard Schenken was one of the latter types. Despite that, he came up with a rather radical way to locate specific aces on freak hands- the Schenken 2D bid.

A particularly strange bidding sequence brought Schenken's brainchild to mind. A casual partner, holding a freak hand, opened a strong club and rebid 3H under the delusion that it must be an even stronger rebid than a game-forcing 2H. Confused, I simply bid 4H. It turned out a laydown slam depended on my having a specific ace. It dawned on me that the rebids of 3H, 3S, 4C, and 4D were "impossible" after a strong 1C opening. There were game-forcing bids available at a lower level in all four suits. However, these unneeded rebids might make perfect asking bids to find specific aces or kings on certain freak hands. The opportunity to use them might come up only once a decade, but it might be the only way to find that grand slam that lets you win the Spingold. Think big!

Here's the simplest scheme I could come up with (to differentiate it from another possibility I'm going to outline, I'll call it Scheme 1): After 1C-1D, an impossible re-bid of 3H, 3S, 4C, or 4D asks for partner's honor holding in that suit. It says *nothing* about the opener's holding in that suit. He can have a singleton, looking for the ace, or AQJ109xxxx, looking for the king. Responses are simple:

- first step = no high honor
- second step = Q
- third step = K
- fourth step = A
- fifth step = 2 of the top 3 honors

Opener then sets the final contract with his next bid, If he can't do that, he had no business asking the question. (That may be too arbitrary. It might be sensible to let opener inquire in a second suit below the 6 level if the first answer is an ace or king. That would require partnership agreement.) There are other possible schemes. For instance, the opener could ask for responder's keycards without specifying the suit in which he needs help. Here is an outline of such a scheme (call it Scheme 2):

Opener	Responder	
1C	1D	
3H (asking for specific aces)	3S/4C/4D/4H =ace of that suit (no others)	
	3NT = 0 or 2 aces	
	If 3NT is the answer, 4C then asks for clarification.	
4C (Do you have 0 or 2?)	4D=0	
	4H= 2 of the same **color**	**C**
	4S= 2 of the same **rank**	**RA**
	4NT= 2 of the same **sh**ape	**SH**

Those who play CRASH will see that the beginnings of each answer to the 4C inquiry spell that word. CRASH stands for **COLOR / RANK / SHAPE**. That serves as a good memory aid.

Since it is remotely possible that responder could have 3 aces (he might have bid 1D with an impossible negative),there is even a way to describe that holding. Responder simply leaps an extra level (4S, 5C, 5D, 5H). This bid shows all of the aces *except* the ace of the bid suit. There should be no problem about getting too high. A small slam should be cold, and a grand slam is likely.

In a slightly more elaborate scheme (call it Scheme 3), one could use a jump to 3H to ask for specific aces and a jump to 3S to ask for specific kings. The responses would be almost exactly the same for both asks. (The only difference would be the need to bid 4S to show the spade king after the 3S ask.)This scheme has the advantage of enabling responder to show specific aces or kings in two suits instead of just one. The simpler one-suit scheme allows you to find out about the whole keycard holding in one key suit.

Anyone serious about using these types of bids can easily come up with a scheme to fit his preferences. Generally speaking, these bids cover freak one-suited hands. As for the exact types of hands which might be suitable for their use, it depends on how strict you want your definition of "freak one-suited hand" to be.(It might be a hand with 7-5 distribution, but with one suit absolutely certain to be named trump.)

If you want to use a very rigid definition, qualifying hands should resemble this description: they must contain a very long suit which will serve as trump no matter what partner may hold. It may be a no-loser suit such as AKQJ10xx or a similar suit missing only one or two key honors. There must be no possibility of any side suit losers except for any missing key cards. It will often contain a void.

The only information opener will need from his partner in order to bid a slam is whether he holds a particular card or cards. Here are some example hands:

♠AKQJxxxx ♥ A ♦ QJ109 ♣ void   ♠ void ♥ AQJ109xx ♦AK ♣AKQJ

These two hands fit our first scheme perfectly. An inquiry in one suit will allow us to bid 4, 6, or 7 confidently.

♠ AKQJ10xx ♥ void ♦ KQJ109 ♣ x   ♠ x ♥ KQJ109xxx ♦AKQJ ♣ void

These two are perfect candidates for the more general asking schemes. Obviously, these hands will make 6 or 7 opposite one or two specific aces. They will also go down in 6 if partner's only ace is in opener's void. The impossible 3H rebid will get the needed information at the 4 level or below. Since this type of hand will occur roughly as often as a monsoon in Death Valley, some pairs will want to loosen the requirements slightly, allowing for suits with a slight possibility of extra losers but still more likely than not to produce slam opposite the right aces in responder's hand. Examples might be:

♠ void ♥ AKQ ♦ KQ10 ♣ KQJ9xxx   ♠ A ♥ void ♦ AK109xxxx ♣ KQ10x

These hands would not be certain to make slam opposite a useful ace, but their chances would be pretty good.

Though the entire discussion so far has presumed a 1C-1D auction, it would certainly be possible to use impossible jump rebids after a positive response to 1C (1H,1S,1NT, or 2C).Some examples might be 1C-1H-3S, 1C-1S-4C, or 1C-2C-4H. This would require partnership discussion. Since 2D and 2H responses to 1C are two-way bids which require further clarification, it would not be practical to use such bids after 1C-2D or 1C-2H auctions.

After a positive response to 1C, it would probably be best to use Scheme 1 for simplicity's sake. Using Scheme 1, an impossible jump rebid would essentially be a super asking bid in one particular suit. For example, 1C-1H-4D would simply say, "What do you have in diamonds?"

If one were insistent about using scheme 2, either 3H or 3S could be used as the all-purpose asking bid for aces, as long as it could not be a natural raise in that suit. The previously outlined sets of responses would apply. At the risk of being redundant, here is a chart of the impossible 3H or 3S scheme which might be used after positive responses:

1C   **1D, 1S, 1NT, or 2C**
3H (impossible)   3NT = 0 or 2 aces
4C= asks clarification   4D = no aces
                                    4H = two aces, same color (♠/♣ or ♥/♦)
                                    4S = two aces, same rank (both minors or both majors)
                                    4NT = two aces, same shape (pointed♠/♦ or rounded ♥/♣)

1C   **1S, 1NT, or 2C**
3H (impossible-asks   3S = spade ace only
specific aces)   4C = club ace only
                                    4D = diamond ace only
                                    4H = heart ace only
                                    3NT= 0 or 2 aces (4C asks- see CRASH answers above)
                                    4S = three aces, no spade ace
                                    5C = three aces, no club ace
                                    5D = three aces, no diamond ace
                                    5H = three aces, no heart ace

1C   **1H**
3S (impossible)= exactly the same continuations described above, except a 4S response could show the spade ace alone, with 4NT showing three aces without the spade ace

Those interested enough to consider using this type of asking bid can work out their own method.

APPENDIX H

Alternative Scheme for 1C-1NT and 1C-2NT
More Artificial Continuations Using Asking Bids And Ogust-like Responses

This is one possible alternative to the natural continuations described earlier on pages 128-138. and 160-162.This structure, which might attract a few mad scientists like myself, is more artificial. It is aimed at getting some useful specific information about responder's holdings in prospective trump suits. This involves making opener's natural suit bids double as asking bids. Responder's answers most closely resemble the Ogust convention's method of describing weak 2 bids.

As mentioned before, this structure actually shares one common set of bids with the natural scheme-the rebids and continuations used when opener has a balanced hand.

When opener bids 2C (Stayman), responder's reply will again either be a transfer showing a 4-card suit or a bid denying a major but describing his hand's strength. Repeating the earlier summary (it saves a lot of looking back), a 2D reply shows 4 hearts. Responder may also have a second suit. A bid of 2H shows 4 spades. It denies 4 hearts, but the hand may have a 4-card minor. A bid of 2S shows no major and a minimum (13–14 HCP). The hand will have 1 or 2 minors. A bid of 2NT shows 4 clubs, no major, and a maximum (15 HCP). A bid of 3C shows 4 diamonds, a maximum, and necessarily 3-3-4-3 distribution.

If opener has a fit for responder's guaranteed suit, he bids it. This bid also asks about the quality of the agreed-upon suit. If no acceptable trump fit is found in the transfer suit, opener bids a different suit. This asks about responder's holding there. If no secondary suit fit can be found, opener can sign off or try for slam in NT.

The same inquiry process takes place when opener bids a 5+-card suit instead of bidding Stayman. Responder's reply indicates his holding in the suit. Depending on the response, his exact strength may be established later if necessary.

The instruments for all this investigation are modified versions of the Ogust convention. Unfortunately, three slightly different versions are needed: one for suits in which responder has guaranteed 4-card length and two others for suits in which his length is unknown. I have tried to make the answer schemes as similar as possible to minimize memory problems.

You'll notice that I haven't given the exact definitions for responder's answers. That's because Ogust is somewhat subjective. It uses terms like "good hand / bad hand" and "good suit / bad suit." In general, our responder will describe his support as poor, fair, good, or excellent. He answers in steps. The pattern will be very similar. The steps will begin with the worst possible hand and culminate with the best. There will also be a follow-up method to get more exact information if slam is in the picture. The definitions I list here reflect my own ideas about what constitutes poor, fair, or good support. Others may use their own standards.

First, when there is a known 4-4 fit:

- first step = poor support (Jxxx or less)
- second step = fair support (Qxxx, Kxxx, Axxx)
- third step = good support (QJxx, KJxx, AJxx)
- fourth step = excellent support (KQxx, AQxx, AKxx)

When opener bids a different suit, needing 4-card support:

- first step = lacking 4-card support
- second step = poor 4-card support (Jxxx or less)
- third step = fair 4-card support (Qxxx, Kxxx, Axxx)
- fourth step = good 4-card support (QJxx, KJxx, AJxx)
- fifth step = excellent 4-card support (KQxx, AQxx, AKxx)

When a 4-4 fit is established, opener can ask about responder's overall strength by making the cheapest continuation bid. The first step shows a minimum (13–14 HCP) and the second step shows a maximum (15 HCP).

When opener bids a 5+ card suit:

- first step = poor support (xx, Hx) (H=high honor, x= small card)
- second step = fair 3-card support (xxx, Hxx)
- third step = poor 4-card support (xxxx)
- fourth step = fair/good 4-card support (Hxxx)
- fifth step = excellent 4-card support (HHxx)
- (H = high honor—A, K, or Q)

When the support is poor, opener can ask about support in a second suit. The same answers would apply.

When responder's answer establishes at least an 8-card trump fit, opener can use the next cheapest bid to ask about general strength. In assessing strength, "minimum"should mean 13 to an average 14 HCP. "Maximum" should mean 15 or possibly a very good 14 HCP—a hand with lots of 10s and 9s.

If opener denies 4 of responder's suit but shows a 4-card suit of his own, the same basic standards apply. However, responder has not guaranteed 4-card support. Therefore, the first step denies 4 cards in the bid suit. The other responses all show varying degrees of 4-card support.

When there is no hope for a 4-4 fit but slam in NT is possible, opener can bid 2NT instead of a suit.(If responder bids 3C to show 4 diamonds, he can bid 3H.) This bid asks about strength only. The answers are simple:

- first step = 13
- second step = 14
- third step = 15

If you're into upgrading, you can add a fourth step for a "super 15" with lots of intermediates. You can also promote a lower answer by 1 step, but only with very good intermediate cards.

When opener bids a 5+ card suit rather than bidding Stayman, our answers have to be adjusted. Responder may have only 2 cards in our suit. The first step has to account for that holding. We then have to have responses for 3-card and 4-card support. The response chart shows those responses.

Here are some sample auctions:

A. ♠ Axxx   ♠ KQxx   1C   1NT (13–15 HCP)
    ♥ Kx   ♥Axx   2C (Stayman)   2H (4 spades)
    ♦ KQxx   ♦Ax   2S (ask)   3H (excellent support)
    ♣ AQx   ♣Jxxx   4C (Gerber or 1430)   X (answer = 2 aces or 3 KC)
                            6S

B. ♠ Kxx   ♠ Axxx   1C   1NT
    ♥ AQxx   ♥ Kx   2C   2H (4 spades, 2-3 hearts)
    ♦ Ax   ♦ Kxx   3C (ask)   3S (4-card support—Hxxx)
    ♣ KQxx   ♣Axxx   4C (Gerber or 1430)   4S (2 aces or 2 KC)
                            6C

C. ♠ AKJxx   ♠ Qxxx   1C   1NT
    ♥ x   ♥ AKxx   2S   3H (4-card support—Hxxx)
    ♦ AKJx   ♦ xx   4C (Gerber or 1430)   4S or 4NT (2 aces or 2KC +Q)
    ♣ Kxx   ♣ Axx   5C (kings?)   5D (1) or 5H- specific K)
                            6S or 7S

D. ♠ x   ♠ Axx   1C   1NT
    ♥ KQJ10xx   ♥ Ax   2H (ask)   2S (poor support)
    ♦ KQx   ♦ Axxx   3H (ask)   3NT (Hx)-Ax, Kx, or Qx
    ♣ AKx   ♣ J10xx   4C (Gerber or 1430)   4H or 4NT (3)
                            5C (kings?)   5D or 5H (0)
                            6H/6NT/7H (?)

E. ♠ A   ♠ Jxx   1C   1NT
    ♥ Kx   ♥ AQx   2NT (5+clubs)   3D (fair support)
    ♦ KJ10x   ♦ Axxx   4C (Gerber or 1430)   4S (2 aces) or 4H (((0 or 3KC)
    ♣ AQJxxx   ♣ Kxx   4S (kings?)   4NT (1 king or 0 side kings)
                            6C

NOTE: *The answers to the queries about aces, kings, or keycards obviously depend upon partnership agreements. I apologize if the fact I have listed 2 or 3 possible responses may be a bit confusing.*

1C-2NT

More Artificial Continuations Using Asking Bids and Ogust-like Responses

This is a corresponding structure for 1C-2NT (16–18 HCP) auctions. This structure also involves the use of Ogust-like replies to inquiries about holdings in opener's suits. Of course, all the bids and replies are one level higher.

Here is the 3-level version of that scheme. When opener is balanced, he bids 3C, looking for a 4-4 fit in a suit. Responder's replies are as follows:

- 3D = shows 4 hearts, possibly with a second suit
- 3H = shows 4 spades, possibly with a side minor
- 3S = shows 4 clubs, possibly with 4 diamonds
- 3NT = shows 4 diamonds, with no side suit (3-3-4-3)

If opener has 4 cards in responder's indicated suit, he bids the suit. This bid doubles as an asking bid, inquiring about trump quality. With a known 4-4 fit, responder answers as follows:

- first step = poor suit (Jxxx or less)
- second step = fair suit (Qxxx, Kxxx, Axxx)
- third step = good suit (QJxx, KJxx, AJxx)
- fourth step = excellent suit (KQxx, AQxx, AKxx)
- fifth step = super suit (AKQx)

If opener does not fit responder's indicated suit, he may bid a different suit, hoping to find a 4-4 fit there. Since responder has not promised 4 cards, a second set of answers is used. They are as follows:

- first step = lacking 4-card support
- second step = poor 4-card support (Jxxx or less)
- third step = fair 4-card support (Qxxx, Kxxx, Axxx)
- fourth step = good 4-card support (QJxx, KJxx, AJxx)
- fifth step = excellent 4-card support (KQxx, AQxx, AKxx)

With a more unbalanced hand, opener may bid a 5+card suit (3D, 3H, 3S, 3NT=5+ clubs). These bids also serve as asking bids. Responder uses a third set of answers.

These are needed because he has to show both his length and strength in the suit. The following are still as similar to the other answers as possible:

- first step = poor support (xx, Hx) (*note-* H= Q, K, or A)
- second step = poor 3-card support (Jxx or less)
- third step = good 3-card support (Qxx, Kxx, Axx)
- fourth step = poor 4-card support (Jxxx or less)
- fifth step = fair/good 4-card support (Qxxx, Kxxx, Axxx)
- sixth step = excellent 4-card support (KQxx, AQxx, AKxx)

If the answer shows poor support, opener can ask about a second suit if he has one. The second suit may also just be a help-suit slam try. The same answers apply. Any continuation is forcing. The cheapest new suit after a trump suit is found may be used to start asking for aces, and the cheapest bid after the answer can be used to ask for kings. Since it is almost certain that you will wind up in slam somewhere, the main purpose of all the exploration is to see if a suit fit may be better than 6NT and whether a grand slam is possible.

Here are some example hands:

A. ♠ KQx   ♠ AJxx   1C   2NT
    ♥ Axxx   ♥ Kx   3C   3H (4 spades)
    ♦ KQxx   ♦ AJxx   4D   5C (good 4-card support)
    ♣ Ax   ♣ Kxx   5D (1430)   5NT (2 KC)
                            6C (kings?) 6S (2 outside kings)
                            7D

B. ♠ Axxx   ♠ KJxx   1C   2NT
    ♥ QJx   ♥ AKx   3C   3H (4 spades)
    ♦ Ax   ♦ KQxx   3S   4D (good suit)
    ♣ AQJx   ♣ xx   4NT (1430) 5H (2 KC, no Q)
                            6S

C. ♠ x   ♠ AKx   1C   2NT
    ♥ AKQxx   ♥ xx   3H   3S (poor support)
    ♦ AKJxx   ♦ Q10xx   4D   5D (good 4-card support)
    ♣ Qx   ♣ AKJx   5H (1430)   6D (2 KC + Q)
                            6H (kings?) 7C (2 outside kings)
                            7NT

D. ♠ KQJxx	♠ Ax	1C	2NT
♥ x	♥ AKQx	3S	3NT
♦ AQx	♦ xxx	4C	5C (good 4-card support)
♣ KQxx	♣ Axxx	5D (1430)	5S (3 KC)
		5NT (kings?)	6D (1)
		7C or 7NT	
E. ♠ AQ	♠ KJ10x	1C	2NT
♥ KQ10xx	♥ Jx	3H	3S (poor support)
♦ x	♦ AKQx	4C	4S (Hxx)
♣ AQJxx	♣ Kxx	4NT	5H (2 KC)
		6C	6NT
F. ♠ x	♠ AKJ	1C	2NT
♥ AK	♥ QJxx	3D	3NT (Hxx)
♦ KJ10xx	♦ Qxx	4C	4S (Hxx)
♣ AQxxx	♣ Kxx	4NT (1430-clubs)	5H (2KC)
		6C or 6D	6NT ?

Note: After 1430, I just used a simple 0,1,2,3 answer for total kings in these examples. In some other sections of the book, I used examples where responder showed specific kings. I have no strong preference. Partners should simply agree on one method or the other.

Final Thoughts

As a great American statesman (I believe it may have been Millard Fillmore) once wrote,"People will little note nor long remember what we have said here." He, of course, was wrong, but his words might well apply to this little literary opus on contract bridge bidding..

It is unlikely that .many players will adopt this system as a whole. It would require a pair of strong, youngish players willing to put in a considerable amount of time on the development of partnership agreements to really make use of it.

However, I'd like to think that there are several ideas presented in this book that deserve consideration by many types of players, even those who have no interest in using a strong club system.

Standard and 2 / 1 players might want to look at the various kinds of major suit raises I've outlined. Among the treatments that might fit into their systems are:

1. Constructive raises with short and long suit game tries
2. Sartor Raises for limit raise and better hands
3. Three-way jump shifts with mini- and maxi-splinters

They might also be able to use my "Little Bit West Of Texas" transfers (with "Invisible Blackwood" and the Sartor Slam Try (the 2S response to 1NT), among other ideas.

Precision players and users of other strong club systems might want to incorporate some of the off beat two-level openings and responses to a 1C opening bid that are outlined in the book.

1. The "1D with muscles" opening
2. The 1C-1D - 2H sequence to show a balanced 20-21 HCP hand
3. The 1C-1D- 2S sequence to describe a standard strong 2C opener with clubs
4. The 1C-1D- 2NT sequence to describe a standard strong 2C opener with diamonds

5. The rebid structure after a 2C opening bid
6. The unusual 2-level opening bids (for use in big unrestricted team events)
7. Ideas for coping with interference over 1C and other openings and responses

I think many of these ideas have real value. I'd love to see some of them actually used in top competition.

Printed in the United States
By Bookmasters